ELEMENTS *of* FICTION WRITING

CONFLICT & SUSPENSE

WD

WRITER'S DIGEST
BOOKS

JAMES SCOTT BELL

Writer's Digest Books
An imprint of Penguin Random House LLC
penguinrandomhouse.com

ISBN 978-1-59963-273-5

Illustrations © Dover Pictura/Art Nouveau

Edited by Melissa Wuske
Designed by Claudean Wheeler

146119709

CONFLICT & SUSPENSE

CONTENTS

INTRODUCTION

Trouble is my business.

—RAYMOND CHANDLER

Once you get a character with a problem, a serious problem, "plotting" is just a fancy name for how he or she tries to get out of the predicament.

—BARNABY CONRAD

You tell stories.

You tell stories because you want people to read them.

You want readers to be moved, entertained, maybe even enlightened.

You want to tell stories that wrap readers up and get them lost in a world you've created, with colorful characters and plots that don't let up.

It doesn't matter what genre you write in. You want all these things happening because that's what makes the magic connection in this alchemy we call fiction.

Yes, that's it. You want to make a little magic.

You can, you know.

Most aspects of the craft of writing fiction can be learned. You can practice them and put them to work for you.

Frankly, I get a little miffed when someone says fiction writing can't be taught. That would come as news to all the young writers who were instructed by teachers, editors, books, and articles. People like John Grisham, who dined monthly on *Writer's Digest* magazine.

Or me, reading Lawrence Block's fiction column as if it were holy writ. And then trying the things he wrote about and seeing how they worked on the page.

I've also taught countless writers in conferences and through books on the craft, and have seen many of them break into print.

So don't buy into the idea that this craft doesn't have tools and techniques that will make you better.

What can't be taught is what you bring to your fiction—your inherent talent, background experiences, passion, and heart. The singular *you*.

But talent and experience mean nothing if they don't find an expression on the page that readers can relate to.

Craft teaches you how to connect with readers so they can get lost in your stories.

And what gets them lost?

It really comes down to one thing: characters who are in trouble.

It doesn't matter what kind of trouble it is so long as it is of great importance to the story people. When a reader describes getting "caught up" in a novel, it's just shorthand for saying that trouble is happening to a character, or group of characters, and the reader wants—no, *needs*—to see what happens.

Alfred Hitchcock said it this way: *A great story is life, with the dull parts taken out.*

A scene without trouble is a dull part. A character who is not caught up in trials and dangers and challenges and obstacles—interior, exterior, or both—is not going to excite us for very long.

It doesn't matter who the character is, either. A quirky, colorful character overstays her welcome after a few chapters, unless trouble comes calling.

So trouble is your business. And conflict and suspense are the tools of the craft that will take your business to the readers.

THE ESSENCE OF STORY

Imagine the first storyteller. I'll call him Og. He has just returned from a hard day hunting meat. He was about to bag him some wolf when he got surprised by a mastodon lumbering by.

Bummer.

He dropped his club and ran. He hid in some rocks. An hour or so later he came back to his prey and found it being devoured by a saber-toothed tiger.

Double bummer.

Then Og had to trek back to the waiting fire. His tribe was sitting there hoping for some steaks (they were quite tired of berries and roots). They looked at Og and grunted something that can be roughly translated, "Where's the meat, man?"

Og was on the spot. His position as chief hunter-gatherer was up for grabs, depending on what he said next.

The last time something like this happened, and the tribe asked what went wrong, Og merely shrugged and threw dirt at them. This didn't help matters at all. They seemed unwilling to give Og more chances.

So now Og gets on his haunches and says, "I was out hunting like always, and had a wolf in my sights. I threw a rock and got him right on the head. He went down. I was about to go get him when I heard this ROAARRRR!"

He pauses to take stock of the reactions around the fire. Every face is turned toward him. He can see consuming interest in their eyes.

He has them hooked.

Good, Og thinks.

Let's see if I can keep them that way while I figure out how to get out of this.

"I spin around," Og says, "and there is a tiger with those long, spiked teeth. There is spit dripping off those teeth. His eyes were huge, as big as lakes! I could smell his fur. It smelled like death."

The audience is leaning forward now. Og thinks, *That went well. If I take time to describe things this way, it stretches out the story and the tension. And that bit about the smell, that was pure genius.*

Og is beginning to develop a style.

He's also searching for an ending, and so he lays out, beat by beat, a story of this encounter with the tiger and the ensuing fight to save his own life. He finally gets to the end and speaks of a mighty battle with the beast, until his ultimate triumph.

Someone in the audience asks, "So where's the tiger?"

Og must think up a twist ending. So he comes up with the speculative fiction genre, and says a god of the mountains came down and took the tiger as tribute. He was about to call down fire from the sky on Og's tribe. Og told him not to, that it would be bad, and he would fight the god if he had to. The god relented.

So Og has saved all their lives. Or so the story goes.

Well, the reaction of the listeners is so good that Og gets a double portion of berries. An attractive woman gives him a blanket of squirrel fur in honor of his exploits. One of the old men gives Og his best club. A couple of the younger tribe members hand over their favorite trinkets and promise more if Og will tell more stories.

And Og thinks, *Maybe I can make a living at this.*

Og's brother, who collects the booty, keeps 15 percent of it.

So Og starts telling stories every night by the fire instead of hunting for food. His tales inspire the other men to go out and hunt. Encouraged by Og's fiction, they become brave and successful. They give Og a portion of everything they gather.

Og buys a new luxury cave with an interior pool.

What Og discovered was that a story with trouble and threat, drawn out and told with a certain élan, is what keeps people interested and willing to pay for more. This is the true essence of story, a record of how a character deals with high-stakes trouble. In the case of Og's first tale it was physical death on the line. Og had a thriller on his tongue.

But Og later told stories about his emotions. How he was having to deal with past demons, like his father flicking pebbles at him when he was a boy, and when he fell in love with a cave girl who later got stepped on by a wooly mammoth. He notices that the women of the tribe—and, in secret, even some of the men—cry during the telling of these tales.

And pay him to tell more.

Og starts calling these "character-driven" stories but knows they are based on the same idea: a high-stakes threat to the characters' interior life and happiness.

And you know what? The essence of story has not changed, from Og to the early myths to the Greek drama to Stephen King to *Lost* and Pixar.

It's all about trouble and its two best friends—conflict and suspense.

EMOTIONS ON A ROLLER COASTER

Go to a theme park and ride a roller coaster. Then go home and write a novel. You might find that one feeds the other.

We all know a roller coaster plays with your body, primarily your stomach. It takes you up slowly, then shoots you down and around. There's a buildup that creates anticipation, then a payoff that is all thrills. Finally, you're let out—we hope—at a smooth, satisfying ending.

A novel is meant to be a thrill ride for the emotions. This doesn't mean only the large charges one would find in an action techno-thriller. Even a quiet character novel, done right, has the same dynamic going for it.

You, the author, are a manipulator of emotions. This is not a bad thing at all. Every artist wants to do that. The key to the art is to make the readers forget they are being played, so they can simply enjoy the experience.

Or maybe your goal is not simply entertainment, but to make people think. Michael Crichton was a novelist of this sort.

Perhaps you want to make people mad, because of an issue that chaps your hide. Edward Abbey wrote *The Monkey Wrench Gang* with sense of environmental outrage.

But in all cases, your ability to weave conflict and suspense into your novel is going to be what determines whether it is successful or not.

A well-structured plot is like that fabled bridge over troubled waters, like the Golden Gate in San Francisco. On one side you have the beginning and on the other side, the end. The solid pylons resting on the bedrock of the bay provide the turning points into each act of the novel. Your organic scenes weave together to form the suspension cables. All of this supports the deck and everything works together so the reader gets a view of the churning waters.

You direct them from one side to the other, from beginning to end. You control what happens at each stage of the journey.

At this point there are usually some protests. "I don't care about rules and techniques! You have to let it flow, man. I'll tell the story my way!"

Fine. Let it flow. But after all that flowing you want to shape your story into something people read, yes? Lots of people?

If you're okay with handing out copies of your experimental flow-novel to five or six people, that's fine, too.

And sell three copies. But you let it flow. If that's your goal, flow on.

But if you want to connect with a wide audience, you learn the fundamentals of the craft that make it happen.

Once you do, you can be as free as you like, knowing each step of the way what works and what doesn't. You now pour your imagination and vision into a structure that readers can relate to.

You have them hooked, just like Og.

DEFINITIONS

Conflict has long been recognized as the engine of story. Without conflict there is no drama. Without drama there is no interest. Without interest there is no reader. And no writing career.

In simplest terms, *conflict* is a clash between at least two incompatible sides. One of these sides must be personal, that is, having the ability to exercise conscious will.

For example, a storm rolling into the pleasant weather of a Midwestern town does not offer us conflict. There is no conscious will exerted by the storm or the nice day in the town.

If, however, a safety inspector for the Midwestern town has only two hours to prepare to meet this natural disaster, and takes steps to do so, there is conflict. He is exercising his will toward solving a problem.

This is the conflict involved in *man vs. nature* stories. Man has the will, nature offers the opposition.

But most dramatic narratives involve at least two human agents opposed to one another. They have opposing agendas. It's two dogs and one bone.

And they each have the ability to think and act toward getting the bone for themselves.

Suspense arises out of conflict. It is a subset of the dramatic question, Will the character involved in the conflict exercise his will in such a way as to overcome?

Suspense is the tightening of the emotional experience of the reader.

Think of it as a boxing match. The two combatants are in conflict. They are exercising their wills in a conscious effort to knock each other's block off.

Now suppose one fighter gets the other against the ropes and starts pummeling. The suspense of the moment is whether the trapped fighter will be knocked out. Or, if he's knocked to the canvas, will he get up?

Or what if the two fighters are circling each other, throwing jabs? The suspense question is who will land a good blow first?

Any number of suspense questions can be raised in the context of the overall conflict.

Your novel sets up a central clash, and suspense is what powers the reader through, turning pages, no matter what the genre.

Conflict lays a foundation. So in Part I we will be looking at how you create the best soil for this combat of wills. Out of that ground comes the suspense, which is the subject of Part II.

A note about my previous books on the craft. There are a few sections, most notably in chapters three and four of this book, that somewhat overlap material I covered in *Plot & Structure* and *Revision & Self-Editing*. This is unavoidable in a book covering conflict and suspense, so I have shaped those sections with the subject matter of this volume in mind. In this way, those who are unfamiliar with the other books will get what they need to improve the conflict and suspense in their writing.

And those who do know the other books will get a slightly different perspective and some essential review. This will deepen their understanding of the previous material, all with the goal of getting readers to say:

I COULDN'T PUT IT DOWN
. . . .

Ever since I started writing, the one compliment I prize most is when a reader says of one of my books, "I couldn't put it down."

That's what we're all about, isn't it? What's the alternative? The reader putting the book down, that's what. And deciding not to buy your next one.

It could even be worse, as when Dorothy Parker observed, "This is not a novel to be set aside lightly. It should be thrown with great force."

Our goal as storytellers is to keep the reader turning pages to the end. Conflict and suspense make that happen.

PART ONE
Conflict

CHAPTER 1
WHAT A GREAT STORY IS REALLY ALL ABOUT

What is the goal of the novel?

Is it to entertain? Teach? Preach? Change the world? Make the author a lot of money?

All of the above?

Certainly there is nothing wrong with entertaining fiction. Nor, if the author truly feels passionately about something, trying to get a message across. Sure, even change society for the better, like Harriett Beecher Stowe and *Uncle Tom's Cabin*.

A writer may care about style and the poetry of words. Or defying convention and experimenting with form.

It's even okay for a writer to make money!

But in the end, none of these objectives will work to their full potential unless they forge, in some way, *a satisfying emotional experience for the reader.*

By satisfying, I don't necessarily mean happy. Tragedy was the original intent of drama. But as Aristotle pointed out, the idea was to create emotion and then *catharsis,* thus making the audience better citizens. So the inner experience of the audience was primary.

Genre and tone don't matter so long as the emotions of the reader are engaged, intensified, and ultimately, after the last page, given a certain release. When you do all that you have a book that lingers in the mind long after it's over and causes people to talk about your fiction.

And that's the best form of marketing there is. Perhaps the only kind that works over the long haul.

Now, what jazzes certain readers may be the power of an idea. Or riffs of style. But those things work for *those readers* by gripping them emotionally.

Take Ayn Rand, for example. She touted a philosophy she called "objectivism," which is based on "the virtue of selfishness." Her novels are full of speeches on that subject. Even though that's directed at the mind, those who respond to her work *feel* she's offering a correct view of the world.

Amish fiction, a popular genre of recent years, appeals to readers who yearn for simpler times and admire strong religious convictions. It *feels good* to leave the chaos of the modern world for a little while.

On the other side of the spectrum is a novel like Elie Wiesel's *Night,* which creates emotions like horror (real-life horror, which is the scariest of all) and deep sadness. It succeeds not because it catalogues bad acts, but because the readers' emotions are yanked through the wringer, by way of identification with the characters.

Why is romance consistently the best-selling genre in the fiction world? Because the readers of that genre desire to *feel* something. Maybe it's because they're not feeling it in their actual lives and romance novels provide a vicarious experience. Maybe some are of a certain profile that loves the idea of love and wants to see it vindicated. Whatever it is, these stories sell because they provide a satisfying emotional experience for a large number of readers.

How about the genre books that are specifically designed to be short and make you cry? Again, it's a matter of emotion. Somebody reading a Nicholas Sparks novel wants to go through a box of tissues. Sparks caters to that market. A big market.

But no matter the type of novel, you have to make it an emotional ride. Conflict and suspense are your tools for doing that.

A WORD ABOUT DEATH

The stakes in an emotionally satisfying novel have to be *death.*

That's right, death. Somebody has to be in danger of dying, and almost always that someone is the Lead character.

This applies to any genre, from light comedy to darkest tragedy.

Here's why: There are three kinds of death: physical, professional, psychological. One or more of these must be present in your novel.

Physical

This is obvious, isn't it? If your Lead character will actually die, as in stop breathing, he had better win in the arena of conflict. Because if he doesn't, he's toast.

Obviously the stakes are the highest here. Win or die.

Choose a thriller at random and you're almost always going to find physical death at stake.

It might be because the Lead character has happened upon a secret that the bad guys don't want revealed, such as the idealistic law student Mitch McDeere in John Grisham's *The Firm*.

Or maybe the Lead character is in the "trouble business," like Jonathan Grave, the covert rescuer in John Gilstrap's series that begins with *No Mercy*. In each book, somebody dies if Grave and his team do not succeed.

But physical is not the only kind of death that creates compelling fiction.

Professional

When the novel revolves around the Lead's calling in life, the failure to win should mean that her career is over, her calling a waste, her training a fraud, her future a cloud. It must mean that there is something on the line here that will make or break the Lead in the area of her life's work.

This is the thread that makes Michael Connelly's Harry Bosch series so compelling. Harry has a working rule that obsesses him. As he puts it in *The Last Coyote*, "Everybody counts or nobody counts. That's it. It means I bust my ass to make a case whether it's a prostitute or the mayor's wife. That's my rule."

For Harry, there's no getting around this drive, so every case becomes a matter of solving it or *dying professionally*. He is in danger of being drummed off the force at times or in not being able to go on.

Make the job and the particular case matter that much. A lawyer with the one client he needs to vindicate (as in Barry Reed's *The Verdict*, made into the hit movie starring Paul Newman); the trainee whose law enforcement career could be over before it begins (as in Thomas Harris's *The Silence of the Lambs*); a cop with a last chance case involving horrific killings (*The Night Gardener* by George Pelecanos).

Psychological

Dying on the inside. We say that about certain events. We should say it about the Lead character. Imminent danger of dying psychologically if the conflict isn't won.

Holden Caulfield in *The Catcher in the Rye*. If he doesn't find authenticity in the world, he's going to die psychologically. (Does he? At the end, we're not sure, but it's close.) In fact, if he doesn't find this reason, we're pretty sure actual death—by suicide—is inevitable.

Psychological death is crucial to understand, as it elevates the emotions of fiction like no other aspect.

This is the key to all romances, isn't it? If the two lovers don't get together, they will each miss out on their soul mate. Their lives will be incurably damaged. Since readers of most romances know they're going to end up together, it's all the more important to create this illusion of imminent psychological death.

This is also the secret to lighter fare. The people in the comedy need to think they're in a tragedy, usually over something trivial. But the "something trivial" has to matter so much to the characters that *they* believe they will suffer psychological death if they don't gain their objective.

For example, Oscar Madison in *The Odd Couple* loves being a happy-go-lucky slob. He loves not cleaning up his apartment, smoking and eating whenever he wants, playing poker to all hours, and so on. When neat freak Felix Unger moves in, that life Oscar loves so much is threatened. In Oscar's mind, it's so bad he gets close to wanting to kill Felix.

Being a happy slob matters to Oscar. We believe it even though it's trivial, and there's the comedy.

Or take any episode of *Seinfeld*. It's always about how important something stupid is to the characters. Like the soup in "The Soup Nazi" episode. Oh, the soup! If Jerry doesn't get this soup, he will die inside. In fact, there comes a moment when Jerry must choose between his girlfriend, who has offended the soup Nazi, and the bowl of soup.

It's a painful battle going on!

He chooses the soup.

Psychological death is powerful in any genre.

Let's say your story is about someone accused of absconding with company funds. He's an embezzler. I wrote such a story, *Watch Your Back*. In the book, Cameron Cates works for a big insurance and investment company. He devises a way to set up a false account and to transfer funds to an offshore bank.

What if there was no way he could get caught? The suspense would be mild: "Gee, how much does he get in the bank before the company stops the flow?"

Is that enough? Hardly. Thus the risk of being caught, not only by the company but the FBI, must be apparent and explicit from the start. Because getting caught in those terms means the virtual death of a long prison stretch.

John Howard Lawson pointed this out nearly eighty years ago in his classic volume, *Theory and Technique of Playwriting*. In it, he says that a conflict that fails to reach this magnitude is a conflict of "weak wills." Lawson says, "In the Greek and Elizabethan tragedy, the point of maximum strain is generally reached in the death of the hero; he is crushed by the forces that oppose him, or he takes his own life in recognition of his defeat."

Yes, death. Physical in classic tragedy. But also professional and psychological today.

Lawson also defines the character of drama as conflict "in which the conscious will, exerted for the accomplishment of specific and understandable aims, is sufficiently strong to bring the conflict to a point of crisis."

This crisis, I would simply add, involves a type of death.

Do these two things:

- Think about what is at stake for your Lead character in the main conflict of the book. Define it right now. Write that down.

- Define what kind of death can be overhanging the action. You have to choose one as primary. You can have another from of death that comes into play during the story, but only one should arc over the story line.

EXAMPLE: You're writing a thriller about hit men chasing a former colleague who has stolen money from the "big man." Obviously physical death is in play. It's possible to include a subplot about the Lead's personal life as a matter of psychological death. Maybe there is someone he has to forgive, or who had to forgive him, in order to make him whole. But the primary mode of death that covers the story is physical.

EXAMPLE: You're writing a legal thriller about a prosecutor with a highly publicized case his bosses at city hall want him to win … only he becomes convinced the defendant is innocent. If he says anything about it, it will be the end of his career. Professional death.

Or it's a defense lawyer who is used to settling cases for easy resolution and fees, who gets a client accused of shoplifting. Does this involve professional death? Not yet. You have to devise the story elements that will make the case so important that it will at least feel like professional death to the lawyer.

How can you do that? You can figure out ways the client means something personal to the lawyer. Maybe it's on older woman, the one who used to take care of him when he was a kid. He's her only hope. She has no money and no family left. The case starts to matter to him.

Or the shoplifter is a kid who is headed down the wrong road, maybe a road the lawyer was once on. He decides to try to be the one to help the kid, who is from a horrible home. The kid does something worse while he's out on bail, something that might mean long imprisonment. Now the lawyer has to save the kid or it will feel like he's failed in his professional duty.

Maybe this is the story of a big-time lawyer who thinks he's lost his mojo as a trial lawyer. Maybe this little shoplifting case is his way back to getting his confidence so he can handle bigger cases again. But if he loses, well, it's all over. He'll never be able to walk into a courtroom again.

The point here is to ratchet up the elements of the story so it feels like a setback is going to be horrible for the work life of the professional.

EXAMPLE: Your story is about a thirty-year-old divorced woman who moves to a small town to start all over again. What in her background makes this essential to her psychological well-being?

Maybe her husband has kept her from pursuing her dream of being an artist. In her new town she's determined to do the thing she loves most. But if she fails, the dream dies. She has limited funds. How is she going to gain the means to live and also fund her art?

What if her father lives in this town and she has come to reconcile with him after years of separation? What if he's dying? If she does not get some sort of closure, she will carry an open wound with her the rest of her life. That's a kind of dying on the inside.

EXAMPLE: You've written a wild, comedic novel about a professional wrestler who decides to become an opera singer. How can you work death into it? In comedy, it's usually something trivial that the character has elevated to enormous importance.

What if he has fallen in love with a woman who is obsessed with opera? She thinks wrestling is only for Neanderthals. To win her love (psychological death at stake), he signs up for opera lessons.

This exercise at the beginning of your novel-writing process will save you a great deal of time and stress down the line. The stronger this foundation in death, the higher the stakes of your story. And the fixes will be easier when it comes time to revise.

THE LINKS OF EMOTIONAL CONFLICT

My working definition of a successful novel is this: *the emotionally satisfying account of how a character deals with imminent death.*

Once you understand that, you can build, organically, the links in the chain of emotional conflict. The chain looks like this:

> CONFLICT (Possibility of imminent death)
> ACTION (Steps to avoid death)
> + SUSPENSE (Unresolved tension associated with action)
> EMOTIONALLY SATISFYING EXPERIENCE

Remember, suspense does not always mean a bomb under a table or a team of bad guys behind the hotel door. Suspense is any unresolved tension in the story that makes the reader want to see what happens next.

If the reader does not care what happens next, she puts the book down and doesn't buy your next one. That's why this change is so important.

You must have emotional connectivity on every page, indeed every paragraph. It must vibrate through the entire book.

CHAPTER 2

BRAINSTORMING
FOR CONFLICT

H ow do you begin to write a story with conflict?

1. You come up with ideas that connect with you emotionally.
2. You nudge them in a direction that offers the greatest possibilities for conflict.

So where do you find such ideas?

Everywhere.

Your problem should never be a shortage of ideas. It should be deciding which idea you will develop into a novel.

Become an idea-generating machine. With a little bit of training, your brain will start generating spark after spark. Your creative mind is a muscle. The more you use it, the more nimble it becomes.

This is what you want. You want an imagination that works even when you're sleeping and when you're just observing life ("the Boys in the Basement" in Stephen King's wonderful metaphor).

By learning to brainstorm for conflict, you'll have your writer's mind on active duty at all times, ready to pick up potential ideas and, even more, begin shaping them into concepts with conflict at the core.

Here are some ways to begin this training process.

1. With a concept, or "What if …"
2. An image
3. A setting

4. A story world
5. An obsession
6. Steal old plots
7. An issue
8. First lines
9. Your passionate center
10. Dictionary game

1. CONCEPT OR "WHAT IF ... ?"

Perhaps the most honored creative game of all is the *What If? Game*. Storytellers from the campfires of Mesopotamia to the screens of the Kindle have come up with tales by asking that question or having their writer's mind ask it for them.

When you engage in the game, train yourself to think in terms of conflict.

Let's say you're driving down the street and you see a man in a nice suit on the corner. He's wearing old tennis shoes. You wonder, what's odd about that?

You continue on, driving and thinking about your idea. You are careful not to crash into the car in front of you, of course (though, if you do, you can use it as material).

So you think in terms of conflict. Why would a man in a suit be in beat-up tennis shoes? Has he been recently fired from a great middle-management job? Or is he a homeless guy who has managed to find a good suit? Was he once a lawyer?

Wait a second. The last idea triggers some interest. Lawyers are always fair game.

What if ... he was once a high-powered lawyer brought down by a trumped-up ethics violation? Framed by his former partner?

And now he's out for revenge.

Revenge is good for conflict.

Or you're driving down the highway (notice how often you're driving and playing this game?) and see a billboard for some sort of sunscreen. A beautiful woman in a bikini and sunglasses is lounging under a hot sun as a bronzed Adonis applies the protective goo to one of her honey-colored legs.

What if ... he is a hit man who is supposed to kill her? What can we do with that? He's fallen in love with her, which brings up all sorts of conflict with those who hired him. His own life may be on the line now.

... she is having an affair with him? Who is she married to? Maybe the most dangerous man in Las Vegas. Or, for a more literary take, an older man she has fallen out of love with.

... he is rubbing her not with sunscreen, but a substance from another planet that will turn her into a half woman/half squid with a thirst for blood?

You take it from there. Come up with at least five other "What if ..." scenarios. Make that your goal each time you get an idea spark. List five to ten possibilities. The last few should be the hardest to come up with but may in fact turn out to be the best.

Let each idea involve a potential Lead character.

Look at each item on your list and tweak them until they are packed with conflict. Come up with an opposition character who has a strong reason to oppose your Lead. Later, choose the top two to develop into a one-page pitch.

My novel *Try Dying* was based upon a news item I read one day. It seemed to be one of those strange stories that happens in a town like L.A. I cut the piece out of the newspaper and threw it in my idea box, where I keep notes and clippings of all kinds.

It was in there for a few years, and I'd see it every now and again. It always intrigued me. I never knew what to do with it. Finally, I just sat down and rewrote the item, as if I were a reporter:

> On a wet Tuesday morning in December, Ernesto Bonilla, twenty-eight, shot his twenty-three-year-old wife, Alejandra, in the back yard of their West 45th Street home in South Los Angeles. As Alejandra lay bleeding to death, Ernesto proceeded to drive their Ford Explorer to the westbound Century Freeway connector where it crossed over the Harbor Freeway and pulled to a stop on the shoulder.
>
> Bonilla stepped around the back of the SUV, ignoring the rain and the afternoon drivers on their way to LAX and the west side, and placed the barrel of his .38 caliber pistol into his mouth and fired.
>
> His body fell over the shoulder and plunged one hundred feet, hitting the roof of a Toyota Camry heading northbound on the Harbor

Freeway. The impact crushed the roof of the Camry. The driver, Jacqueline Dwyer, twenty-seven, an elementary school teacher from Reseda,
died at the scene.

And that's all I had. I felt this could be the opening of a novel, but then what?
What kind of novel? Who was it about? How could this bizarre occurrence
lead me to a compelling story?

I started to ask "What if ..." and the third or fourth thing that came to
me was, "What if this was being narrated by the man who was engaged to
the driver, Jacqueline Dwyer? I found myself writing the next lines:

This would have been simply another dark and strange coincidence, the
sort of thing that shows up for a two-minute report on the local news—
with live remote from the scene—and maybe gets a follow-up the next
day. But eventually the story would go away, fading from the city's collective memory.

But this story did not go away. Not for me. Because Jacqueline Dwyer was the woman I was going to marry.

This became the first page of the novel and hardly changed at all. I didn't
know who the *I* was yet, but I saw the possibility for huge conflict to come.
And it did.

So play "What if ..." all the time. If you start doing it consciously, pretty
soon your writer's mind will run on automatic pilot, feeding you story idea
after idea. Any "What if ..." idea can be noodled into a conflict situation.
You don't even have to be driving:

1. Find an ad in a magazine or tabloid that has two or more people in it.
2. Jot down five "What ifs ..." that harbor conflict between characters.
3. Choose the best one and write a one-page scenario on the develop-
   ing story. It may be one you want to keep.

2. AN IMAGE

We are a visual culture, moved and shaped by what we see. In the brainstorming for conflict stage, getting images uploaded to your writer's
mind provides an infinite supply of story material. Here are some ways
to tweak it:

Music

I once imagined almost an entire screenplay from a scene that came to me listening to a movie soundtrack. It was a piece that gave me a picture of a father and a son together, on a hillside. The son was fourteen years old. The man was troubled about the son. And then the son burst into tears.

The music gave me the image and the emotion. I used this to imagine the conflict between the son and the father and then the inner conflict in both.

Other scenes started falling into place. All from a little music.

Make playlists of mood tunes. Mine are almost entirely film soundtracks. I have them subdivided into things like *heartfelt, adventurous, suspenseful, fighting*. If I'm about to write a particular scene and I know the mood I want, I'll go to that playlist.

To generate material I sometimes put my soundtracks on a random mix, letting images play in my mind until something comes up that demands to be dramatized.

You never know what you'll come up with when you switch from *Ben-Hur* to *Dirty Harry*, but I guarantee it will be interesting.

When an image really grabs you, stop and write about it for five minutes. Let the music play as you write, with the scene reeling like a movie in your mind. Keep an eye out for the points where characters are opposed to each other.

You don't have to know what's going on right away. Record to discover.

Dreams

What are your dreams trying to tell you? You don't have to be Dr. Freud to let dreams suggest story material.

Keep a pad by your bed so you can record your dreams if they awaken you.

At the very least, write notes in the morning.

Some people say they can't remember their dreams when they wake up. I've been told that if you get back into your sleep position for a while, the dreams might come back to you.

It's worth a shot because dreams can give us subterranean material we can't get at any other way.

Movie Mind

Your mind will play you a movie if you let it. And it's free.

Carve out some time in a quiet place for this exercise. The only direction you are going to give your mind is to come up with some conflict.

Imagine two characters and set them down in a scene. The more vivid you imagine the setting, the better.

Let the characters suggest who they are but don't settle for plain vanilla. Keep watching until the characters develop some originality. Begin to see them.

Sometimes it helps if you cast these characters, letting actors from the past or the present "audition" for a part in the drama.

Once you've got the setting and the characters, watch the scene until conflict occurs. It can be an argument, a physical confrontation, points of confusion, other characters entering the scene, random events, an obsession, an odd action.

Keep the scene going until it grabs you. At some point, it will. Guaranteed.

Nurture this idea by setting down a little bit of the backstory, how these two characters got to be who they are.

You may find yourself caught up in the beginning of a tale packed with the clash of conscious wills.

3. SETTINGS

What physical locations offer possibilities for novel length conflict? Answer: Anywhere! If you know how to look at it.

I live in Los Angeles. I've rarely used any other setting because there is such a wide variety of places right here in my hometown, each one offering a unique kind of conflict.

Take Skid Row. I set a novel there because every corner offers a sense of dread and danger. From the seedy transient hotels to the sidewalks where drug deals go down. It's hard to find anywhere there isn't some form of illegality or craziness on Skid Row.

I've also used the lovely San Fernando Valley, which at one time was the ideal suburb for all of America. Mostly Caucasian in population. Now there are at least one hundred different languages spoken in parts of the Valley. And almost as many gangs to go with them.

But a big city is not the only place to find conflict.

Consider the lovely, rural climes of Washington's Puget Sound. Ideal for a tourist getaway? Not for Gregg Olsen, who places the grisliest of serial killers there, and then plays off the forbidding nature of the undeveloped setting.

Here's Olsen's description from *Victim Six*:

> Even in the midst of a spring or summer's day with a cloudless sky marred only by the contrails of a jet overhead, the woods of Kitsap County were always blindfold dark. It had been more than eighty years since the region was first logged by lumberjacks culling the forest for income; now it was developers who were clearing the land for new tracts of ticky-tacky homes. Quiet. Dark. Secluded.

Notice the words Olsen chooses: *marred, blindfold dark. Quiet. Dark. Secluded.* And then notice what happens by adding another element to the setting—the killer:

> The woods were full of dark secrets, which is exactly what had attracted him in the first place. He'd noticed the brush pickers when he'd been out of the hunt several weeks before, when he had an urge to do *something*. A crammed-full station wagon was parked on the side of the road as close to the edge as possible without going into the ditch. They poured from their vehicle, talking and laughing, as if what they were about to do was some kind of fun adventure.
>
> He sized up the women.
>
> Most were small.
>
> Good.

City or country, rural or populated, every setting holds the possibility not just for conflict between characters, but for being part of the conflict itself.

That's where you need to take your mind.

In *Good in Bed*, Cannie Shapiro's infant daughter is in critical condition at a Philadelphia hospital. The circumstance has rubbed raw all sorts of issues for Cannie, from her father relationship to her fitness as a mother.

Author Jennifer Weiner uses this as an opportunity for the setting to conflict with Cannie:

> I walked and walked, and it was as if God had fitted me with special
> glasses, where I could only see the bad things, the sad things, the pain
> and misery of life in the city, the trash kicked into corners instead of
> the flowers planted in the window boxes. I could see the husbands
> and wives fighting, but not kissing or holding hands. I could see the
> little kids careening through the streets on stolen bicycles, scream-
> ing insults and curses, and grown men who sounded like they were
> breakfasting on their own mucus, leering at women with unashamed
> lecherous eyes. I could smell the stink of the city in summer: horse
> piss and hot tar and the grayish, sick exhaust the buses spewed. The
> manhole covers leaked steam, the sidewalks belched heat from the
> subways churning below.

Try This:

1. Start with your own living situation. Write a page of straight description of your immediate setting—work from your residence outward to neighboring homes, streets, town centers, parks, undeveloped land, and so on.

2. Take apart the individual settings and give them their own page. For example, maybe your original page had this:

> The main highway is about a mile from my apartment. I can hear the
> trucks at night, hauling whatever it is they haul up north toward Stockton
> or down south toward San Diego.

Put those lines at the top of a fresh page.

3. Now make up a character alone, in trouble, in that setting, and write a couple of paragraphs where the setting, not another character, adds to the conflict:

> She stumbled up to the shoulder of the main highway. The gravel bit into
> her knees. How had she gotten here?
> The honk of a giant truck kicked her heart. Then the lights of the
> oncoming monster blinded her. She threw herself backward, falling on

the incline. Above her the truck slammed by, showering her with bits of tiny rock.

Try that for every one of the settings you've described. What you're doing is training your mind to be on the lookout for ominous locations, which are anywhere you choose.

5. Now pick a location you're unfamiliar with. Do you live in New York? Try Sioux City, Iowa, or Kent, England. Do some online research. Familiarize yourself with the place via travel sites, blogs, firsthand accounts.

6. Now repeat steps 1 through 3 for this new location. You will be pleased, if not downright amazed, how these exercises get you juiced about writing. That's the magic of conflict.

7. Look at your Work in Progress (we'll just call it WIP from now on). Go to every passage where you describe the physical location. Highlight in yellow each line that is neutral in description—that is, where the description is not adding to the tone you're after.

   Example: You're writing about a runaway teenager arriving at a house in the dead of winter:

   Icicles were under the eaves.

   That's okay as far as it goes, but you can do more:

   The icicles pointed down like accusing fingers.

   Highlight in red every passage that does "double duty," that sets up a feeling or tone of conflict as well as describes.

8. Eliminate or change every passage in yellow until there are only passages in red.

Note that the conflict does not have to be outright dread (though there's never anything wrong with that!). Even a feeling of discomfort in the character can be enhanced, thus adding to the inner conflict of the passage:

The sun beat me with unforgiving heat.

> The car still smelled like Henry. She could almost hear his accusing
> voice from the passenger side.

You don't have to stay at home. You can read about a setting. When something catches your eye, do a little research. One day I read a news report in *The New York Times* that began with this paragraph:

> New cracks in Hawaii's surface continued to spew lava on Monday in
> the latest punctuation of Kilauea Volcano, the mythical home of the
> Hawaiian fire goddess Pele ... The fissures prompted the closing of parts
> of Hawaii Volcanoes National Park, including Chain of Craters Road
> and other trails and a campground in the area. The observatory also
> warned of lethal levels of sulfur dioxide near the vents. However, be-
> cause the eruptions were in a "very remote area" of the park, they did
> not pose a threat to people or towns, said Janet Babb, a geologist with
> the observatory.

But in my brainstorming, there very definitely will be a threat to people and towns.

Now I can do some research on volcanoes, the campgrounds mentioned, and so on. That doesn't mean I have to stay in Hawaii.

What if there's an eruption of something under the earth in a campground in Arizona?

Why not? What does that suggest?

Brainstorming will tell me.

4. STORY WORLD

Related to setting is the *story world*. This takes not just the physical locale, but describes what happens within a certain milieu.

For example, if you are writing a legal thriller, your story world will include law offices, courtrooms, and places where lawyers hang out. You want to do research on what happens in these places, looking for natural conflict points.

If you want to write about the CIA, get to know the culture.

If you want to write about a church choir, get to know what happens behind the pulpit. Plenty of conflict points can be found there, as well.

A great place to find out about story worlds is on specific blogs. I once wrote a series of thrillers where the hero had to hide out at a Benedictine monastery. I found a couple of blogs written by Benedictine nuns. Their description of the day-to-day in the monastery was invaluable.

Story world is different from setting, which is strictly the physical locale. Instead we're talking about what goes on in a character's sphere—what social, professional, and personal contacts she has and how they affect her.

Historical Settings

If you write in a historical genre you simply move the search for conflict to the past. You can do double duty here by giving a sense of place and, most important, how a point-of-view character perceives it.

In a historical novel dealing with Los Angeles in the 1920s, I had a character from the Midwest arrive in the City of Angels:

> He passed through the depot, getting stares from some of the passengers and well-wishers there. He was dirty to be sure, but hadn't they seen a guy down on his luck before?
>
> He walked on and found himself in a place that looked like Mexico after all. A plaza and active marketplace marked the spot. Most of the people were brown skinned. A street sign announced that Doyle was on Olvera Street.
>
> Further on he walked and seemed to pass through a curtain into a completely different realm.
>
> Streetcars and automobiles clanged and chugged down busy thoroughfares. A thick river of people ebbed and flowed on the sidewalks— men in suits and straw skimmers, women in walking dresses and wide-brimmed hats. Signs attached to every building announced businesses and amusements—Boos Bros. Cafeteria, Loews State Theatre, Nerney's Grocery and Meat Market, Woolworth's Five and Dime Store, the National Hotel, Moline's Auto & Supplies, F. W. Pierce Furniture and the towering edifice of the U.S. Post Office.
>
> What manner of place was this?
>
> Doyle stopped at a corner and fished a crumpled newspaper out of the trash can. It was a few pages from the *Los Angeles Times*. Some listings about real estate in a place called Lankershim—Many lots at

> $1450! A wonderland to come! Gateway to the beautiful San Fernando
> Valley!—and a caricature of a man calling himself Saving Sam, who sold
> automobile tires. He had a little mustache, this cartoon character, which
> made him look like one of those snake oil salesmen from the Old West
> dime novels. Doyle supposed Los Angeles was where the new hucksters
> were flooding. It was wide open, and there were plenty of sheep ready
> for fleecing.

The description is filled with detail but also the character's feeling of being a fish out of water and perhaps a mark for con artists.

Let the readers know how your characters internalize the setting.

Social

What sort of demographic does your Lead character inhabit? If it's an upper-crust, Ivy League educated set, does she belong there? Is she rebelling against it? Or has she come from the "wrong side of the tracks" and can't quite fit in?

Create a background for your character that is in conflict with the current social setting. In Tom Wolfe's *I Am Charlotte Simmons,* a girl from a conservative Southern town enrolls in an elite college. Her first encounter with fellow students at Dupont is when her father, who has a mermaid tattoo on his forearm, is helping Charlotte move her things into the dorm. The mermaid stands out prominently:

> Charlotte caught two of the boys in the mauve shirts sneaking glances
> at it. One said to the other in a low voice: "Nice ink." The other tried to
> suppress a snigger. Charlotte was mortified.

It becomes immediately apparent that the manners and customs at Dupont are completely foreign to Charlotte. When she is finally back in her dorm room with new roommate Beverly, Charlotte observes Beverly dressed up for a night out:

> She was wearing black pants and a lavender silk shirt, sleeveless and
> open three or four buttonholes' worth in front. It showed off her suntan ....
> She had put a peach-colored polish on her nails; it looked great on the
> tips of her perfectly tanned fingers.

> "I'm meeting some friends at a restaurant," she explained, "and I'm
> late. I'll put away all that stuff when I come back." She gestured toward
> a mountain of bags and boxes piled this way and that.
>
> Charlotte was astonished. The very first day wasn't even over, and Bev-
> erly was *going out to a restaurant*. Charlotte couldn't imagine such a thing.

But that's nothing compared to her first visit to the co-ed bathroom, where she hears a *prodigious pig-bladdery splattering sphincter-spasmed bowel explosion, followed by, in rapid succession,* plop, plop, plop *and a deep male voice ...*

Then another male voice from an adjoining stall comments on the noises, and the two voices go back and forth. When she tries to wash up and scurry out, she sees in the mirror two guys:

> Each had a can of beer in his hand. *But that was not allowed!*

And so on. Wolfe wastes no opportunity for Charlotte to run up against some strange practice brought on by her new situation. Explore those areas in your own character's life. Social conflict is some of the best material in fiction, because it affects the inside of the character as much as the outside.

5. OBSESSION

Come up with a character who has an obsession. This is the advice of Ray Bradbury, who then counsels that you follow the character wherever he starts to run.

And he will run into obstacles. He will run into people who want to stop him, throw him off his game, maybe even kill him. (Remember, there are three kinds of death. Start thinking about those now.)

What are the chief obsessions? Love, sex, money, power, fame, validation, and revenge.

For each of these there are innumerable variations on the theme. A ten-year-old girl and a fifty-year-old man can both be obsessed with fame, but for entirely different reasons. Getting deep into those reasons provides fertile soil for a story with conflict.

Make a list of the types of characters who would oppose the character's obsession: family members, rivals, friends, enemies. From this cast, you will be able to select the best opposition for your Lead character.

6. STEAL OLD PLOTS

I once read a thriller about a small town where people were being trans-
formed into animal-like creatures who feasted on human flesh. One of the
characters in the town, a child, was convinced her parents were not really
her parents anymore.

As I read that I thought of one of my favorite movies, *Invasion of the
Body Snatchers* (the 1956 version). At the beginning a little boy is running away from his mother because he doesn't believe she is his mother
anymore.

And I'm thinking, this novelist is liberally borrowing from the movie.

Then a bit later in the novel, it's revealed that the animal-people are the
result of biological experiments by a mad genius.

And now I'm thinking, the author has borrowed H.G. Wells's plot for
The Island of Dr. Moreau.

I thought I'd caught this author, but then he gave me one last twist. He
had a character think that the whole thing reminded him of *Invasion of the
Body Snatchers*, and another referred to *The Island of Dr. Moreau.*

He was winking at readers like me, who knew what he was doing!

And this author does know what he's doing. His name is Dean Koontz.
The book is *Midnight.*

Do don't be afraid to borrow, steal, update, or combine old plots and
pack them with conflict.

7. AN ISSUE

What issue in life really gets you mad? Maybe it's political. You have plenty
of issues to choose from here! It could be social or legal or spiritual.

Make a list right now of those issues that you find yourself thinking
about most of the time. Now think about making that issue either the central element of your plot or a subplot strand in your novel.

But here's the secret: You must be fair to both sides. If you aren't you'll
get preachy and melodramatic.

Let's take a hot-button issue like abortion. It hard to imagine something
that makes for a more contentious debate.

No matter what your view, you task as a writer is to "walk in the other person's shoes." To see things from both perspectives and justify each position in the minds of the characters. You are not arguing before Congress. You're writing stories about complex human beings.

If you are fair to both sides, even while advocating for one position, your book is going to be much more meaningful than if you made things pure black and white. Trust me on this. Real conflict over an issue is found in the gray areas.

8. FIRST LINES

Dean Koontz, in his 1981 book *How to Write Best-Selling Fiction*, had some advice for creating story line:

> Sit at your typewriter [yes, he used the word typewriter] and, without a great deal of cerebral exercise, pound out a gripping opening sentence or paragraph. It is not necessary or even desirable to think about where the story will go or what it will be about before you type that opening. Just do it. The less planning you put into this exercise, the more freely you allow these narrative hooks to just roll off the top of your head, the greater the likelihood that the experiment will succeed.

As an example, Koontz tells how he was doing this exercise one day and typed the words: "You ever killed anything?" Roy asked.

He stared at the line for a moment and it seemed to him that Roy would be a boy of fourteen. Suddenly everything seemed to unfold in his writer's mind, and he wrote two pages in ten minutes, a conversation between Roy and a younger boy named Colin. The ideas just kept flowing and Koontz wrote a quick outline. The book, *The Voice of the Night*, became a hit under one of Koontz's numerous pseudonyms.

All because of playing the first-line game

Joseph Heller wrote this line, without knowing anything else: "In the office in which I work there are five people of whom I am afraid." This became the genesis of his massive satirical novel, *Something Happened*. (The line was moved further in by Heller once the book was finished, but it was the line itself that suggested the larger work.)

1. Carve out half an hour of time for this game.
2. Write a string of first lines on a page, leaving a space between them.
3. Try various ways of opening, from dialogue to character actions.
4. Feel free to expand an opening line into a paragraph.
5. When you've done ten or more, stop and look them over. Which ones grab you?

9. YOUR PASSIONATE CENTER

Criminal defense lawyers are particularly reviled these days. But they have an essential part to play in our justice system. Their job, especially for public defenders, is a hard one, because, in fact, most clients are indeed guilty.

So the question they'll get most often is, "How can you defend someone you know did it?"

The answer is, they believe in the Constitutional right to trial. That is what they are defending. So most criminal defense lawyers I know are passionately sold out to the guarantees affording those accused of crimes. This lets them do their job to the utmost, which they must if the system is to work. The Constitution of the United States is their passionate center.

What is yours? In every idea you come up with, there is the seed of your own passion if you dig down deep enough.

Let's take a homeless lawyer for a moment. What if he is particularly upset about the way the homeless are treated in his city? How do *you* feel about it? Define that for yourself and then heat up the passion. Or you can substitute in the feelings you get about something else.

Do This:

Make a list of the ten things you care about most. Then take some time to write a paragraph or two about *why* these things matter to you. Use this list as a springboard for ideas to write about.

10. DICTIONARY GAME

When all else fails, there is one idea-generating game you can play anytime, anywhere. In fact, you can use this game when you're in the middle of a project and don't know what to write next.

You simply open a dictionary at random and plop your finger down on the page. Take the word you find and write for two minutes on whatever it brings to mind.

Then step back, analyze, and turn those notes into a basis for conflict. I'm going to do this right now, totally spontaneously.

The word I turned to was *flash*. I wrote this:

> There's a flash of lightning. It illuminates someone in the rain. I'm standing outside a little shack in the woods and it seems like a horror movie. A clichéd horror movie. So the hulking presence that comes toward me might look like a serial killer to my mind, but he's really a woman. A very large woman who is lost. Why is she lost in the rain? She's crying. She's not all there. She is in a plain dress, like a farmer's wife. Maybe I'm in Kansas. Where am I? I haven't got time to find out, because she has fallen to her knees. I help her up and bring her into the cabin, where I've got a fire going. I get a blanket to put around her shoulders but when I get back to her she is standing up and says, "I know where Bugsy Siegel buried a million dollars."

Now I step back and look at this thing, all inspired by the word *flash*. Is there an idea lurking here that gives me a little juice?

Well, yes, the idea that Bugsy Siegel buried a million dollars somewhere.

I think I am going to leave this poor, wet woman in the cabin all alone. I hope she finds a story to be in someday.

But for now, I'm thinking there's an ex-cop whose father knew Bugsy Siegel and on his deathbed whispered about the million bucks. Suddenly, out of nowhere, some very bad people want to talk to this ex-cop.

And I'm off to story nurturing.

This process took all of five minutes. There is no way I would have arrived at Bugsy Siegel's millions on my own. The word *flash* led to a scene that led all the way to a random comment, which became the plot idea.

That's the fun of the dictionary game. You never know where you're going to end up. Once you have a trove of plot possibilities, it's time to think about creating the solid foundation you need for conflict to be at its peak in your story. That's the subject of the next chapter.

CHAPTER 3
THE FOUNDATIONS OF CONFLICT

When you begin to construct a novel full of conflict, tension, and suspense (and why write any other kind of novel?), you work from the bottom up.

That is, if you want individual scenes with conflict, and individual beats with tension, you don't plug those things in at random.

You construct a solid foundation that will yield the conflict you need at every point in the story.

Without the right foundation, your story will lean away from interest, like that tower in Pisa. The poor architect, once construction started, couldn't do anything about the too-soft soil. He couldn't prop it up or counterbalance.

It was doomed to lean forever.

Don't let that be true of your novel.

There are four elements that will make your foundation solid. I summarize these with the acronym LOCK:

1. **L**ead worth following
2. **O**bjective (with death overhanging)
3. **C**onfrontation
4. **K**nock-out ending

Now some of you are NOPs, No Outline People. You are also called "Pantsers," as in Seat-of-the-Pants writers. You like to frolic freely through the tulips of your imagination. Every morning you prance feral and wild in the fields, falling in love with your writing, enraptured with the wonder of it all.

And some of you are OPs, the Outline People. Your spiritual father is the Prussian military strategist Carl von Clausewitz. Everything regimented and in place, for that is how you win the war!

Both sides have something to commend them, and it's possible to dwell in between. No matter what your preference, however, you still can't shirk the foundation.

That means you, Pantser. Even you. And believe me, if you get these right at the start, your dancing will be a whole lot more satisfying and your novel a whole lot stronger.

A LEAD WORTH FOLLOWING

You can't just throw random people together and think up some trouble and call it conflict. That may work for a page, but only because the reader is asking: Who are these people and why should I care about their trouble?

That's the first, nonnegotiable key to conflict in fiction: The reader must care about the people it's happening to. That creates an emotional investment in the characters and a desire to see where the trouble leads.

So you begin with a Lead worth following.

Readers become tied to the world of a story not through ideas or setting or style, but through characters. And the most important character is your Lead (or protagonist). The successful novel has at least one Lead character readers think is worth following.

First you need to know what kind of Lead you're creating. You have three choices.

Positive Lead

The positive Lead is what we would traditionally call the hero. He or she, broadly speaking, represents the values of the community. The community in this case is us, the readers. We support the Lead in his pursuits.

This was the purpose of the heroic myths. By going out into the dark world and conquering the monsters, the hero was representing the audience and their collective conscience.

This does not mean the Lead character is perfect. It only means that we are on his side. We want to see him victorious.

Robin Hood, even though he's an outlaw in the world of his story, is positive because he's on the right side. He stands for justice and protects the weak.

David Copperfield and Oliver Twist. We root for them. Clarice Starling in *The Silence of the Lambs*. Mitch McDeere in *The Firm*. Luke Skywalker. Each of these characters is in the midst of troubles, trying to do the right thing.

Negative Lead

A negative Lead is one who is doing things that are antithetical to community values. He might be a total misanthrope, like Scrooge, who spends his days counting his own money, exploiting poor clerks, and railing against charities and Christmas.

Or she might be a self-centered coquette like Scarlett O'Hara, who wants what she wants when she wants it.

The question here is, how do you hook the reader with an emotional investment in such characters? Why, for example, would we be willing to follow a man as unpleasant as Scrooge through an entire story?

The answer is in the emotions of hope and desire.

If you introduce your negative Lead correctly, you can raise the hope that he will change his negative ways. This is, in fact, a hope for redemption. One of the most powerful emotional moments we can have in our lives is when we are shown mercy for a wrong committed, and change as a result.

Take a recent movie example. Walt Kowalski as played by Clint Eastwood in *Gran Torino*. Walt is an old, crotchety, short-tempered bigot. He hates the "slopes" who have moved in next door. Hates what's happened to his formerly all-white, working-class neighborhood.

So why should we care to watch a character like this?

In a word, *redemption*. We watch a negative Lead to see if he will be redeemed or receive the "just desserts" of his actions.

But we must be given reasons to watch up front.

That's why Eastwood begins his movie with Walt standing by his wife's casket. He's just lost her, so there is an immediate sympathy factor. That is intensified as his granddaughter comes into the church dressed inappropriately, and we hear Walt's two sons talking in ways that indicate family estrangement.

Then there's the scene where Walt opens up just a bit to the young priest, telling of his time in Korea, the horror of it, and how intimately he knows death. He admits that he may not know as much about life.

That's enough to carry us through all the antisocial acts and utterings.

So the conflict in Act One between Walt and his neighbors, the local gang, and the boy is set in the context of a man who has decency inside him, waiting to get out again.

The other strong emotion relating to a negative Lead is the desire to see the character get what she deserves. In other words, wanting to see justice done. In this way, once again, the values of the community are vindicated: When bad people do bad things they are ultimately caught and punished. Our world is restored to order.

Of course, you can have a negative Lead "get away with it" at the end, which is another statement about the world. Just know that the number of successful novels written with that sort of ending is not very many.

Antihero

The antihero Lead is one who does not care about the community. He is living apart, according to his own code, and does not wish to get involved in anyone else's troubles.

Unlike the negative Lead, the antihero is not actively pursuing goals that would have a deleterious impact on others, except occasionally by chance.

The antihero may actually live apart from others, as does Ethan Edwards, the character played by John Wayne in *The Searchers*. He comes out of the wilderness, alone, and goes back to the wilderness, alone.

But an antihero may also be among people, yet still not caring to get involved with the real troubles of the community. Rick in *Casablanca* runs a popular saloon in French- occupied territory in World War II. He is allowed to run it because he takes no sides in the war effort. In fact, he says, "I stick my neck out for nobody." That is the quintessential guiding philosophy of the antihero.

Or think of Dirty Harry Callahan, the San Francisco police detective. He is a professional. His community is the law enforcement community. But he doesn't like their rules and regulations, so he "lives apart" from them. Which is why he is in constant trouble.

The conflict in an antihero story comes when he is dragged into the troubles of others and is forced to deal with it. Then, at the end, he can either rejoin the community or reject it once more.

At the end of *Casablanca*, Rick has rejoined the community. Having been dragged into the trouble involving Viktor Lazlo and his wife (Rick's former lover), Rick resolves matters and walks off with his new friend, Louis, to get involved in the war effort again.

Dirty Harry, on the other hand, rejects his law enforcement community. At the end of the film, having caught the bad guy by going outside the book, Harry takes his badge and throws it into San Francisco Bay, symbolically resigning from the community. (However, a studio executive ran down and recovered it and gave it back, because the film made too much money for Harry to resign permanently.)

The antihero is popular with American readers and audiences. He appeals to their frontier spirit and rugged individualism.

Creating the Give-a-Hoot Factor

What makes a character worth following? How is the reader calculating the benefits of reading the whole book?

Since the novel is an emotional experience, it follows that the Lead character must create emotion in the reader. Your ultimate task as a novelist is to play on that emotional investment—keep the reader hooked by heart.

Without that emotional investment, nothing you do with conflict, action, or suspense is going to matter. The reader simply won't care.

Some call this the give-a-hoot factor.

From whence comes the hoot?

The approach to creating a Lead character varies widely from writer to writer. Some advocate the filling out of dossiers that ask numerous questions about background, social life, beliefs, physical characteristics, family, and so on.

Others prefer to create characters on the fly and get to know them only as the writing progresses. In this way characters grow organically to fit the needs of the story.

Most writers, I suspect, are somewhere in between. They like to do some initial work on character background, then get to the writing and fill in as needed.

Whatever your preferred method, I am going to suggest that you begin to use the element of conflict at each stage. In this way you'll create that trouble factor that will make your Lead worth following. (Note: This approach can be tweaked and used for all your main characters.)

A Feeling

Begin by asking yourself what sort of feeling you want your character to engender in the reader.

Do you want the reader cheering? Feeling sorry? Getting angry along with the Lead? Loving the Lead? Or looking at her like she's a train wreck waiting to happen?

Who are some of your favorite Lead characters in fiction or film?

Make a list, then mine that list for a clue to what you want the reader to feel.

My own list would include: Philip Marlowe, Harry Bosch, Aram Garoghlanian, Shane, Kinsey Millhone, Martin Riggs, Roger Thornhill, and Spartacus.

Each of those names creates a certain feeling in me. Martin Riggs (Mel Gibson's character in *Lethal Weapon*) evokes sympathy and fascination with his suicide wish. That mixes with his extreme competence at his work. He's a man who wants to die in action but is so good at that action he keeps winning.

Therein lies your first clue to using conflict to create an unforgettable character: Find two feelings that don't generally go together and fit them into your Lead. This initial conflict immediately makes the character more compelling.

Even if you did nothing else before you started writing, this exercise will be a huge step in your writing.

Let's try one from scratch.

We'll be writing a suspense novel about an ordinary man who is mistaken for a long-idle serial killer. That's your "What if ..." concept.

So what sort of feeling do you want? I'd say we want to feel sorry for this guy. He will be like that Hitchcock hero Roger Thornhill in *North by Northwest*. Perfectly innocent, successful, enjoying life. Until a mistake makes the bad guys think he's an agent for the U.S. Government. He's kidnapped, almost killed. And then he goes to the U.N. looking for answers from a diplomat who gets a knife in the back.

We choose feeling sorry and scared for our hero, and then we'll add to that a certain sympathy factor because he's got attitude in the face of danger, even a little humor.

In homage to Hitchcock, I'll call him Roger Hill. He's thirty years old.

Occupation

What sort of work or vocation does your character engage in that is a field for possible trouble?

For our ordinary man hero, what kind of work shall we think up for him?

What if he's an accountant? You pluck that out of the air and think about it for a moment.

Where can we find conflict in his work? Let's make him an associate with one of the big four accounting firms. Working horrendous hours. Maybe he's been assigned to a major corporate client, using up half his billable hours every year on this one entity.

What does the stress of that work do to his family life? What if he discovers malfeasance in the corporate books and has to disclose it? What if he's got a rival who is set on bringing him down a few pegs so he doesn't make partner?

That's how you do it. Brainstorm the conflict possibilities right off the bat. Don't stop with Occupation: Accountant.

Background

Let's try some more on Roger's past.

Where did he go to school?

Roger grew up in a nice burb of Los Angeles, upper end of the middle class. Went to a private high school on the west side.

What sort of conflict can we mine there?

What if Roger was into sports? Say he was on the basketball team. But he had a coach who hated him for some reason. What reason? Maybe Roger reminded the coach too much of his own wayward son, who ran away from home and died in the streets during a robbery attempt. Maybe Roger had the same sort of what-the-hell attitude the coach's son had. The coach was determined to get Roger to submit to his will through attacks on Roger's manhood. (Remember the drill instructor in Stanley Kubrick's *Full Metal Jacket*?)

Just this one imagining beyond the fact that Roger went to a private high school has given us a rich vein of background to mine.

What sort of a man is Roger now, after going through that experience?

One more dossier question: What's Roger's romantic life like?

Well, after a few relationships Roger became engaged to the beautiful Katrina Honerkamp. She came from money. She was everything Roger wanted in a woman. But two months before the wedding she announced it was off. She'd fallen for somebody else, an actor who thought himself the next best thing to Johnny Depp.

What has this done to Roger's insides? Whatever it is, make it full of conflict. Especially when he meets the mysterious Belle Duncomb. Does Roger keep his distance? Or use her? Or love her? Or something else?

Your call.

The point is you can play this game with as many questions as you want. Each time you do, you will find rich sources of plot material growing like kudzu on the side of a bridge.

And when you are finished here, try one thing more:

Yearning

What is it that your Lead does not have, but yearns for? A yearning is a desire for something without which a person feels life will be incomplete.

It is a thing that predates the story. The Lead brings this to the tale from her past. What this does is enable you to hit the ground running when you start your novel. The character already has trouble inside, in the form of yearning unfulfilled.

A yearning will give you a store of character actions that are not predictable, creating interest from the outset.

Some people say that what you wanted to be when you were twelve is where your true yearning lies. It's true for me. I still wish I could have played center field for the Los Angeles Dodgers. What does that say about me?

I will leave that to others.

Instead let's take our Roger. He's in this grinding accounting firm. This is not what he saw himself doing when he was twelve.

Make a list of possible things Roger wanted to be or do when he was a boy:

> Take a raft down the Mississippi. (He did read *The Adventures of Huckleberry Finn*.)
> Become a movie star.
> Live on a beach in Hawaii and surf every day.
> Become a spy for the CIA.
> Work the rodeo circuit.
> Drive NASCAR.
> Write a novel.

Make the list as long as you like, then choose one that grips you. Play with it. I usually like the ideas that come further down the list, and in this case it's going into Ultimate Fighting.

Now I ask why would twelve-year-old Roger want to do that? Maybe it was because he was being picked on at school. He yearned to be somebody who could defend himself, anytime, anywhere.

Give us some backstory on this:

> Roger was twelve when he first got beat up by a bully. It was while he was on his way to PE, and he was met in the hall by a kid two years older, with actual hair under his arms. The kid told Roger to give him a buck, and Roger said he didn't have one. The kid slapped him. Before Roger could react, the kid pushed Roger into a locker and Roger fell on his butt. Roger wasn't exactly big for his age, a little on the skinny side. but he had a fire raging inside him that he couldn't put out.
>
> What to do?
>
> Become like one of those cage fighters that were coming into pop culture. But when he asked his dad if he could take lessons, his dad told him to get serious about his studies. He wouldn't pay for lessons. So Roger went on being "practical."

And so on.

The last step in this yearning process is to designate ways that yearning can still mean something to Roger today and become a source of inner conflict.

For example, the root of Roger's yearning was a hatred of injustice. The bully, an unjust punk, needed his face mashed in. As Roger has gone on with life, he's seen many such punks who need retributive justice. But Roger has always left that to others.

Now, in the trouble to be developed in the novel, he's going to feel that tension between being "practical" like his father told him to be and doing something about justice.

Don't ignore this deep soil for conflict. It's your chance to play amateur psychologist with your Lead character and make him all the richer because of it.

Jumping Off the Page

When you hear agents and editors talk about characters that grip them, you'll sometimes hear the phrase "jump off the page." It means the character is more than what they've seen before. Even if it's a familiar type, there are things going on that give way to some happy surprises.

In *Revision & Self-Editing* I talked about three aspects of character that attract readers. I called them *grit, wit,* and *it.* Briefly:

Grit is guts. Strength. Courage. This is what a character needs in the death struggle of the plot. She may not have it at the beginning, but you better make sure you show the reader she has the capacity to develop it, and soon.

Wit is a sharp mind. The ability to laugh at yourself occasionally or to simply not take yourself too seriously.

It is a sort of magnetism that draws other characters (and the reader) to the Lead.

You can see it in the following characters:

> **GRIT:** Carol Starkey, LAPD bomb squad vet in *Demolition Angel* by Robert Crais
> **WIT:** Myron Bolitar, in the series by Harlan Coben
> **IT:** Scarlett O'Hara and Rhett Butler in *Gone With the Wind* by Margaret Mitchell

You can easily find other examples just by thinking about these three characteristics as you read or revisit your favorite titles.

Another jump-off-the-page factor is *unpredictability*. This one is useful in that it almost always causes conflict for the very reason that the other characters can't anticipate what's going to happen.

Think of the character of Ronny Cammareri in the movie *Moonstruck*. When we first see him, he's with the ovens below a bakery. Loretta Castorini, who is engaged to Ronny's brother, has come to invite him to the wedding. There's been bad blood between the brothers and Loretta wants to discuss it.

But her attempts to communicate like an adult are met with completely unpredictable responses:

> RONNY
>
> You going to marry my brother Johnny?
>
> LORETTA
>
> Yes. Would you like to go someplace so we could ...
>
> RONNY
>
> I have no life.
>
> LORETTA
>
> Excuse me?
>
> RONNY
>
> I have no life. My brother Johnny took my life from me.

Not exactly handling the question in the way one might expect, Ronny goes on, asking loudly, "What is life?"

Loretta just wants to talk, but Ronny interrupts:

> RONNY
>
> They say that bread is life! And I bake bread, bread, bread, and I sweat and I shovel dough in and out of this hot hole in the wall, and I should be so happy, huh, sweetie? You want me to come to the wedding of my brother Johnny? Where's my wedding. Chrissy, over by the wall, bring me the big knife.
>
> CHRISSY
>
> No, Ronny!

RONNY
Bring me the big knife, I'm gonna cut my throat.

We have traveled a bit far afield from a civil conversation, have we not? But it's pure conflict, of an operatic sort—which is part of Ronny's character.

Another jump-off-the-page aspect is *nobility*. When a character is acting according to high ideals, it's a natural he will run into trouble. Conflict arises when two sides clash over the right thing to do.

In *To Kill a Mockingbird,* for example, Atticus Finch must face off against men who have come to lynch his client, Tom Robinson. He sets up outside the jail, alone, and awaits the confrontation.

Flaws

Perfect people are not interesting to us. We need to sees flaws in the characters as well as strengths. Flaws will give you even more areas for possible conflict.

Scarlett O'Hara is selfish, and therefore doesn't have any qualms about marrying men she doesn't care about, so long as they serve her purposes.

Scout Finch is not a model child. She gets into fights at school and speaks her opinions at inopportune times.

Give your characters flaws that will rub up against other flawed characters.

Strength of Will

Great characters are marked by "strength of will." The stronger the will, the more attractive the character.

Why this works: We all believe, or want to believe, that the free acts of a person have an effect. We want to believe that we can make the world better, or can carve a piece of success for ourselves, or any of a number of other things, by acts of will. We get corrected and set back, but we learn (this is called wisdom) and then we act again.

So we bond with characters who are acting with conscious will toward a specific end.

OBJECTIVE

We've already discussed the stakes of a successful novel involving death overhanging—physical, professional, psychological.

A story *objective* takes one of two forms: to get something or to get away from something. The "something" should have death overhanging.

Take *The Fugitive*. The title suggests the primary objective: Dr. Richard Kimble has to *get away* from the lawman trying to capture him. Physical death is on the line because if he is caught he's going to be executed for the murder of his wife. But there's also psychological death at play: He knows the real killer of his wife is out there, free, living life. To deny justice to the woman he loved would be an unbearable burden on death row.

Let's look at professional death. It's sufficient that it *feel* like professional death to the character. In *The Silence of the Lambs*, FBI trainee Clarice Starling is given a crucial assignment by the head of the Behavioral Science Unit at Quantico: Get the notorious serial killer and cannibal-about-town Dr. Hannibal Lecter to give up some information about himself.

For Starling this is a huge opportunity for advancement. It's crucially important to her. A fact that Dr. Lecter eerily knows by sizing her up in their first meeting. From within his cell Lecter observes:

> You'd like to quantify me, Officer Starling. You're so ambitious, aren't you? Do you know what you look like to me, with your good bag and your cheap shoes? You look like a rube. You're a well-scrubbed hustling rube with a little taste. Your eyes are like cheap birthstones—all surface shine when you stalk some little answer. And you're bright behind them, aren't you? Desperate not to be like your mother. Good nutrition has given you some length of bone, but you're not more than one generation out of the mines, *Officer* Starling. Is it the West Virginia Starlings or the Okie Starlings, Officer? It was a toss-up between college and the opportunities in the Women's Army Corps, wasn't it?

Not only has Lecter pegged her, but by letting her know that he has done so in such direct terms, the stakes are already raised. If she fails to get him to give up information, it will be a humiliating defeat to her confidence. Perhaps fatal to her future with the FBI.

At least, that's how it *feels* to her when Lecter ends the interview:

> Starling felt suddenly empty, as though she had given blood. She took longer than necessary to put the papers back in her briefcase because she didn't immediately trust her legs. Starling was soaked with the failure she detested.

And there you have the stakes of professional (and psychological) death raised in an early chapter of the book. The table is set for emotional conflict.

Honing Your Lead's Objective

1. What is your Lead character's primary objective in the novel? Define it. It should be one thing, to get or to get away from.
2. How is death involved? Name one kind of death—physical, professional, psychological—that is primary.
3. Write a page or two of voice journal (i.e., first-person narration) explaining why death is on the line. Make up any backstory you need to justify this outlook.
4. Edit the paragraph into a form that you can place in your novel. For example, you could place some of the first-person narration in dialogue.
5. Find a place before the midpoint of Act Two in your novel to place this material.

The reason for this placement is that your character must realize, with full force, what the stakes are before the midpoint. Because after that midpoint he's totally committed, can't resign from the action, and must spend the rest of the book in a full throttle attempt to avoid death.

For our character, Roger Hill, let's put down the essential information. Roger's main objective is going to be to *get away* from the law and a vengeful relative of someone he's supposedly murdered. The stakes here are obviously physical death. If the relative finds him and exacts revenge, that's it for Roger here on earth. If the law catches him, it will either be execution or life in prison without parole.

But what if he does get away? What if Roger managed to live on the lam for years and years? Wouldn't that be a kind of psychological death? A man without a home, dead to his past? Without his family? I think so.

And certainly his profession is gone. He can't just waltz in and start being an accountant for big bucks somewhere.

The stakes are really high for Roger.

Now let's have Roger give his viewpoint in the voice journal:

> They think I did it, that's why I'm on the run. You have to ask? I know exactly what'll happen if that crazy redneck brother, what's his name

again? Rudy? If he finds me it's going to be lights out. I saw him on Nancy Grace. I saw the look in his eyes and the hatred pouring out of him. He doesn't care what the cops say, he's going to do things to me.

And by the way, the cops don't seem to care. It's almost like they'd like it if he got me.

Where do I run? How long can I keep this disguise going?

What kind of life is this?

I miss my family. My brother and sister. My mom.

They all think I did it, too!

We are building a solid foundation for conflict here. When you have a Lead readers want to follow, and the stakes are death in some form, you're at the highest level of grip there is.

And now you need to add one more element to ratchet up the reader interest—an opposition force.

The Voice Journal

The voice journal is one of the most effective writing tools I know, useful in all stages of writing your novel. It's a document that is a free-form, stream-of-consciousness journal in *a character's voice,* talking about things you prompt them with. The idea is to write for at least five to ten minutes without stopping, letting the character speak for herself.

In the early stages, the voice journal will help you "hear" the characters talk in a way that is unique to them. This is essential for making your cast of characters different from each other.

During the writing, you may also stop and ask what a character is thinking or feeling about the story. This deepens the emotions in the character and helps solidify and intensify conflict.

You should have voice journals for all your major characters and use them freely as you make progress in your novel.

CONFRONTATION

The third letter of LOCK—C for confrontation—is the crux of your novel. The major conflict between your Lead character and the force that opposes him takes up most of the book.

Almost always that opposition should be embodied in another character. Jean Valjean vs. Inspector Javert. Dr. Richard Kimble vs. U.S. Marshal Sam Gerard. Randle Patrick McMurphy vs. Nurse Ratched.

Sometimes the opposition force is larger than one person but is embodied in a representative. In John Grisham's *The Firm,* the opposition is the mafia (via the law firm that represents it covertly). But when the hammer needs to come down on the Lead, Mitch McDeere, it is in the form of a man named Devasher, the enforcer.

In *Gone With the Wind,* Scarlett is fighting against psychological death—if her Southern way of life goes, she's lost. So she must save Tara and find a way back to high society.

What opposes her in this quest? Many characters arise, such as the carpetbagger Jonas Wilkerson, who thinks he can retake Tara through tax manipulation. Or the Union soldier who comes to Tara with rape and death on his mind.

And of course, Rhett Butler, who keeps battling for her heart.

All of this struggle is subsumed under Scarlett's psychological need to get her Old South way of life back.

The elements can be an opposition force, of course. This is as venerable as *Robinson Crusoe* and as simple as a girl lost in the woods (*The Girl Who Loved Tom Gordon* by Stephen King).

However, most of the time your opposition will be a single character who is directly opposed to the Lead.

The Opposition Character

You must pay as much attention to your opposition character as you do to your Lead. The biggest mistake you can make here is to paint your antagonist in broad strokes and one color. There are few things less compelling than a one-dimensional bad guy.

Let's take a look at your two basic options.

1. The bad guy opposition

When you have a traditional hero for the Lead, you basically have a character who is upholding the values of the community. He is doing things we would normally approve of. His goals are noble.

That doesn't mean he's perfect, but in general he is someone the community would root for.

The villain is one who opposes the Lead and therefore, by extension, the community itself. We root against him. We want him to fail.

But we can't stack the deck.

The pure evil, mustache-twirling villain of the old melodramas was a cartoon character. Readers will feel manipulated.

So you have to be fair.

In fact, you have to love your villain.

Playing Fair With Your Bad Guy

I like what Harlan Coben said in an interview with *Writer's Digest*: "I like to see the difference between good and evil as kind of like the foul line at a baseball game. It's very thin, it's made of something very flimsy like lime, and if you cross it, it really starts to blur where fair becomes foul and foul becomes fair. And that's where I like to play."

That's where you should play with your bad guy. To do that:

- Do a complete backstory for your villain. Look for those places in his past that explain why he does what he does in the present.

- Allow yourself to find a sympathy factor. If you can make the reader feel this, it lends a powerful current of emotion to the experience. It's not that you're approving of the actions of the bad guy, but you're forcing yourself to see him as less than pure evil.

- Justify the bad guy's position. No matter how bad it seems to you, the bad guy thinks he's in the right. He does what he does because he believes he's entitled.

- Give at least one beat in your story where the justification is made clear. Again, this will create a crosscurrent of emotion in the reader, and that is what you want.

Why Do You Love Your Villain?

One question that can truly force you into great territory for conflict is: Why do I love my villain? How can I love someone who is doing such terrible things?

Because it's going to be tough love. It's going to be as if the villain is your brother or father or son. Or sister, mother, daughter.

2. The good guy opposition

What matters in the confrontation phase is an opposition character who has strong reasons to be opposed to the Lead character. The opposition does not have to be evil.

A perfect example is U.S. Marshal Sam Gerard in *The Fugitive*. He is not a bad man; quite the contrary. He is dedicated to the law and is very good at what he does.

He has one job: to bring in fugitives.

Dr. Richard Kimble is a fugitive.

It does not matter to Gerard what the facts of the case are. That's for the court system. Gerard is law enforcement, and the law says that Kimble is an escaped prisoner.

When Kimble has that one chance to plead with Gerard, telling him, "I didn't kill my wife!" Gerard has only one response: "I don't care!"

Is this not similar to Inspector Javert in Victor Hugo's *Les Misérables?*

The Bonding Agent

A final consideration for the confrontation element of your novel is the arena of conflict. Sometimes this is called *the crucible.* I prefer to think of it as the *bonding agent,* the factor that keeps the two sides locked in mortal combat. The reason neither one can walk away.

This is crucial, because if the reader feels the trouble can be solved by simple resignation, there will be no true worry factor.

Consider the following: A woman is married to a man who beats her. She stays with the marriage as long as she can. Finally she makes the decision to get out. One day when her husband is at work she packs some things and takes the car and drives to another state. There she gets a job and begins a new life.

Where's the confrontation? Other than a few legal papers back and forth, it isn't there. Why not? Because the wife solved her problem by moving away from it.

So when Stephen King wrote *Rose Madder,* he knew he had to create a situation that bonded the two together. The husband became a psychopath and a cop to boot. He tells his wife if she ever tries to leave he will kill her. He knows how to get away with it. And he can track her, too, no matter where she goes.

He has kept his wife a virtual prisoner for years. She doesn't drive, doesn't know how to look for a job. She's vulnerable.

When she finally does leave, we know this is not a resignation, but a "death overhanging" quest to get away from her husband.

So what are some ways to create this bond?

1. A Reason to Kill

If the opposition has a strong reason to kill the Lead, that is, of course, an automatic bond. In a thriller, this might be represented by a secret the Lead has found out, as in *The Firm*. This mafia front cannot allow the secret to get out. Young lawyer Mitch McDeere is on their hit list.

Psychological death can also come into play. In the Bette Davis movie *Now, Voyager*, the domineering mother seeks to "kill" the nascent independence of her daughter, which is brought about by her falling in love. She tries all sorts of manipulation to make this happen.

2. A Professional Duty

When a lawyer takes a case, she is duty bound to see it through. A detective assigned to a murder can't just walk away. There are professional duties that tie the Lead to the action.

The readers know and accept professional duty as a bonding agent. Just make sure you show how important the job is to your character.

3. A Moral Duty

A daughter is kidnapped. A father will move heaven and earth, and any number of bad guys, to get her back (e.g., *Firestarter* by Stephen King). This is a moral duty, and no one would expect the father to resign from the action.

A friend can have a moral duty to another friend. This is what makes Neil Simon's play, *The Odd Couple*, work. The obvious question raised about Oscar letting Felix upset his happy life as a slob is this: Why doesn't Oscar just kick Felix out of his apartment? It belongs to Oscar, after all. The living situation isn't working out. In other words, why can't the problem be solved (and the bond of confrontation removed) by simply asking Felix to go?

Simon's brilliant answer was Oscar's moral duty to his best friend, because Felix is suicidal. His wife has left him. All his friends are worried Felix might harm himself. So Oscar has Felix move in so he can keep an eye on him and cheer him up.

Moral duty is a strong bonding agent.

4. A Physical Location

Sometimes the locale itself may hold the confronting parties together.

Casablanca is such a location. People cannot get out of Casablanca without the proper papers, and intrigue swirls around within the walls of Rick's café.

A snowbound hotel full of ghosts is another example (*The Shining*).

A city where a person's life work is located may be another such bond. A cop, for example, is bound to his venue.

Ask yourself this question before you begin plotting in earnest: Is there an obvious way out of the "death struggle"?

Can either side solve the problem by resigning, relocating, or making some other simple change?

Close off all avenues of escape. This is the only way confrontation and suspense can build.

Known or Unknown?

One aspect of the opposition we haven't mentioned is whether we know who it is or not. In a mystery or thriller, it is common for the opponent to be hidden from the Lead until the final battle.

Mysteries traditionally bank on the unknown. Think of the clever criminal trying to avoid the little gray cells of Hercule Poirot. He gathers his clues then gathers the suspects to reveal the truth.

But the same riff can be part of a thriller where the Lead has no idea where the danger comes from, or why it's focused on him. The "reveal" can happen well into the book, or even at the end.

Hollywood movies usually show us both sides, as in *Speed*, which cuts back and forth between those on the "bus that cannot slow down" and the crazy bomber played by Dennis Hopper. From the perspective of the cop and the passengers, they are dealing only with a voice.

In a novel, you have the choice of what to reveal.

Orchestration

When you go to a concert, after shelling out for tickets and dressing up in your evening best, you don't want to sit down and listen to an orchestra of oboes.

Nor do you want to have every instrument play exactly the same note.

What you hope for is the pleasing sound of different instruments coming together in just the right ways, creating the notes and resonance that add up to a great musical experience.

That's what we call orchestration. It is the assembling of parts for a desired effect.

In a novel, the parts you use to orchestrate conflict are called characters.

That's where it all starts. If you create bland, undistinguished characters, your chances of building page-turning conflict will fail.

One of the great strengths—perhaps the greatest—of Janet Evanovich's Stephanie Plum novels is her orchestration of characters for conflict. It begins right in the first chapter of the first book, *One for the Money,* where we meet Joe Morelli, a literal bad boy who grows up into more bad boyness. *He'd grown up big and bad, with eyes like black fire one minute and melt-in-your-mouth chocolate the next.*

Notice that Evanovich builds conflict right into the description of Joe Morelli. This will show up in Stephanie's own conflicted feelings about him as the stories progress. Within three pages we're told that Morelli, who "specializes in virgins," has his way with Stephanie behind a case of chocolate eclairs in the Tasty Pastry.

Then disappears from her life for three years.

Until the day Stephanie sees Morelli in front of the meat market. She is driving her father's Buick and guns it, jumps the curb, and bounces Morelli off the hood. She gets out and asks if anything's broken. He says his leg. She says, "Good," gets back in the car and drives off.

Now that is how you characterize for conflict! In just the first few pages we have a distinct description, action, and confrontation. Running a car into someone is sort of the definition of conflict, wouldn't you say?

But Evanovich doesn't stop there. Even as Stephanie must deal with Morelli, there's another man in her life, another bad boy named Ricardo "Ranger" Mañoso. Orchestrating for conflict, Evanovich makes Ranger

Cuban-American, former Special Forces, slick black hair in a ponytail, and a buff don't-mess-with-me body.

The first time they meet, it's to establish a working relationship. Ranger is going to train Stephanie in the ways of the bounty hunter. And their first case is brining in, you guessed it, Joe Morelli.

Now we have a triangular conflict, set up from the very start.

Of course, the Plum novels are peppered with great supporting and minor characters, who add up to endless possibilities for conflict. Plum herself is "the blue-eyed, fair-skinned product of a Hungarian-Italian union." The other characters she runs across are cast to be different.

Like Lula, African American filing clerk, large and in charge, crammed into Spandex.

Or Grandma Mazur, seventy-something grandmother who, in her skivvies, resembles a soup chicken.

And all down the line. Evanovich gives us all the color and spice and potential conflict because of her great characterizations.

Assembling a Stable

In the old movie studio days, when actors were under contract, it was said they were in a stable. Not very flattering, of course, but close to the truth. Actors under contract didn't have a say in the projects they were cast in. They were, indeed, somewhat like cattle.

The days of the old studio contracts are long gone, but that doesn't mean you can't have a stable of your own. No one's going to know!

So start assembling.

Actors

Think of all the characters you really like in the movies. I mean major and minor characters. Who were the actors?

That starts your list.

For example, I always liked the old character actor Alan Hale. Not Junior, who played the Skipper on *Gilligan's Island*, but Senior, who was in numerous classics including *The Adventures of Robin Hood* and *It Happened One Night*.

Hale was versatile and always brought a jaunty stamp to his roles. I want him around for some comic relief on occasion.

I can make him old or young, but he'll still be Alan Hale.

My favorite actor of all time is Spencer Tracy. He could play a wide variety of roles, and at different ages. The young Tracy could be a tough criminal type or a priest, a crusty fisherman or a doting father.

So I'll keep him in mind for certain roles.

Go ahead. Make your own list.

Fictional Characters

Did you know that fictional characters in other books can slide right over and start working for you?

No one has to know: You're going to change enough about them to make them your own.

Let's say you're reading the latest thriller from one of your favorite authors. You really like the character he created, the eccentric cab driver who happens to be a psychic. You like the voice and you like the quirk.

Steal it and shape it to your own use.

Is this legit? Stealing from other authors?

Not only is it legit, it's one of the best ways to get material.

This is not plagiarism. This is you observing the collective creative mind out there and snatching what you need.

When you read a book with great characters, don't waste them. Hire them.

Change their sex or age. Or keep them the same and make up a fresh backstory for them.

Real People

It's a time-honored writers' practice to base characters on real-life folks. You have to be careful here, of course, not to present a thinly veiled portrait that is defamatory.

So if you take a character from real life, consider changing her around a bit. First, can you make *her* a *him?* Yes, you can, and that will often deliver great results. Surprising and fresh. Or you can combine a primary trait of the real person with another person or character.

Play around, but don't feel shy about borrowing from real life. That's what it's there for.

Putting It All Together

Now that you have a stable of actors and types you can conduct auditions.

I mean it. You have a story you're creating, now put out the call to the actors and let them come before your mind's eye and try out for the parts.

Think up scenes in your mind and let several of your actors improvise.

Create a Character Grid

A useful tool for orchestrating your cast is through the *character grid*. You lay out the names of the main characters in a column on the left-hand side. Across the top put in any information you'd like to see at a glance, with one column dedicated to *Conflict*. Here's what mine might look like:

Main Characters	Dominant Impression	Objective	Past Wound	Secret	Personality Type/Tags	Conflict With Others	Emotion Evoked	Casting

Minor Characters	Dominant Impression	Role	Unique Tags	Conflict With Others	Casting

Now, for each set of character interactions, find points of conflict from the past, present, or future.

Let's look at our example. In the conflict box for Mary, you might put something like this:

Dated Sean in high school. Sean still bitter about breakup.

So when Sean suddenly shows up in Mary's world, there is going to be some residual tension there. The grid allows you to see this relationship at a glance.

Then there is Mary and Hillary. They're friends, they work in the same office. How might there be tension between them?

Friends for five years with Hillary, who can irritate Mary at times. Also in a bad relationship with someone who can't stand Mary.

KNOCKOUT ENDING

It was Mickey Spillane, one of the all-time best-selling novelists, who observed, "Your first chapter sells your book. Your last chapter sells your next book."

The ending is the most challenging part of your novel. It needs to satisfy without predictability and leave the reader wanting more.

It must solve the conflict and relieve the suspense. It must tie up loose ends and make sense of the story.

You know what's easy? Throwing in twists and shocks and surprises.

What's hard is justifying these in a way the reader will appreciate.

Many a book has been a breathless read up to the final chapters, only to be let down by answers that don't make sense or are too far-fetched to be taken seriously.

Is it necessary to know your ending before you start writing? Yes. But not like it's carved in marble.

It's good to have a general idea of how you want the story to come out. Then you can write toward that point, knowing that it's flexible. You can even conceive of the climactic scene in detail. No one's going to hold you to it and it will guide your writing.

What you should be looking for is a final battle, a last point of conflict where the stakes are highest and the outcome in doubt.

The battle can be inside or outside, or both.

Inside the character might be a battle for identity. Who is the Lead really? Will he grow and become the person he needs to be?

Take Rick in *Casablanca*. He's basically a cynic and a drunkard who has given up caring about the world. He doesn't care if he spends his last days in Casablanca and shrivels up and dies. He thinks he's been betrayed by a woman who looks remarkably like Ingrid Bergman, and that's not something a guy easily gets over.

When the woman, Ilsa, shows up in Casablanca with her husband, war hero Viktor Lazlo, Rick has a choice to remain as he is and to withhold help from Ilsa and Lazlo, or he can grow past his hurt and become a decent human being again.

But then a twist. Ilsa declares that she still loves Rick and wants to go away with him. For Rick possesses two letters of transit that mean escape from Casablanca.

Now Rick has the woman of his dreams, but inside a battle begins. Would it be the right thing to do?

And outside there is a battle, too. Rick and the Nazi Major, Strasser, have been playing cat and mouse over the presence of Lazlo. One false move and Rick could lose this battle and his life.

Sacrifice

A powerful ending trope revolves around sacrifice.

Think back through the cultural memes of civilization.

Abraham is asked to sacrifice his son. He offers him up but is stopped at the last moment, and rewarded with the promises of God.

Go to the Athenian democracy and a playwright named Euripides. He offers a play called *Alcestis*. In this play a king named Admetus is given a gift. He does not have to die if he can find someone to die in his place.

He cannot, except for his wife, Alcestis, who takes his place out of love.

Off she goes with Death.

But Heracles (the Greek name for Hercules) hears of this and vows to battle Death and bring Alcestis back from the dead.

Which he does.

Alcestis has given the ultimate sacrifice but now has been resurrected. This theme remains powerful.

In Hammett's *The Maltese Falcon*, Sam Spade has within his reach the woman he's fallen for, Brigid O'Shaughnessy. They belong together. Spade knows he's in love with her. She's a liar and manipulator, but maybe he can knock that out of her. Maybe he can believe in her and find rest with her.

But Spade has to sacrifice this, because someone has to "take the fall" for the murder of his partner.

> "I don't care who loves who I'm not going to play the sap for you … . When a man's partner is killed he's supposed to do something about it. It doesn't make any difference what you thought of him. He was your partner and you're supposed to do something about it."

After Spade justifies his position to Brigid he says,

> "Now on the other side we've got what? All we've got is the fact that maybe you love me and maybe I love you."
>
> "You know," she whispered, "whether or not you do."
>
> "I don't. It's easy enough to be nuts about you." He looked hungrily from her hair to her feet and up to her eyes again. "But I don't know what that amounts to. Does anybody ever?"

In this sacrifice, Spade "wins" because he has upheld the moral order of his universe. When a partner's killed, the other partner has to "do something about it." And he's not going to play the sap.

In Mel Gibson's film *Braveheart*, William Wallace dies at the end. And not in a pretty way. He can end his torture just by confessing to treason. But he does not. And in his death he "wins" by inspiring his followers, and most notably Robert the Bruce, to fight on like free men.

Remember Rick, the saloon owner we left back in Casablanca? He's now at the airport with Ilsa, his great love, and she's ready to go with him. But then he stops and tells her no, this is wrong. We'll regret this, maybe not now but soon and for the rest of our lives.

But we'll always have Paris.

Rick sacrifices the thing he wants most. He has become human again. He has won the inner battle, and also the outer. For though he has killed the Nazi major, his new best friend, the little French captain, Louis, lets him go.

In return for his sacrifice, Rick is resurrected. He's no longer a dead man walking (or drinking). He and Louis go off to join the war effort.

Sacrifice is powerful because it cannot exist without high conflict. It's no sacrifice to give up your seat on a bus. But to give your life for a cause, or another person, that's conflict of the highest kind.

Or to give up a cherished dream. Scarlett O'Hara finally realizes her dreams of Old South respectability, and love for Ashley Wilkes who embodied those dreams, has to be sacrificed (though it may be too late for her to get Rhett back).

Avoid the Expected

When you get to thinking about the ending, suspense is weakened in direct proportion to the expectancy of outcome.

In other words, the longer you can keep the reader from guessing the ending, the better. You should be compiling events in such a way that the reader is wondering how on earth this thing will end. And then, end it in a way that, looking back, makes perfect sense.

This is not an easy task.

1. Write down how *you* would expect this tale to end.
2. Come up with five alternative endings.
3. Choose the best one to end on.
4. Choose one of the other endings as a possible "twist" at the very end. Sometimes this works, sometimes not. But it's good to have the option.

The Knockout Factor

Do these things to head your ending toward a knockout:

1. Keep track of all questions that are raised and need to be answered. Keep these on a separate sheet of paper or in a dedicated file. Or place comments right there in your document so you can scroll through them later. Let's say you have a guy show up in your Lead's car with a knife in his back. Why? You don't know. Your comment might be as simple as this:

Who killed this guy? Connect it up later.

Or you can use the comment to brainstorm:

> Maybe this is an agent who was trying to help Roger. But the bad guys
> found out and set it up to look like Roger murdered him. Or maybe it's
> a homeless guy the bad guys thought was Roger. If it's a homeless guy,
> maybe he's not homeless after all—he could be someone Roger once
> knew. Who? I don't know, figure it out.

2. When you've written the final chapters, see how many threads you left dangling. Are there some you can do without, plot developments that seem, upon reflection, to be tacked on? If so, cut them.

But if there are threads that need explanation, consider having them handled by a minor character. Someone you've planted earlier in the book (or that you do so upon rewrite) who can come in at the end and explain what happened.

3. Go for a final resonance. By that I mean your very last paragraphs. Work these until you have just the right sound, the right mood. Some examples that, if you know the book, feel just right:

> It's funny. Don't ever tell anybody anything. If you do, you start missing
> everybody. *The Catcher in the Rye.*

And there you have the foundations for a novel of conflict and suspense. Know these elements as best you can before you begin. Your story—not to mention your readers—will thank you for it.

Now we have one last question to answer: Where do we put these elements on the time line of our book?

You do it in three acts.

COVER COPY

Now you've got the solid foundations for a novel full of conflict and suspense.

Take a stab at writing your own cover copy.

It's not as hard as you think.

What is cover copy? It's what marketing people put on the jacket or back cover of a book to try to generate enough interest that a consumer will buy it.

And here is their secret: It contains both conflict and suspense. It awakens in the reader (or potential buyer) the desire to know *what happens.*

You should do this even before you write your book.

First, this will be gold to you, a way to keep you on track as you write your book. You will know if you have all the elements you need for a successful book if you have killer cover copy.

Second, this copy will eventually become the main paragraph of your query letters. It'll be lean and mean by then.

Third, you can always tweak the copy as you go along and things develop in the book.

The main thing you want is to capture the *conflict* that your novel needs to have to succeed.

So how do you learn to write such copy?

Simple: You study how the pros do it.

You look at books in your genre and read a bunch of copy. You get the feel and the rhythm.

You can do this also by going to Amazon.com and reading the book descriptions there.

Let's say your genre is contemporary suspense. You find a book like *The Sentry* by Robert Crais. And the product description that goes like this:

> Dru Rayne and her uncle fled to L.A. after Hurricane Katrina; but now, five years later, they face a different danger. When Joe Pike witnesses Dru's uncle beaten by a protection gang, he offers his help, but neither of them want it—and neither do the federal agents mysteriously watching them. As the level of violence escalates, and Pike himself becomes a target, he and Elvis Cole learn that Dru and her uncle are not who they seem—and that everything he thought he knew about them has been a lie. A vengeful and murderous force from their past is now catching up to them ... and only Pike and Cole stand in the way.

See the conflict? Gangs. Federal agents. Crime. Family betrayal. Vengeful, murderous forces.

And the suspense: Pike is a target. Will he get it in the back? Pike and Cole "stand in the way."

Here is a foundation for a page turner.

Or maybe you're writing romance. You find a book like *Taming Rafe* by Susan May Warren:

> Hotel heiress Katherine Breckenridge just wants to make a lasting difference in her world by running her late mother's charity foundation. But she fears she lacks the passion and courage to be as successful as her mother was—a fear that's realized when money from the foundation goes missing and Katherine's one shot to recover it is ruined by Rafe Noble. Two-time world champion bull rider Rafe Noble is at the top of his game when tragedy hits. Guilt stricken over the loss of his best friend, Rafe accidentally drives his truck into the lobby of the Breckenridge Hotel during Katherine's fund-raiser. With a broken knee, a ruined reputation, and the threat of several lawsuits, Rafe goes back to his family's ranch—the Silver Buckle—to recover. Desperate to save the foundation, Katherine heads to the Silver Buckle to talk Rafe into helping her raise the needed funds. But a few days under the bright Montana skies give her more than she bargained for, and Kat discovers there's more to both herself and Rafe Noble than she realized.

Notice also that the copy is usually the material up to the first doorway of no return. You've already nailed that in your planning, so it's simple enough to draft copy up to that point.

Then you drop in a line that gives the gist of the continuing conflict.

See that? You're a marketing genius all of a sudden.

Not bad.

One more example. This is from a literary novel. It may be a bit harder at first to find the juice, but you can do it if you try. Here is the description of John Grisham's literary novel, *A Painted House:*

> Until that September of 1952, Luke Chandler had never kept a secret or told a single lie. But in the long, hot summer of his seventh year, two groups of migrant workers—and two very dangerous men—came through the Arkansas Delta to work the Chandler cotton farm. And suddenly mysteries are flooding Luke's world. A brutal murder leaves the town seething in gossip and suspicion. A beautiful young woman ignites forbidden passions. A fatherless baby is born ... and someone has begun furtively painting the bare clapboards of the Chandler farmhouse, slowly, painstakingly, bathing the run-down structure in gleaming white. And as

young Luke watches the world around him, he unravels secrets that could shatter lives—and change his family and his town forever ....

Now it's your turn.

You have your LOCK elements and know your doorways.

Write your cover copy now, and then get ready to structure your novel.

CHAPTER 4
THE STRUCTURE OF CONFLICT

Structure is as important to conflict as a suspension bridge is to commerce. If you don't have the Golden Gate Bridge, you don't have enough trucks bringing in *pâté de foie gras* to San Francisco.

If you don't have solid structure in your novel, the tension in your novel will dissipate and never be as strong as you'd like it to be.

Here's why: What makes a novel is confrontation. The struggle against an opposing force with death on the line. For that confrontation to matter to the reader, the reader has to care. For the reader to care, there has to be a proper setup. Setup has to happen early, or the reader might set the book aside.

The setup is Act One, the confrontation is Act Two.

Then the book has to have a strong payoff at the end, Act Three, or the whole thing will feel like a letdown.

Structure is not there to hamper you; it's there to help you create the kind of stories people can't put down.

There are some who say structure is restrictive and unnecessary. They say there are other ways to write a novel. Just think of incident after incident. Just let yourself flow.

The books produced by this method are of two kinds:

A. They end up using structure without knowing it, because it is so natural and ingrained they can't help it; or
B. They don't sell.

Are there exceptions? Of course.

When you toss out structure, when you move toward more experimental forms of storytelling, you begin to confuse the reader. Confusion does not mix well with conflict.

It's not that it can't work, strictly speaking. But it will be a lot harder, and the audience for such a book will be much smaller.

That's your call.

"But this is formulaic!" you might shout. That's okay. Get it out of your system. Now think about it.

Why does a formula become a formula? Because it works.

When you're sick, do you want a shot of what works? Or something experimental the doc has been working on in his spare time?

Structure is formulaic only in the same way a suspension bridge is formulaic. You can design it however you want. You can put in whatever elements please you. You can create your characters with wild abandon and make up twists to your heart's content. You can have voice and style and everything else.

ACT ONE: THE BEGINNING

Where do you begin the story? With a disturbance. With something that happens—on the first page, mind you—that is something *different* in the Lead's ordinary world.

As John le Carré once put it, "The cat sat on the mat is not the beginning of a story. The cat sat on the dog's mat is." Begin your novel at the point of disturbance, because disturbance is conflict.

It doesn't have to be something big. You don't have to use a car chase or a grisly murder in the point of view of the killer. It can be anything that is a ripple in the waters of the Lead's ordinary world. Like someone who is asleep, when this happens:

> Dr. Jonasson was woken by a nurse five minutes before the helicopter was expected to land. It was just before 1:30 in the morning. (Stieg Larsson, *The Girl Who Kicked the Hornet's Nest*)

Or this:

> She heard a knocking, and then a dog barking. Her dream left her, skittering behind a closing door. It had been a good dream, warm and close,

and she minded. She fought the waking. It was dark in the small bedroom with no light yet behind the shades. She reached for the lamp, fumbled her way up the brass, and she was thinking, *What? What?* (Anita Shreve, *The Pilot's Wife*)

When you begin with a disturbance, you're doing the most important thing you can in the beginning of your book: You're starting to bond the reader with a character.

That's why readers read (see the section A Lead Worth Following). Trouble for a character arouses immediate interest.

The Doorways of No Return

When I was going through a lot of trial and error to learn about structure, starting with Aristotle and working my way to Syd Field, one question defied explanation. In the three-act structure, especially in the world of film, the first "plot point" was absolutely crucial. That's the point that happens just before Act Two.

The diagram looks like this:

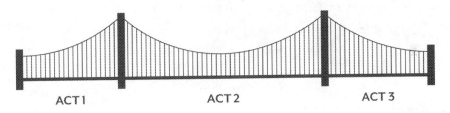

ACT 1   ACT 2   ACT 3

Doorway 1

The most I could find on the first plot point was that it "turned the action around" in some manner or other. Some people called this the *inciting incident*, though that term has been used to cover other parts of a story as well.

My question was always *Why does this work?*

And then one day it came to me, and it revealed the ancient wisdom of the three-act structure. If you think about the plot of your book being that "death struggle" in the middle, the natural question to ask is *Why does the Lead character engage in that struggle?*

Think about it. It's death on the line! In mythic structure terms, the Lead character is out in the "dark world" where he can get killed.

Who wants to go out there if they don't have to?

So here's what has to happen: Something needs to *force* the Lead character into Act Two, into the death struggle, into the dark world. He wants to stay in Act One if he can. That's home. That's safe.

But there's some occurrence pushing him through a *Doorway of No Return.* The Lead is forced through the doorway, and—most important of all—the door slams behind him. He is then *forced* into battle, the conflict, the confrontation, the trouble.

See how that will make the reader worry?

What the reader won't worry about is a Lead who wanders out into the dark world because he's not watching his step. Or says, "Oh, I think I'll take a stroll in the dark world and see what happens."

So the strength of your plot momentum is dependent on that first doorway of no return.

Let's look at some examples.

In *Star Wars,* Luke is on his home planet, living with his aunt and uncle, helping them farm. He dreams of adventure but has no reason to go.

Until his aunt and uncle are killed and the farm destroyed.

This pushes Luke into Act Two, where he can fight the opposition that caused this.

In *Gone With the Wind,* Scarlett would be content to sit at home and flirt and scheme to get Ashley to marry her.

But then something happens that is going to force her to deal with all sorts of trouble, a little something called the Civil War. Scarlett doesn't want this, but there it is. She is pushed through the doorway and it slams shut behind her. The old life will never return.

About one-fifth into *To Kill a Mockingbird* comes Scout's first doorway of no return: Atticus has taken on the defense of a black man, Tom Robinson. Scout is taunted about this at school. At first she denies it, but then Atticus tells her it's true. And once more, Scout will have to confront prejudice, observe attitudes, and figure out which way she is going to grow up.

As a rule of thumb, that first doorway should happen no later than one-fifth into your novel.

Pace

Where you place the first doorway is a matter of momentum.

The closer you put it to the opening, the faster the book takes off.

In Dean Koontz's *The Good Guy*, Timothy Carrier is the quintessential ordinary man, having a beer in a bar. A stranger comes in and thinks Tim is the hit man he's hired. Which is why he slips him ten grand in cash and gives him a photo of the woman he is to kill. And then takes off.

This is not the first doorway yet, because at this point Tim can just walk away. Give the money to charity. Warn the victim, and so on.

But then the real hit man comes in and mistakes Tim for the guy who hired him. Tim offers to give the man half the money as a "no kill" fee to save the life of the woman marked for death. But when the killer walks out of the bar Tim knows the gears are in motion. He has been pushed into the confrontation, which is going to be a struggle to save the life of the woman.

This happens at the end of chapter two. Koontz, as he often does, sets a rapid-fire pace. That's perfectly in keeping with the style of this particular story.

Other stories will have that first doorway come in a little later. So long as there's an opening disturbance, and we have characters in some kind of trouble, we can wait. But not too long.

In film structure terms, the first doorway usually occurs just under half an hour into a two-hour film. About one-quarter of the way in.

In a novel, I like to see it earlier than that. But no later. That's when things start to drag.

Doorway 2

At some point your story has to end. That's the function of the second doorway. It's the event that enables the Lead to engage in the final battle and settle things once and for all. Usually this event is some major clue or discovery that provides the essential information to proceed toward the climax. Or it may be a major setback or crisis that forces the Lead to dig deep and make a final push toward resolution.

In *To Kill a Mockingbird,* the major setback is the guilty verdict in the trial of the obviously innocent Tom Robinson. The pure unfairness of it hits Scout and Jem like a thunderbolt. And it unlooses a series of events that leads to Bob Ewell's attempt on the childrens' lives.

This setback happens with about one-fifth of the novel to go.

In the film *The Wizard of Oz,* Dorothy is captured by the witch and taken to the castle. This makes inevitable the final showdown when the three friends break in to save her.

In *Lethal Weapon,* Riggs (Mel Gibson) and Murtaugh (Danny Glover) are partners trying to bring down a drug ring. The major crisis occurs when the bad guys kidnap Murtaugh's teenage daughter. There is no way to avoid a showdown now.

And that really is all you need to know about basic structure.

In fact, if you know your LOCK elements (see chapter three), and design your disturbance and two doorways, that is often the only *outline* you need.

Even those of you who like to wing it every day (by the seat of your pants, as they say), having at least an idea of these factors will keep you more on track than you've ever been in your writing life—and still leave you plenty of that breathing room you so dearly love.

And, of course, if you like to do more extensive outlining, you are perfectly free to do so. You can lay out your scenes on the proper sides of the two doorways.

CHARACTER DRIVEN VS. PLOT DRIVEN

In a character-driven piece, the most important thing is what happens *inside* the character, how he changes or fails to change (as in a tragedy).

In a plot-driven piece, the most important thing is what happens *to* the character from *outside events.*

Both need plot. The events of the story cause the character-driven Lead to confront himself, his past, his wounds, his secrets, and so on. The events of the story cause the plot-driven Lead to keep alive in some sense, either physically or professionally.

In a *plot-driven story,* the first doorway is an *event.* Something happens that virtually *forces* the Lead into Act Two. He doesn't want to go. No one wants to enter a dark world of conflict and potential death unless he has to.

So ... when Luke Skywalker's aunt and uncle are murdered, it is the event that forces him into the conflict with the Empire. When the cyclone takes Dorothy to Oz, she is forced to find a way back home while fighting against a wicked witch who is hell-bent on killing her. When Dr. Richard Kimble (*The Fugitive*) is being bussed to death row, a botched takeover leads to his near-death escape, forcing him to stay ahead of the U.S. Marshall, Sam Gerard, until he can find his wife's real killer. When John Mc-Clane (*Die Hard*) witnesses a terrorist murder the head of a corporation in a building that has been taken over, he must find a way to stay out of their clutches while trying to get the attention of the police.

Thus it is an event that forces the Lead into the conflict of Act Two.

But what about a character-driven plot? Here, the triggering event is something *emotional* that forces the Lead to look at himself and risk the danger of *change*.

So ... in *On the Waterfront*, Terry Malloy is content to live the life of a strong arm for the local mob boss, until the death of a childhood friend at the hands of the mob brings the victim's sister back to the neighborhood. She wants Terry's help in solving the murder, but Terry tries to tell her he can't possibly do that—until he's moved by her tears. Instead of walking away from her, he allows himself to be drawn to her humanity. He will be forced to choose what kind of person he is going to be from now on—living like an "animal" or being "part of everybody else."

That first emotional prompt happens at the first doorway point.

In the character-driven plot, the Lead is forced by a strong emotional push to look at himself and wonder who he is, and if he has the courage to change. The first step in that change is a small step, but it leads through that first doorway, and makes the conflict of Act Two inevitable.

No one can go back through the "doorway of no return." The Lead in a character-driven story will have to fight through the second act, facing obstacles that force him to confront his own being. By the end of the story he will be a new person or will have failed in the attempt and "died inside" in some manner.

In a plot-driven story, the Lead will fight to survive in some vital way—physically or professionally, or both.

In a character-driven story, that second doorway is going to be something with a huge, emotional wallop. Why? Because it has to lead to the character having the courage to make his change complete.

In *On the Waterfront,* it's when Terry's brother Charlie is killed as a warning to Terry not to testify. Of course Terry is torn apart by this. He initially seeks violent revenge. But the priest gets to him and convinces him that his testimony to the crime board is much more effective. Terry summons the courage to live as a human being, and not an animal.

ANALYZING THE KING'S SPEECH

Let's take a close look at a character-driven film that won the Academy Award for Best Picture of the Year.

In *The King's Speech,* Prince Albert is a British Royal with a terrible hardship: He stammers. Because he will be expected to give speeches, this is no small thing. The film opens with a disturbance, a speech that he has to give to a large assembly at Wembley Stadium. He fumbles it. We can see in his face, and also the face of his loving wife, Elizabeth, what a horrible experience this is for him.

We know from the start, then, that this is going to be a story about psychological death. We see how important it is to Albert that he is able to fulfill his royal duties. If he does not, he'll not only suffer the disapproval of his family, from his austere father on down, but let down the people of Great Britain, too. As the threat of war begins to become more real, the question becomes, How will he be able to inspire his nation if he can't speak to them?

So "death overhanging" is certainly present here. Inner death. You can make the case that it is "professional death," too. His ability to perform his kingly duties is on the line.

You can have more than one type of death hanging over the story.

Remember, the *thing* that is at stake for the character can be something we might view as relatively trivial. But if we can *justify it in the life of the character,* it will work.

Quite often in a character-driven story like this, the first doorway of no return is an *emotional* push. It is something that happens inside the character that gets him through that door to confront the opposition in Act Two.

And what is that opposition for Prince Albert? Again, when we are dealing with a character-driven narrative, you must look inside the character himself. In this case, the confrontation is the very handicap he suffers from. He is not opposed by any one person. People do show up to exacerbate his physical problem. His brother, David, makes fun of him and looks down upon him in a way. The Archbishop of Canterbury and others of that ilk have little confidence in him. And his father, of course, truly disapproves and doesn't know how to handle Albert's stuttering.

So the confrontation of Act Two will be a series of incidents showing Albert trying to avoid the psychological death of his stuttering. The stakes will increase, culminating in the large final battle: a major speech just after England enters the war with Germany.

The first doorway of no return, then, happens about a quarter of the way into the film when Albert listens to the recording that his speech therapist, Lionel, made at their first session. Albert read a bit of Hamlet's soliloquy while listening to Mozart on headphones. To his shock, the recording is almost flawless.

Inside, Albert is moved emotionally toward a glimmer of hope. He consents to go for speech therapy. In this he shows courage, because all other therapists have been useless to him.

We have tremendous sympathy for Albert at this point. We have seen a "care package" early on. He is truly a loving father. He does not let his handicap stop him from telling his little girls stories.

And so this reveals another key that we've talked about. A reader or viewer must feel invested in a Lead character. They need to have some reason to want to keep reading about this person.

When you have a character who is so likable and sympathetic because he is both an underdog and facing hardship with courage, you are almost home free. Now it is a matter of constructing scenes that show the lead taking steps—trying actively to overcome the obstacles.

The second doorway of no return comes when England formally enters the war with Germany. Now Albert will have to face a final battle with his stammering, at the most crucial time. The stakes are the highest they can be. What he says will either inspire or disappoint the nation.

Do you see how psychological death is revealed here? We see it in the fine acting of Colin Firth. His face is reminiscent of the acting job done by Gary Cooper in *High Noon*. That is another film about a man facing his own fears, as the clock ticks toward a final battle and he has only himself to face the challenge.

Or almost only himself. Because *The King's Speech* is also about the friendship between Prince Albert and Lionel Logue. That is a major part of Act Two.

How does one show conflict here? Remember, this is about two allies. In that sense it is somewhat reminiscent of a buddy film. The key to making it work is to show points of conflict between the allies. And that happens several times in *The King's Speech*. There is a tussle between Albert and Lionel about what names they would call each other, what exercises they would undertake. The conflict escalates to a point where Albert doesn't want to listen to Lionel anymore and splits from him. There is also a moment when Albert has been confronted with the fact that Lionel has no credentials, and the two duke it out. There are little arguments that go on between them. That conflict is part of the fabric of the film. Without it, you'd just have two happy friends and a bored audience.

Albert is also in conflict with his family, of course. And with those who doubt him. So all of the elements are set up in exactly the same way we would set up the structure in a plot-driven story. It's just that this time the action is driven by the Lead character's need to overcome and grow.

Is there a character arc? Of course there is. Albert grows from someone who is captive to his fears and his stammer to someone who has found the courage and the means to overcome. And he exercises that courage at the moment his country needs him most.

In a way it's also like a sports movie. The little team that nobody thought could win the big game. But they work hard to face challenges and then when the big game comes they are ready to play.

The climactic radio address in *The King's Speech* is like the big game. There are moments when you think maybe he won't come through. But with Lionel helping him, he delivers the speech and becomes victorious. Just like the little guy on the underdog team who sinks the basket at the last second to win the game.

CHAPTER 5
POINT OF VIEW
AND CONFLICT

Choosing a point of view (POV) for your novel is one the most important decisions you can make. But many writers—even those who are published—are flummoxed about POV. They may have a surface understanding of the differences, but that's about it.

Getting a grip on POV is essential for any novelist because it has bearing on conflict and suspense, the two things your novel needs most to become successful.

Reading about POV can also be confusing. Some writing teachers themselves are not so clear on the crucial distinctions.

So let me make it real simple for you.

You have two choices: first person or third person.

Under first person you have two further choices: present tense or past tense. Under third person you also have two further choices: limited or unlimited.

I will explain these choices below.

"But what about *second person?*" you might be thinking.

Second-person POV is this: *You walk into the room and see the crowd. They look back at you. All of them seem to know what you've just done. You ignore the stares and walk up to Robert. "Hi buddy," you say, holding out your hand.*

Yes, some novelists have used second-person POV. My advice is not to follow their lead.

If you really, really want to, then heed this advice: *You sit down at your desk and begin to write in second person. It seems a good way for you to stretch your literary style. You know that it reduces the chances you'll be published, and also that most readers find it frustrating. But you decide to learn all you can about it and write it and see how it works. And you wish yourself luck.*

What about *omniscient POV?* The word means *all-knowing*, and that's why omniscient POV is sometimes called the "godlike" perspective. The narrator is free to go wherever she wants to go, into any character's thoughts at any time (even within the same scene) or into the sky above so she can describe the events like a camera.

The omni voice can comment on the events (*It was the best of times, it was the worst of times)* or can keep opinions out of it. Since it is the "God's-eye view" it is highly flexible in the amount of intrusion.

Omniscient narration is little used anymore, though it may be a good choice for some longer styles of fiction, especially historical epics. It allows the author to give the readers large-canvas background information. But keep in mind this can be ponderous if done without restraint. And it is by no means required that writers use omniscient POV for epic-length fiction. The more intimate POV of third person can work as well or better.

You can, on occasion, begin a chapter with an omniscient perspective and "drop back" into the POV. Here's what I mean:

> The forests of Sherwood were long known to the villagers as a dark and somewhat scary place. They could hide robbers who waited for the unsuspecting horseman. Tales spread from the stables to the inns. Be on guard lest ye be robbed was always the end of the refrain.
>
> Robin of Loxley stood beneath the Major Oak tree, longbow in hand. It felt good and strong. I will send Prince John a message, he thought.

The first paragraph gives us the large-angle view, then drops into our POV character, where it will remain.

Note that in either case, the use of the omniscient voice doesn't run to commentary, as in the nineteenth-century style. Who cares what you, the author, thinks about the times? Give us the characters.

It's also possible to write in omniscient *without* ever rendering the inner thoughts of a character. While rare, it can be effective in certain genres.

Think of it as being like a movie camera. It only captures what an audience can see. Here's an excerpt from Dashiell Hammett's *The Maltese Falcon:*

> Spade sank into his swivel-chair, made a quarter turn to face her, smiled politely. He smiled without separating his lips. All the Vs in his face grew longer.
>
> The tappity-tap-tap and the thin bell and muffled whir of Effie Perine's typewriting came through the closed door. Somewhere in a neighboring office a power-driven machine vibrated dully. On Spade's desk a limp cigarette smoldered in a brass tray filled with the remains of limp cigarettes.

This is the camera view because if we were in Spade's head he wouldn't have been able to see the Vs in his face grow longer. Nor do we get Spade's thoughts. And notice how the description of the cigarette on Spade's desk is like a camera zooming in.

Finally, the more overt authorial voice in omniscient might be good in some genres, such as speculative fiction.

In Douglas Adams's *The Hitchhiker's Guide to the Galaxy*, the Adams voice is readily apparent. As in the prologue to *So Long, and Thanks for All the Fish*:

> Far out in the uncharted backwaters of the uncharted backwaters of the unfashionable end of the Western Spiral arm of the Galaxy lies a small underregarded yellow sun.
>
> Orbiting this at a distance of roughly ninety-eight million miles is an utterly insignificant little blue-green planet whose ape-descended life forms are so amazingly primitive that they still think digital watches are a pretty neat idea.

Likewise, Joe Haldeman's crisp little speculative novel, *The Hemingway Hoax*, begins by telling readers it's the beginning:

> Our story begins in a rundown bar in Key West, not so many years from now. The bar is not the one Hemingway drank at, nor yet the one that claims to be the one he drank at, nor yet the one that claims to be the one he drank at, because they are both too expensive and full of tourists. This bar, in a more interesting part of town, is a Cuban place. It is neither clean or well-lighted, but has cold beer and good strong Cuban coffee. Its cheap prices and rascally charm are what bring together the scholar and the rogue.

CREATING CONFLICT IN FIRST-PERSON POV

First person is the character telling what happened.

> I went to the store. I saw Frank. "What are you doing here?" I said.

Obviously this POV requires everything to be seen through the eyes of one character. The Lead can only report what she saw, not what Frank saw or felt (unless Frank sees fit to report these items to the Lead). No scene can be described that the narrator has not witnessed—although you can have another character tell the narrator what happened in an "off-screen scene."

You can use past or present tense with first-person POV. The traditional is past tense, where the narrator looks back and tells his story.

But the narrator can also do it this way: *I am going to the store. I see Frank. "What are you doing here?" I say.*

There is an immediacy of tone here that, when handled well (as Steve Martini does in his Paul Mandarini legal thrillers), is compelling. But it is not the stylistic innovation it used to be, and you won't hurt yourself if you never use it.

First person makes for a very intimate, and potentially memorable, tale. But to maximize the potential for conflict, you have create a strong voice for the narrator. Think *attitude*. The reason is this: Attitude runs into trouble. There is always going to be someone who thinks differently and doesn't like the Lead's view of things.

So starting with a clear attitude creates a sense of conflict to come.

The opening lines of *The Catcher in the Rye*, for instance, immediately tell us we're listening to someone with a unique view of his own life and is ready to get in your face about it:

> If you really want to hear about it, the first thing you'll probably want to know is where I was born, and what my lousy childhood was like, and how my parents were occupied and all before they had me, and all that David Copperfield kind of crap, but I don't feel like going into it, if you want to know the truth.

Does Janet Evanovich's Lead character Stephanie Plum have an attitude, a voice? Judge from the opening of *High Five:*

> When I was a little girl I used to dress Barbie up without underpants. On the outside, she'd look like the perfect lady. Tasteful plastic heels, tailored suit. But underneath, she was naked. I'm a bail enforcement agent now—also known as a fugitive apprehension agent, also known as a bounty hunter. I bring 'em back dead or alive. At least I try. And

> being a bail enforcement agent is a little like being bare-bottom Barbie.
> It's about having a secret. And it's about wearing a lot of bravado on the
> outside when you're really operating without underpants.

One can also choose to write first-person POV for various characters, in different chapters. Some authors put the name of the POV character at the start of the chapter, then proceed to write in that narrator's voice.

This requires a lot of skill, of course, because each voice must be different, each perspective unique.

KEEPING THIRD-PERSON POV FOCUSED

Third-person POV is when the action is described by the writer *as seen through* the perceptions of a character. Instead of *I saw* it's *she saw*.

The biggest problem I see in third-person narration is the author keeping that POV consistent throughout a scene. It's easy to lapse and suddenly have the POV switch to a different character or to a perspective the character can't see. I'm reading the second novel of a "hot" young thriller writer now, and he makes this mistake. You're cruising along in the head of a character, then suddenly you drop into the head of a secondary character, before going back.

It sounds something like this:

> Ramsey ran around the corner, feeling the heat of the bricks against his
> skin. Nick was keeping up with him, but he could hear the boy huffing
> and puffing. *I hope he's up to this,* he thought.
>
> "Come on, kid," Ramsey said. "You can make it."
>
> "I'm ... trying," Nick said.
>
> Ramsey slowed and put out his hand. When the kid took it, a new
> charge of adrenaline shot through Ramsey's body. He was going to pro-
> tect this boy no matter what.
>
> Nick squeezed Ramsey's hand. He wanted to say he now trusted
> Ramsey, but the words stuck in his throat. He was too tired to talk but
> was determined to show Ramsey he could run fast.
>
> Up ahead, Ramsey saw two men standing at the corner, watching.

Notice that we are in Ramsey's head up until Nick *wanted to say* ... Ramsey can't know what's going on in Nick's mind.

When this kind of "head hopping" occurs, it reduces conflict because it removes the reader from the one who is experiencing it: the POV character. It's really a move that only an omniscient narrator can make, but it's ill-advised here. Even though readers might not consciously think about what's going on, it creates a little bump in the reading experience.

Enough of those bumps and the trip is going to be less satisfactory.

In the limited variety of third person, you stay with one character throughout. You never take on another character's POV. Done well, this can be nearly as intimate as first person.

If you allow other characters to have a third-person POV (this is called *unlimited third person*), you obviously spend less time in the head of a single character. You spread the intimacy around.

But adhere to the discipline of "one scene, one POV." If you need to change POV, you should start a new chapter or leave white space to signal the switch.

HOW DO YOU CHOOSE A POV?

It's mostly a matter of feel, but here are a few things to keep in mind:

1. Don't use first person unless your Lead character's voice is distinct, original, and has plenty of attitude.

2. A temptation in first-person POV is the Lead talking too much about irrelevant things or going off on tangents. These could dissipate conflict.

3. It's easy to relate interior thoughts in first person, but when you do, make sure there is inner conflict reflected there.

4. Third person can be almost as intimate as first, so long as you write the narrative in a way that sounds like the character's own voice:

> John saw Mary across the room. He almost dropped his wine. She was gorgeous. A blonde, too.

Change to:

> John saw Mary across the room. He almost dropped his Bordeaux. A Greek goddess with golden hair had stepped down from Olympus.

5. If you're just starting out as a writer, it's long-standing advice that you start with third-person POV and learn to keep it consistent (one POV per scene). That discipline will serve you well.

6. Character-driven, or so-called literary fiction, is often more hospitable to first-person POV, as it delves most deeply into the inner conflicts of the Lead.

7. Plot-driven fiction, especially thrillers, often use third person because it allows the author to "cut away" from one POV to another, leaving the readers hanging.

8. If you're still in doubt, write the first three chapters in third person, then go back and do them in first person. Get some feedback on which style resonates with potential readers. This exercise won't be wasted because, at the very least, the different perspective will give you greater insight into your characters.

CHAPTER 6
OPENING WITH CONFLICT

Writing does not feel the same from day to day. Sometimes you are in the flow of creative discovery and the words seem to pour out effortlessly. Other times it's like you're playing tennis in the La Brea Tar Pits. Regardless of your "flow state" or the place you are in the novel, there is one unifying theme: conflict.

Alfred Hitchcock said that a good story is "life, with the dull parts taken out." Hitchcock's axiom holds for everything you write.

No conflict=dull. No trouble=readers are tempted to put the book down.

Let's talk about the elements of the three-act structure and how they relate to conflict and suspense.

In brief, beginnings should have a disturbance and portend major trouble to come. Middles show the main confrontation and how it escalates as the story goes along. The final act keeps readers in suspense as the conflict heats up until the final resolution.

In each of these acts there are things you need to keep in mind. You don't want the ghost of Alfred Hitchcock coming to you with a reminder to cut your dull parts.

BEGINNINGS

The majority of manuscripts I've seen by new writers over the years begin too calmly, slowly, or sometimes DOA. The three biggest reasons for this are the myth of exposition, the black hole of happiness, and the lure of the lyrical.

The myth of exposition holds that a reader needs to know a whole bunch of backstory and explanatory material at the beginning of a novel. After all, the author has spent all this time coming up with character background, setting, and so on. At the very least, the writer will have a picture of the character and may make up the background as she goes along.

In either case, the writer reasons that the reader must know all this material to understand what's happening in the story. But this is a myth.

Readers, in fact, will wait a long time for exposition. What grabs them is a character in motion and something that is stirring the placid waters of existence. I call this the *opening disturbance*, which is further explained below.

For now, memorize this rule: Act first, explain later. You will never go wrong delaying exposition.

This is not to say you cannot include some backstory or exposition, in light doses, in the opening chapter of your novel. You can "marble" it in as you go along, but err on the side of restraint.

One way of insuring conflict in your openings is giving us a real scene; that is, something happening on the page in real time—not a summary.

Also a scene in which dialogue is possible helps bring conflict to the surface. By having at least two people with different agendas in dialogue, you have an automatic scene with confrontational possibilities:

> "Any thoughts that you'd like to start with?"
>
> "Thoughts on what?"
>
> "Well, on anything. On the incident."
>
> "On the incident? Yes, I have some thoughts."
>
> She waited but he didn't continue. He had decided before he even got to Chinatown that this would be the way he would be. He'd make her have to pull every single word out of him.

This is the opening of Michael Connelly's *The Last Coyote*. It's immediate conflict. We know as the scene goes along that Harry Bosch, LAPD, is being examined by a psychologist over some of his actions on the job. The psych wants answers and Harry doesn't want to give them.

Different agendas.

This scene goes on for a long time, back and forth, thrust and parry. Every now and then, through the dialogue itself or in narrative form, Connelly drops in a little bit of exposition:

Harry Bosch just looked at her silently He wanted a cigarette but would never ask her if he could smoke. He would never acknowledge in front of her that he had the habit. If he did, she might start talking about oral fixations or nicotine crutches. He took a deep breath instead and looked at the woman on the other side of the desk. Carmen Hinojos was a small woman with a friendly face and manner. Bosch knew she wasn't a bad person. He'd actually heard good things about her from others who had been sent to Chinatown. She was just doing her job here and his anger was not really directed at her. He knew she was probably smart enough to know that, too.

Sometimes that exposition is through dialogue:

"Everybody keeps calling it the incident. It kind of reminds me of how people called it the Vietnam conflict, not the war."

"Then what would you call what happened?"

"I don't know. But incident ... It sounds like ... I don't know. Antiseptic. Listen, Doctor, let's go back a minute. I don't want to take a trip out of town, okay? My job is in homicide. It's what I do. And I'd really like to get back to it. I might be able to do some good, you know."

"If the department lets you."

The point is this opening scene never bogs down because it is, from the start, one of confrontation. And that makes for immediate reader interest.

But what if you're writing some other sort of novel, like a sweeping historical, that requires you to take a broader view of the opening? Follow your instincts, but see if you can put some hint of conflict to come somewhere on that first page.

Here is the opening of Dennis Lehane's historical novel, *The Given Day:*

Due to travel restrictions placed on Major League Baseball by the Department of Defense during the great War, the World Series of 1918 was played in September and split into two homestands. The Chicago Cubs hosted the first three games with the final four to be held in Boston. On September 7th, after the Cubs dropped Game Three, the two teams boarded the Michigan Central together to embark on the twenty-seven hour trip, and Babe Ruth got drunk and started stealing hats.

Lehane lulls us into thinking this opening paragraph is merely a documentary-style setup. But the last phrase hits us out of nowhere and, most important, hints of conflict to come. Not just getting drunk, but stealing hats? Babe Ruth? Why? Who from, and what will they do about it?

Of course, a historical novelist can begin with a character in crisis right off the bat:

> The gale tore at him and he felt its bit deep within and he knew that if they did not make landfall in three days they would all be dead. Too many deaths on this voyage, he thought. I'm Pilot-Major of a dead fleet. One ship left out of five—eight and twenty men from a crew of one hundred and seven and now only ten can walk and the rest near death and our Captain-General one of them. No food, almost no water and what there is, brackish and foul. *(Shogun* by James Clavell)

There are innumerable ways to open with conflict or the portent of conflict. There are also many ways *not* to open your novel. Here are a few of them.

HAPPY PEOPLE IN HAPPY LAND

Many times an author lays out a scene of domestic bliss or perfect harmony, thinking that the readers will get to like the characters involved. Then, when the trouble starts, they'll be hooked in with these nice folks and be oh-so-worried about them.

But the opposite is usually true. The reader is wondering why bother? Life is good! These people can get along just fine without me.

Remember the first shot of *The Wizard of Oz*? It's not of Dorothy waking up in her nice, warm bed, the sun shining, the birds singing. If that were so, and she started singing about some land over some rainbow, we'd be wondering, *What's her beef?* She's got it good. Quit whining already.

No, the opening shot is of Dorothy running down the road, Toto at her heels, looking over her shoulder in fear. And then, back at her farm, she tries to tell her aunt and uncle, and the farmhands, about the terrible Miss Gulch and her plan to ice little Toto. And no one will listen!

Okay, now we see not a happy girl in happy land, but a girl with problems. Now when she sings about escaping over the rainbow, we're with her.

Here is my rendition of the type of thing I see all too often in beginning manuscripts:

As Janet prepared breakfast for her girls, she paused at the kitchen window and thought how lucky she was to have April and Dakota. They had it all, it seemed. They were both pretty and smart. April had recently won first prize for her third-grade essay, "The Weimar Republic and Why it Matters to Children Today."

And little Dakota, what could one say? At four she was already reading Proust. The countless hours spent reading to her in the womb had paid off.

Janet sighed contentedly as she poured the organic wheat flakes into the bowls.

"Thanks ever so much for the breakfast, Mommy," said April.

"I like wheat flakes," said Dakota.

"I know you do," Janet said.

"Where's Daddy?" Dakota asked.

"He's still on his business trip," Janet said. Her thoughts turned to Frank. What had she done to deserve such a wonderful husband?

And so it goes. The girls are readied for school, Janet thinks about her day, and then at the end of the chapter there's a knock at the door:

Janet opened the door.

A deputy sheriff stood there. He was about thirty and had a stern expression on his face.

"Janet Robinson?" he said.

"Yes. Is something wrong?"

"This is for you." The deputy held out a trifolded paper. She took it.

"Have a nice day," the deputy said and walked away.

Janet unfolded the paper. Her eyes scanned the official-looking heading: *Petition for Divorce.*

This is indeed a disturbance to Janet's placid world. But it has come too late. Enduring Happy People in Happy Land for this long is too much. The harried reader won't get past the first page.

Instead, I would do something like this:

Janet looked out the kitchen window as the Sheriff's cruiser pulled to a stop in front of her house.

Now what could that be about?

"Where's my cereal!" Dakota shouted.

"Be quiet," Janet said, "I'm going as fast as I can."

The disturbance happens in the opening line. A Sheriff's car stopping in front of your house is not ordinary. It's usually going to be bad news. Now the scene can unfold with the reader worrying, along with Janet, about the meaning of the vehicle.

Also, having crabby kids adds to the conflict.

No dull parts.

THE LURE OF THE LYRICAL

You'll often hear editors and agents warn about opening with weather. It's a standard complaint. Because most often when it's done it is merely descriptive and doesn't set a tone of trouble to come.

Now it's true that many excellent novels begin with lyrical passages. Most often this is done in so-called literary novels, where style is as important to the author as story. Readers who respond to such writing are patient if the style is pleasing to them.

The only caveat I would offer here is not to be lured by the lyrical in a desire to show what a good writer you are. You may be the best writer since Shakespeare, but always serve the needs of the story and the reader first. One exception: If you write solely for yourself, without concern for connecting with an audience, you can of course write whatever you like.

The best of both worlds is if you can combine your style with portents of trouble or a mood that mirrors the novel as a whole.

Ken Kesey's famous opening to *Sometimes a Great Notion* is exactly like this. The novel is a big, lusty story of men in the logging business. The setting is key to the story, as a background for the major conflicts to come:

> Along the western slopes of the Oregon Coastal Range ... come look: the hysterical crashing of tributaries as they merge into the Wakonda Auga River ...
>
> The first little washes flashing like thick rushing winds through sheep sorrel and clover, ghost fern and nettle, sheering, cutting ... forming branches. Then, through bearberry and salmonberry, blueberry and blackberry, the branches crashing into creeks, into streams. Finally, in the foothills, through tamarack and sugar pine, shittim bark and silver

> spruce—and the green and blue mosaic of Douglas fir—the actual river
> falls five hundred feet ... and look: opens out upon the fields.
>
> Metallic at first, seen from the highway down through the trees, like
> an aluminum rainbow, like a slice of alloy moon.

I don't want to discourage you from playing with the language and exploring style. Just be intentional about it and know that style is not about being admired. It's about weaving rich language into the conflict.

VOICE AND POINT-OF-VIEW FUZZINESS

"A pet peeve of mine is ragged, fuzzy point of view," says literary agent Cricket Freeman. Fuzziness means either not knowing whose POV the story is in or having a narrative voice that is not distinctive. Let's take each problem in turn.

Here's a common opening mistake I see:

> The trees were ghostly skeletons against the night sky. In the distance the
> wail of a nocturnal bird seemed to signal trouble to come. Getting stuck
> in the woods was not in anyone's plans. But that's just the way it was.
>
> Liz drew the blanket around her and said, "This place creeps me out."

The problem here is that we don't know whose head we are in at the start. While the description gives us some indication of the mood, it is removed from a "hot" POV. That makes the start less intimate for the reader. It becomes a wasted opportunity.

The fix is simple. Just set us in a POV at the start:

> Liz drew the blanket around her and said, "This place creeps me out."
>
> The trees looked like ghostly skeletons against the night sky. In the
> distance Liz heard the wail of a nocturnal bird that seemed to signal trouble to come. Getting stuck in the woods was not in her plans. But that's
> just the way it was and now she'd have to deal with it.

By tweaking this opening we are inside a character. Since character is what fully engages a reader, we get that from the start.

Is it ever okay to begin with a large-canvas type of opening? Sure, if that fits the need and mood of your novel. It's a time-honored move to begin with an omniscient POV and then to "drop" into a character POV.

But times and tastes change, and the sooner you get a reader bonded with a character, the better.

Fuzziness in POV can also occur in first person, when the voice lacks distinction or attitude.

> The pebbled glass door panel is lettered in flaked black paint: *"Philip Marlowe ... Investigations."* It is a reasonably shabby door at the end of a reasonably shabby corridor in the sort of building that was new about the year the all-tile bathroom became the basis of civilization. The door is locked, but next to it is another door with the same legend which is not locked. Come on in—there's nobody in here but me and a big bluebottle fly. But not if you're from Manhattan, Kansas.

There's no mistaking the attitude in Marlowe's narration of Raymond Chandler's *The Little Sister.* It's the sort of voice that makes a reader sit up and take notice.

When writing in first person, don't open bland.

INFORMATION DUMPS

I have a rule: Act first, explain later.

This is especially crucial in the opening, when you want the story to grab the reader. That's why you ought to make this a rule of thumb. In the first thirty pages, don't give any more than a short paragraph of exposition at any one time.

And when you do, don't make it pure informational lard, like this:

> Joseph Doakes worked at McKinley, Gunther & Katz, the second largest law firm in Chicago. The first largest, Ketchum, Kellum & Skinnem, was in the building directly across from McKinley, Gunther. The two firms had long battled for supremacy in the city. In 1954, when Steve McKinley started the firm, there was still money to be made representing the big railroads. McKinley's first major client, Union Pacific, made it possible for the rising lawyer to commission his own building on Michigan Avenue, for which he hired a hot young architect named James Ingo Freed. Freed had only recently graduated from the Illinois Institute of Technology and was working with the legendary Miles van der Rohe. McKinley had met him quite by chance one day on the shore of Lake Michigan.

What's happened here is too much information in too short a time, covering too many tangents. All the while we've forgotten poor Joe Doakes up at the top of the paragraph.

TOO MUCH BACKSTORY

Backstory refers to any essential information about the characters that happens before your novel begins.

Sometimes this information comes in later via the flashback, which we'll talk about later.

There are those who advocate no backstory in the opening chapters, but I think that goes a little too far. Backstory can help us bond with a Lead character, our most important task in those first pages.

So the rule is, don't put in too much or none at all.

What you do put in, marble in with the action (as one observes the "marbling" of the fat within a fine piece of red meat. Or, for you vegetarians, in an artfully designed piece of cloth).

David Morrell's *First Blood* (the basis of the Rambo franchise) starts off immediately with the conflict of the principles, John Rambo and Madison Police Chief Wilfred Teasle. Teasle determines Rambo is a vagrant and escorts him out of town. Rambo comes back for a bite to eat, and Teasle drives him out of town again, warning him not to come back.

We're in chapter three before we get any significant backstory. Rambo has just finished eating a hamburger on the outskirts of town, setting fire to the paper bag it came in:

> Six months back from the war and still he had the urge to destroy what was left of what he had eaten so he would not leave a trace of where he had been.
>
> He shook his head. Thinking about the war had been a mistake. Instantly he was reminded of his other habits from the war: trouble getting to sleep in the open, waking with the slightest noise, needing to sleep in the open, the hole where they had kept him prisoner fresh in his mind.
>
> "You'd better think of something else," he said out loud and then realized he was talking to himself. "What's it going to be? Which way?" He looked where the road stretched into town, where it stretched away from

town, and then he was decided. He grabbed the rope on his sleeping bag, slung it around his shoulder and started hiking into Madison again.

Morrell limits himself to one paragraph of backstory, choosing only the most significant details. We now know Rambo is a war vet with issues and was once a prisoner.

Then Morrell gets right back to the action, which is Rambo heading back to the town where all the trouble is.

HERE WE ARE IN SUNNY SPAIN

An old cliché that often happens in TV sketch writing is for the writer to begin the piece with the characters giving the setting right off the bat. To do it, the two participants might walk on, look around, and one says, "Well, here we are in sunny Spain."

Or any of a number of variations on that.

It worked for sketch comedy but won't work in your novel. Why? Because readers know when you're slipping them information rather than having two characters talk to each other naturally:

"Hey Rachel," Tom said. "Which way is it to the Via Delorosa again? I swear, these Triple A maps of Jerusalem aren't doing us a heck of a lot of good on our one vacation this year."

"Oh Tom," said Rachel, "you were complaining about that the whole trip over here, on the cruise ship Enchanted."

"Don't remind me. The cruise was totally your idea. When you gave me those tickets for my forty-fifth birthday last February, what was I to do? Now it's six months later and I still don't know what to do. Except I want to find that doggone Via Delorosa so I can send some pictures back to our daughter, Elizabeth."

"Who just turned sixteen."

"Yes."

Good for sketch comedy, not for novels.

CHAPTER 7

KEEP IT MOVING IN THE MIDDLE

I do a lot of writing at my branch offices. The offices are in cities all over the world, and each has a round green sign outside. They have free Internet and pricey coffee, but they also have something else: the human parade.

For many years, before remodeling, I had a regular table at my local Starbucks. It was by the window, with a view of the parking lot, and afforded me a wide-angle window to the entire store.

I have seen my share of the human condition. And that condition is made up of conflict.

One day a woman came in wearing shabby clothes and a thatch of hair that had not seen a brush in days. She did not order coffee. Instead, she sat at one of the tables and began shouting at the top of her lungs, "Where is Jimmy Hoffa? Where is Jimmy Hoffa!"

The manager of the store came out and engaged the woman in conversation, the primary object of which, I gathered, was to get her to keep her voice down.

She inquired about Hoffa again, her voice heading up in decibels. The manager reached for his cell phone and went outside. The woman accused the store of having Jimmy Hoffa in the back. The accusations went on for several minutes.

Presently, the manager of the store came back in, accompanied by a security guard. The woman told the security guard that Starbucks was hiding Jimmy Hoffa's body in the back of the store. The security guard escorted the woman outside. And that's the last I saw of her.

Now consider this scene in dramatic terms.

A normal morning in a low-key environment is interrupted by a surprising character shouting about a well-known mystery.

It disturbs the patrons—conflict. Attempts to quell the tirade fail, generating more conflict with the manager. The stakes are raised when the security guard enters. And we are left in suspense, wondering what the fate of the woman might be.

Oh, and we still didn't solve the mystery of where Jimmy Hoffa is.

So there you have it—surprise, conflict, mystery, and suspense. It all adds up to a scene working on all cylinders.

Those are the kinds of scenes you want to write throughout the middle of your novel. Or, as one wag put it, the "muddle." Because it's all about trouble.

THE JOURNEY SO FAR

Do you remember the scene in *Lawrence of Arabia* when Lawrence (Peter O'Toole) has convinced Sherif Ali (Omar Sharif) that his band of Arab soldiers can attack Aqaba from the desert side?

Only to do it they'll have to cross an expanse that has never been crossed before, the Nefud.

Just before they begin, Ali points to the vast wasteland before them and warns that from here there will be no water. And if the camels die, the men die.

It looks like hell's stove and goes on forever. Which is how some writers view the middle of their novels. It stretches out like an arid desert, and they wonder if indeed they'll get across it without frying.

Well, you can. And not only that. Your camel will survive, and you'll hit plenty of water. Because you've got conflict to guide you.

If you have laid out your map properly, you will have reached the edge of your desert by passing through the first doorway of no return. All the elements are strong.

We have a Lead worth following. Death is on the line. A stronger opponent is waiting to stop the Lead.

On the other side of the desert is the Knockout Ending.

How should you begin? By getting to the next scene. Then proceeding to the scene after that.

But what scenes are they? How do you know which oasis to head for?

Because you know your LOCK elements (Lead, Objective, Confrontation, Knockout Ending), you can lay out your scenes organically. You never have to worry about a wrong turn or getting lost in a sandstorm.

You do it with action and reaction.

ACTION AND REACTION

There are two basic beats in fiction: action and reaction. If you understand these dynamics you'll know 90 percent of what it takes to write scenes packed with conflict and tension.

Remember our definition of a novel: *the record of how a character deals with the threat of imminent death.* When these stakes are established, you raise a question in the reader's mind: What things will the character *do* in order to prevent his death?

The character has to do something. If he doesn't, death will happen. And your character will be a spineless patsy who lets it happen.

Thus the action element in fiction; that is, a record of those things the character does to gain the objective (which will prevent death).

Thus, in *The Fugitive*, we see what Richard Kimble does in order to keep from being captured by the law and also to find out who killed his wife.

In *The Catcher in the Rye*, we see what Holden Caulfield does in order to find authenticity in the world (if he doesn't, he'll die inside, and maybe kill himself as well).

What about reaction beats? These are moments, perhaps even whole chapters, where a character is reacting to the events, and feeling or ruminating about them. But these feelings and thoughts must be organic, tied to the overall objective (avoiding death). They will then have tension attached because it's still an open question whether the character will win and live, or lose and die.

Action Scenes

You are now armed with the knowledge of how to construct a "perpetual plot machine." You can create an almost never-ending stream of scenes relating to the objective. Your job is to select the best ones to include in your novel.

Each action scene should involve steps to solve problems relating to the overall objective. (Note: We cover subplots on page 125.)

Let's take *The Fugitive* as an example. Richard Kimble is facing certain death: execution because he has been found guilty of murdering his wife. Unless he solves this problem, he's done. There's also a psychological death involved. If he doesn't find the real killer, there will be no justice for his dead wife.

A botched escape attempt on the prison bus leads to a horrific accident that enables Kimble to escape.

Now the perpetual plot machine provides all the action material needed. The author simply has to design scenes where Kimble is taking steps to avoid being caught, while finding clues about his wife's murder.

Let's consider the structure of an action scene. It has three components: objective, obstacles, and outcome.

Objective

The scene objective is not the same as the main story objective. It is anything the character needs to accomplish in order to further his goal of avoiding death.

In *The Fugitive*, Kimble is wounded and dressed in prison clothes after his escape. Before he can do anything else, he has to take care of his wound and change his appearance.

A scene objective.

Now we provide some obstacles. The main obstacle is other people who will see him and report him.

Kimble finds a rural hospital. Nearby is a tow truck with some coveralls in it. He steals them (remaining unseen).

Now he has to get into the hospital to stitch himself up and shave his beard. How is he going to do that with other people around?

He goes to the back of the hospital, the loading dock, where he can blend in with the workers. He unloads something and takes it inside the hospital.

Now what?

He has to get to a room with antiseptic and stitching material. He finds one with a comatose patient (whew).

He then cleans and dresses his wound.

But he's got to get rid of the beard. He uses shaving gear that he finds in the bathroom to shave … just as a nurse enters the room to check on the patient and get him some water from the bathroom.

Obstacles

Kimble hides behind the door and manages to remain unseen.

He needs food (the obstacle of physical hunger). Luckily the comatose man just got his meal served and Kimble wolfs it down.

He also puts on a white smock and walks out of the room, pretending to be a doctor … just as a state trooper, holding a picture of the bearded Kimble, comes toward him.

Obstacle!

The trooper asks if he's seen a man fitting Kimble's description. Kimble solves this problem the only way he can, humor. "Every time I look in the mirror, pal. Except for the beard of course."

The trooper lets him go.

Is the scene over? Not yet! The writer squeezes even more tension out of the scene. A prison guard whose life Kimble saved is being brought in on a gurney. He looks up and is about to say, "Hey, that's Richard Kimble," when Kimble puts the oxygen mask over his face and tells the paramedics to check the guy's sternum (the medics wonder how he knew that just from looking at him).

Still not over. Kimble has to get away. An ambulance seems like a good idea. He takes the one that just came in with the prison guard.

Outcome

All scenes end eventually, and there are two basic outcomes: 1) the character realizes his objective; or 2) the character fails to achieve the objective.

Within these two outcomes there are variations. In general, you want the outcome to make the character's situation worse than when he started.

Why? Because of our old friend *worry*. Readers want to worry about the character, and you're going to help them do that.

In the scene from *The Fugitive,* Kimble gets out of the hospital without being stopped (a successful outcome) but immediately he encounters more trouble.

First, the medics are just bringing in the guard Kimble saved on the prison bus. He's on a gurney, looks up and is about to say something. Kimble clamps the oxygen mask on him. But not before telling the medic exactly where the guard has been stabbed.

Then he gets into the ambulance and drives away.

But that gets reported almost immediately, communicated to Gerard, the U.S. Marshall, and he hops in a helicopter for the next big chase, another action scene.

Reaction Beats

I call this section reaction *beats* because reaction does not have to take up an entire scene.

Imagine that your character has just been dealt an outcome in an action scene. Usually it's going to be a setback of some kind because that's best for dramatic purposes.

So the first thing that happens inside the character is an emotional reaction. If the bad guys start shooting, the person being shot at is not going to start calculating the geometric parameters of his position. He's going to feel the jolt of adrenaline as his body tries to keep him alive.

Likewise, if a woman sees her spouse in the arms of another, she's not going to coolly note the time and go have coffee. She's going to seethe, burn, explode, dissolve, break down—or something like it.

Only after the emotion has subsided do human beings attempt to figure out what to do next.

We will spend some time, then, cogitating. What's the next move?

Do I run farther down the alley with the bad guys in pursuit? Wait, this alley ends at a brick wall. No good. What about that Dumpster? Jump inside? Rats. Garbage. Yuck.

Idiot, would you rather be shot?

All of which may take place in mere seconds, or fractions thereof.

Finally, a decision is made. The character has to act.

He decides on the Dumpster, which leads to ... another action beat.

See how that works?

In a way, it's a logical unpackaging of how we live our messy lives without realizing it.

So after an action scene is over, the outcome realized, inside the character figure out:

1. Emotion
2. Analysis
3. Decision

The great thing about understanding reaction beats is that they are the key to controlling the pace of your novel.

And you do need to control it, even if you're writing a full-on, adrenaline-rush novel. You need to give the readers some breathing space.

The reaction beat is a chance to get us into the character and slow things down for a bit.

EXAMPLE: Roger has just escaped being gunned down by the bad guys and is taking refuge in an apartment he broke into. Whose apartment? He has no idea:

> He was thankful no one was there. He sat on the sofa and let his pulse calm. Unbelievable! There were people out there actually trying to kill him. The nearest thing to real trouble he'd ever gotten in was when he was sent to the principal's office in seventh grade. And even that was a misunderstanding.
>
> Kill him? Who? Why?
>
> He breathed in and out. In and out again, slowly.
>
> Okay, he told himself. You're Mr. Goal-Oriented Guy. You can figure out what to do here.
>
> Call the police. Why not?
>
> Because you know how they operate. Word would get out. He'd be walking around with a big neon target on his back.
>
> Who else? His brother, maybe? Steve had contacts. Not the kind Roger would ever want to associate with. Until now.
>
> Steve. Hadn't spoken with him five years.
>
> They'd never been close. When they were kids ...

The scene continues with reflections from the past and finally a decision to contact Steve, leading to the next action scene.

On the other side of the action coin, you can speed things up by shrinking the reaction beats. You can move from action to action with only a flash of emotion or analysis, sometimes leaving them out altogether and filling in blanks later:

> He was thankful no one was there.
> Steve. He needed to contact Steve.
>
> No one was there.
> He called Steve.

WRITING THE SCENE

Let's write a scene with conflict and tension. First, our three Os.

OBJECTIVE: Roger's objective in this scene is to walk unnoticed down Broadway in downtown Los Angeles and get to the little store on the corner of Sixth and Broadway. There's a man there who may know the identity of the real serial killer. This is definitely information Roger needs.

OBSTACLES: The main obstacle in this scene will be the man at the store. We'll call him Mr. Kim. He is not going to want to give Roger the information he needs.

Other obstacles? The setting will seem forbidding to Roger. He'll think there is someone watching him. Maybe there's a cop car parked right outside the store for some reason. This could happen before or after Roger is in the store.

Let's decide on after, because that way Roger has an extra reason to be careful when he comes out.

OUTCOME: At the end of the scene, will Roger have the information he needs or not? In other words, will he achieve his scene objective?

Almost always, you want the scene to end in frustration, trouble, or setback. That makes sense in view of the "worry factor" we've already talked about. Or you can have the Lead achieve the scene objective, but doing so results in some other event that makes the character's situation worse.

Let's keep the serial killer's identity hidden from Roger at this point. More suspense. So we know Mr. Kim will not give up that information. Maybe he can issue Roger a warning of some kind, a place to avoid.

Or maybe he just gets angry as Roger continues to press him.

We're brainstorming here. Make a list of possible scene outcomes. Maybe Mr. Kim pulls out a shotgun and tells Roger to get out of the store. Maybe Mrs. Kim comes out of the back with the gun.

Maybe a guy chooses that moment to rob the store.

What if the cops pull up outside and Mr. Kim screams at them to come in and get this guy?

I could go on. The secret to creativity is to get lots of ideas then choose the best one. Part of that is cutting the ones you don't like.

I decide I don't like the robbery scenario, as it seems too much of a high-concept coincidence. Even though coincidences that make the situation worse for a character are generally okay (as opposed to rescuing the character, usually a no-no), this one seems too far-fetched.

But the cops rolling up looks good. I like that one. Roger is going to be in a heap of trouble if the cops get wind of who he really is.

Now I've got my three elements lined up. Next I want to find the right place to start the scene.

SCENE OPENINGS

There are, in general, two ways to open a scene:

1. Establish the location and proceed to the action.
2. *In media res,* in "the middle of things," starting with action and dropping in location details as needed.

Your decision will come down to pacing. The first option slows things down a bit, while the second gets things moving fast. You can control the pace further depending on how many words you use for each.

I want a fast pace in the scene I'm writing, so I won't spend much time with location. I'll drop in details as the action proceeds:

> Roger got out of the subway at Pershing Square. For a moment he was disoriented. He didn't know which way was north or south. He could have been trapped in the middle of a maze.

Okay, we have Roger in a location and some of what he's feeling. Remember, emotion is the key to character bonding with the reader. This glimpse into Roger's inner life—feeling like he's lost or trapped—sets the mood.

Finally he got his bearings and headed to Broadway. The sun was hidden by the concrete canyon formed by buildings. Some old, some new, some needing work like right now.

He pulled his hat down lower, snapping the brim. He could have been Bogart. No he couldn't. He was no PI and this was no forties film noir. He was an accountant and this was real. All it would take was one person recognizing him and the reality would become the end point of his life.

Or something to that effect. This is all first drafting and playing with mood. And that's what you should do, too.

Try things, but make it consistent with the tone of the scene. Because you know your three Os, you can play in the right ballpark.

The liquor store guy, what was his name again? Kim, that was it. Sixth and Broadway. If Thompson was correct, Kim would be the key to ending Roger's nightmare.

It took him five minutes to get to the place, tucked in between a cafeteria-style eatery and a cheap clothing store blasting salsa music.

Roger saw a black-and-white prowling the opposite side of Broadway. He turned into the alcove of the clothing store.

Try not to look suspicious, he thought. But is there anything more suspicious than a guy in a hat trying not to look suspicious?

He gazed at the T-shirts in the window. Mexican soccer and Telemundo babes were apparently the big seasonal items.

When the cop car was a good block away, Roger ducked into the liquor store.

The man who Roger assumed was Mr. Kim stood behind the counter looking at a newspaper spread in front of him. He was about fifty, with thick black hair and black-framed glasses.

He gave Roger a quick look then went back to his paper.

"Are you Mr. Kim?" Roger said, approaching.

The man looked up. "Eh?"

"Mr. Kim?"

The man's eyes narrowed. "Who are you?"

And now I'm into the scene and obstacles as described.

WHY FEAR IS THE ESSENCE OF SCENES

It is reported that once upon a time, Muhammad Ali was on a plane when turbulence hit. The pilot ordered all passengers to buckle their seatbelts.

Ali did not comply. A flight attendant came over and politely asked Mr. Ali to fasten his seatbelt. Ali said, "Superman don't need no seatbelt." The flight attendant, without missing a beat, said, "Superman don't need no airplane, either."

There are no supermen in novels. Everyone needs to feel something along the fear continuum.

Fear of the Unknown

The thread of fear that runs through *To Kill a Mockingbird* is of the unknown phantom, Boo Radley:

> Had Jem's pants been safely on him, we would not have slept much anyway. Every night-sound I heard from my cot on the back porch was magnified threefold; every scratch of feet on gravel was Boo Radley seeking revenge, every passing Negro laughing in the night was Boo Radley loose and after us; insects splashing against the screen were Boo Radley's insane fingers picking the wire to pieces; the chinaberry trees were malignant, hovering, alive.

But fear can also manifest in simple worry, another form of fearing the unknown (the future).

In *Stone Cold*, a Jesse Stone novel by Robert B. Parker, Jesse is alone on Paradise Beach, thinking about the murder he's trying to solve. But rather than just rehearse the facts, Parker weaves in several strands of worry:

> The town beach was empty, except for a woman in a pink down jacket running a Jack Russell terrier. Jesse stood for a moment under the little pavilion that served, as far as Jesse could tell, no useful purpose. Twenty feet to his left Kenneth Eisley's body had rolled about at the tidal margin, until the ocean receded. The first one. Jesse looked out at the rim of the gray ocean, where it merged with the gray sky. It seemed longer ago than it was. They'd found him in November, and now it was the start of February. Dog was still with Valenti. Too

long. Dog shouldn't be in a shelter that long. *I got to find someone to take the dog.*

Jesse is worried not just about the length of time the investigation is taking, but for the murdered man's dog that was put in a shelter:

Beaches were cold places in February. Jesse was wearing a turtleneck and a sheepskin jacket. He pulled his watch cap down over his ears, and pushed his hands into the pockets of his coat. *I know who killed you, Kenneth.*

Jesse "knows" but has no proof. It's all instinct. And that bothers him, of course. He can't even serve a search warrant. There are other murders he "knows" about, including one of his lovers, Abby Taylor:

He stepped off the little pavilion and onto the sand. He was above the high tide line where the mingle of seaweed and flotsam made a ragged line. Ahead of him the Jack Russell raced down at the ocean as it rolled in and barked at it, and dodged back when it got close. He was taunting the ocean. *I know who killed the lady in the mall, and the guy in the church parking lot and I know who killed Abby.* Jesse trudged along the sand, feeling it shift slightly beneath his feet as he walked. *Now me?*

Now he has the added worry that he has become a target himself. That leads to a deeper reflection on his own life:

He'd gotten their attention. They were reacting to him. It was a start. *If I stay with them maybe they'll make a run at me, and I'll have them.* He smiled to himself. *Or they'll have me.* He stopped and looked out at the ocean. High up, a single herring gull circled slowly above the ocean, looking down, hoping for food. Nothing moved on the horizon. *I guess if they get me I won't care much.*

There is more of this reflection, then the passage ends:

When he got to the aimless little pavilion Jesse paused again and looked out at the ocean again. Nothing alive was in sight. He was alone. He breathed in, and stood listening to the quiet sound of the ocean, and the soft sound of his breathing. *I wonder if they will succeed.*

When you get to a section of your manuscript where the character is alone, reflecting, do the following:

1. List all of the story elements that the character is worried about.
2. List life issues the character may have (as when Jesse Stone considers that it might not matter much if he's killed).
3. Weave those into a long section where the character is observing a setting that does double duty (not the gray, isolated setting for Jesse Stone's thoughts).
4. Overwrite this section. Put in all the emotion you can.
5. Edit the section down to get just the tone you want.

These reflective passage can be some of the most powerful in your novel. When readers get a look into the conflict within a character, there is an immediate increase in interest.

Why do readers respond emotionally? When does it happen?

Readers respond when the character experiences disequilibrium as a result of his actions—in particular, when he expects change and instead frustration is the result.

Frustration is a key element in a novel. Not as in, "Gee, I'm frustrated," but frustration as a noun of outcome. A turning back off what the character wants or expects.

This gives us the dynamic of every scene as well.

FICTION IS NOT REAL LIFE

Some time ago I participated in a panel discussion with three fellow thriller writers. During the Q & A we got this question from the floor: How can I learn to write a good action scene?

I answered first. I told the questioner that it's what happens *inside* the character that's the key, and you can make that implicit or explicit by using all the elements of fiction writing—dialogue, internal thoughts, description, and action.

I recommended he read how Dean Koontz does it, especially in what is considered his breakout bestseller, *Whispers* (1980). There Koontz has an action scene (an attempted rape) that lasts seventeen pages (that's right, seventeen pages!), all taking place within the close confines of a house.

Another panelist protested (in a good-natured and professional manner). He said action needs to be "realistic." For instance, when a gunshot is fired nobody has time to think. It all happens too fast. If they're shot, the pain comes, and they will not be reflecting on anything. They'll just be in pain.

Now this was grist for a great discussion. I licked my chops but, unfortunately, we were at the very end of the panel and time was called. I never had a chance to respond.

Now I do.

I would have said, first, that a gunshot does not cover the wide spectrum of action. In the Koontz scene from *Whispers* we have someone stalking the Lead. No guns. So that example is of limited value.

But further, and even more important: Fiction is not reality! Fiction is the stylized rendition of reality for an emotional effect.

That's so important that I'll say it again: *Fiction is the stylized rendition of reality for an emotional effect.*

Reality is boring. Reality is not drama. Reality is to be avoided at all costs ("We must stay drunk on writing," Ray Bradbury once said, "so reality does not destroy us").

Hitchcock's axiom holds that a great story is life with the dull parts taken out. Reality has dull parts. Lots of them. Fiction, if it works, does not.

A thriller writer wants the reader to believe she is vicariously experiencing the story. We use techniques to engage the reader's emotions all along the way.

If there is no emotional hook, there is no thrill, no matter how "real" the writing seems.

Let's have a look at a couple of clips from *Whispers*. Hilary Thomas, a successful screenwriter, comes home to discover that Bruno Frye, someone she'd met once, is waiting for her, and not for a game of cribbage:

> She cleared her throat nervously. "What are you doing here?"
>
> "Came to see you."
>
> "Why?"
>
> "Just had to see you again."
>
> "About what?"
>
> He was still grinning. He had a tense, predatory look. His was the smile of the wolf just before it closed its hungry jaws on the cornered rabbit.

Koontz breaks into the dialogue exchange for some description. The effect is like slow motion, which is another key to a good action scene. In essence, you slow down real time to create the feeling and tone you desire:

> He took a step toward her.
>
> She knew then, beyond doubt, what he wanted. But it was crazy, unthinkable. Why would a wealthy man of his high social position travel hundreds of miles to risk his fortune, reputation, and freedom for one brief violent moment of forced sex?

Now Koontz inserts a thought. In real time, when a rapist takes a step toward a victim, there would probably be no reflection, no pondering. But fiction enhances moments like this. Koontz is stretching the tension. He wants the reader taut while furiously flipping pages.

But seventeen of them? Is Koontz insane? Or is he one of the best-selling writers in history for a reason?

In fact, Koontz is a consummate pro who knows exactly what he's doing. He even names it a couple of pages in:

> Abruptly, the world was a slow-motion movie. Each second seemed like a minute. She watched him approach as if he were a creature in a nightmare, as if the atmosphere had suddenly become thick as syrup.

That, my friends, is stylized action for an emotional effect.

CINEMATIC TECHNIQUE

We live in a visual age. Movies and TV and YouTube and the Internet have shaped the way we process information and entertainment.

That wasn't the case in the nineteenth century. There novelists like Dickens and Eliot had to spend lots of ink on describing locations, building up the settings, pulling the readers in. Those readers, who had little to distract them from their reading time, were patient with this.

Not so today. We move fast. We form pictures in our minds as quickly as we can. We jump from task to task, and sometimes to two or three things simultaneously. We live our lives like a series of jump cuts in film.

Fiction, then, can profitably emulate cinema. By using techniques such as cuts, close-ups, and slow motion, we meet readers where they are. Our technique becomes translation software for the imagination.

Let's look at another action sequence, this one from master thriller writer David Morrell. In *The Protector,* a private security cop named Cavanaugh has been retained to protect a brilliant biochemist named Daniel Prescott. Some very bad people want Prescott and are willing to kill to get him.

In this scene, Cavanaugh meets Prescott, who is holed up in a warehouse rigged with security cameras, monitors, and electronic consoles. Cavanaugh barely has time to begin instructing Prescott before an explosion blows up the nondescript Taurus he arrived in:

> The roar from the speaker was so loud that the entire room shook. On the screen, chunks of the Taurus crashed onto the concrete, smoke and fire swelling.
>
> Prescott gaped.

Morrell takes a moment after the explosion to give us a close-up of Prescott's reaction. This "establishing shot" will be repeated:

> A second explosion rocked the room. On a different monitor, the door through which Cavanaugh had entered the building blasted inward, smoke and flames filling the area at the bottom of the stairs. Three men rushed in, but although their hair was matted and their faces were beard-stubbled and filthy, their eyes had neither the blankness of the homeless nor the desperation of drug addicts. These men had eyes as alert as any gunfighter Cavanaugh had ever encountered.

In "real life" a second explosion like this would not give a character any time to think. But remembering that fiction is stylized reality for an emotional effect, Morrell rightly gives us a couple of beats to describe and draw out the effect of the action on Cavanaugh: He observes the men and their faces, and especially their eyes. This is the meaning of the action to Cavanaugh:

> "Is there another way out of here?"
>
> Prescott kept staring at the screen, which showed one of the men aiming a pistol at the elevator door while the other two aimed pistols upward and stormed the stairs.

> "Prescott?" Cavanaugh repeated, drawing his weapon.
>
> Prescott kept staring at the screen.

Returning to the "shots" of Prescott's face, we get the sense of impending dread, the same way we would have in a movie.

There's a famous shot in Hitchcock's *The Birds* where the character played by Tippi Hedren watches in horror as a flame shoots across spilled gasoline toward the tank that will inevitably explode. Hitchcock goes back and forth between the flame and Hedren, who each time has a different expression and head angle (with no movement within the shot). It's pure style and pure creation of emotion for the viewer.

So think of your action scenes in cinematic terms, and you'll be on your way to creating the emotion you desire in the reader.

STYLE AS ACTION

But action scenes and techniques are not just for writers of thrillers. If you're of a literary bent, and pure style is one of your priorities, you can do the same thing with reality as the thriller set—stylize it for an emotional purpose.

In Pat Conroy's *The Prince of Tides*, the narrator, Tom Wingo, and his brother, Luke, attend a poetry reading given by their sister, Savannah, in a Greenwich Village church:

> The church was almost full when Savannah walked out of the vestibule. She was introduced by a supercilious bearded male who wore a poncho, a beret, and leather-thonged sandals. According to the program, he was a leading spokesman of the New York School and taught a course called "Poetry, Revolution and Orgasm" at Hunter College. I hated him on sight but changed my mind instantly when his introduction of Savannah proved so heartfelt and generous.

Why so much time spent on the description of a secondary character? Because the essence of action is what it does *inside* a character. Conroy continues:

> I have always loved my sister's voice. It is clear and light, a voice without seasons, like bells over a green city or snowfall on the roots of orchids. Her voice is a greening thing, an enemy of storm and dark and winter. She pronounced each word carefully, as though

> she was tasting fruit. The words of her poems were a most private
> and fragrant orchard.

The lyrical prose here creates an emotional effect even for the simple action scene of a woman reading her poetry. Conroy thus creates not only mood but a glimpse inside the soul of the narrator.

Turnabout is fair play, so I will note that heightened style can also play well in the action scenes of those who write thrillers, crime, mystery, and suspense. Once again, not being tied down to reflecting some notion of reality, we can stylize it for our purposes.

That's why being a writer is so much fun.

As it was for the hardest of the hard boilers, Mr. Mickey Spillane. He is Exhibit A for the use of style within action, to slow things down and move *inside* the character, where the essence of action resides.

In *One Lonely Night*, Spillane's hero, Mike Hammer, is armed with a tommy gun as he goes to rescue his secretary, the beautiful Velda, who is being tortured in a room by Commie rats. Just before going in, Hammer, a World War II vet, wonders about himself, why he likes killing so much, why he's dark and twisted by society's standards and, indeed, why he has been allowed to live.

Hammer gets close and sees the bad guys inflict more pain on innocent Velda. But does Spillane have him burst right in? Not yet!

> And in that moment of eternity I heard the problem asked and knew the answer! I knew why I was allowed to live while others died! I knew why my rottenness was tolerated and kept alive and why the guy with the reaper couldn't catch me and I smashed through the door of the room with my tommy gun in my hands spitting out the answer at the same time my voice screamed to the heavens!

So Hammer is firing away. Spillane still does not render this "realistically." He now gives us Hammer's inner thoughts:

> I lived only to kill the scum and the lice that wanted to kill themselves. I lived to kill so that others could live. I lived to kill because my soul was a hardened thing that reveled in the thought of taking the blood of the bastards who made murder their business. I lived because I could laugh

> it off and others couldn't. I was the evil that opposed other evil, leaving
> the good and the meek in the middle to live and inherit the earth!

Only now, after giving us the essence of the action inside Hammer, does Spillane get to the outer action:

> They heard my scream and the awful roar of the gun and the slugs tearing
> into bone and guts and it was the last they heard. They went down as they
> tried to run and felt their insides tear out and spray against the walls.

This last paragraph would have been the only one written by a lesser writer (and Spillane is a much better writer than critics ever gave him credit for).

By using heightened language, run-on sentence structure, and a slow-motion look inside the character, Spillane has given us not merely action, but an enduring character.

Do This:

Turn to an action scene in your manuscript. This is any scene where your Lead character is after an objective that will help solve the death problem in the story.

- Read your scene over once. Now open up a new document and write for ten minutes without stopping. Write only the inner thoughts of the character. Feel free to explore every aspect of these thoughts: current feelings, philosophies, self-reflection, thoughts about the past, flashback glimpses, and anything else that occurs in the writing. Don't stop and don't censor yourself. This is stream of consciousness. Go.

- Put the document aside for at least an hour. You can also wait a day or two, depending on your writing schedule. When you read it over, highlight the lines or words that jump out at you because they are fresh and insightful.

- Put these highlights into your scene. You might combine them into one paragraph or place them strategically throughout. The point is that you get us inside the character's head.

- Remember, the more intense the action, the more of this style the reader will accept. Be sure the inner life matches the outer intensity.

TYPES OF SCENES

In fiction there are certain types of scenes that tend to recur, and they also offer great opportunities to intensify the action. Here are a few with some suggestions for getting the most out of them.

Chase Scenes

Long a staple of action movies, chase scenes are no less valuable in fiction. They usually occur in thrillers but can appear in any kind of genre if used in the right way.

One can imagine a character-driven novel where the Lead is being followed by someone for an unknown reason. Maybe she's walking down the street of her hometown and suddenly notices a man following her in the shadows.

Is it some random guy with something on his mind?

Or is it an old friend?

Whoever it is, you can use the chase to increase the sense of dread. You'll need:

1. The chased
2. The chaser
3. A narrow margin of escape
4. A view of character emotion

Here's a bit from "Rage Road," a story I wrote for the collection *Watch Your Back*. A man and his fiancée are driving along a nice stretch of road together. But a jerk in a truck has decided to make things personal after the man blasts his horn at him:

> "Tricia, we can't let—" John saw in the mirror that the guy was speeding up, starting to pass him on the left. The left was the opposite lane. For a moment there was no oncoming traffic.
>
> "No way, pal," John said and pushed hard on the gas. He put the 9 mm Beretta between his legs and grabbed the wheel with both hands. For a few brief seconds he and the truck were going the same speed. John's Altima was doing fine with its 3.5 V-6, keeping the pickup half a car length behind and to the side.

Then John saw, up ahead on the long strip of straight road, a big truck heading their way.

The pickup guy would have to get his butt back in line or die.

But the guy sped up. He was going to try to pass anyway.

John pushed the Altima.

"Let him pass!" Tricia said.

John said nothing, swiveling his head, watching the guy's truck and the big monster up ahead.

The pickup was almost even with John now.

John gave more foot to the gas.

"Let him in!"

The monster trunk was howling now, the sound of the horn spitting vicious warning.

John shot another glance to the side. The guy in the truck locked eyes with him. They were dark, squinty eyes, deeply set in a twenty-something face under a shaved head. He looked like he wanted to crash into John's car just for spite. For a second, that's what John thought he'd do.

But at the last possible moment, Squinty Eyes dropped back and got behind John.

The truck honked past.

John felt sweat and heat, like a fever, breaking out on his face. He heard Tricia crying softly.

"Don't," he said.

"Shh."

"Come on."

"Don't talk."

He put his hand on her left leg. "Baby, please, I need you to be with me on this."

In the mirror John saw Squinty Eyes staying close, about a car length behind.

Tricia issued a pitiful sob. Then put her hand on top of his. "I trust you, John. I promise I do. I just don't want anything to happen."

For the first time in miles John allowed himself to look at the rolling green hills. They always looked nice after a hard rain. "Nothing will, babe. Not as long as you're with me."

But what about Squinty? Would he have something to say about that?

Maybe, because here he came again, fast on the side.

John took his hand off Tricia's leg and grabbed the gun. Time to make things plain. Just show the guy what would happen if he messed with them anymore.

Of course, John would never use it, not for real. Now it was just for show. But a good show. A hard show.

Left hand on the wheel, John reached over with his gun hand and used his index finger to lower the window.

Wind whipped in.

"What are you going to do?" Tricia said.

"Scare him."

"But you can't point a gun at someone."

"If you're threatened you can."

And here came Squinty, almost even.

Okay, John thought. Let's see if I can get his squinty little eyes to open wide.

He waited, timed it, increased speed just a little.

Squinty had his passenger side window down. When they were side-by-side Squinty shouted an F-bomb. John smiled, raised the gun.

He pointed it at Squinty.

For your chase scenes, consider the following:

1. Is there sufficient motivation for the chaser to go after the chasee? It could be based on a mistake, but you must then justify the mistake.
2. How does the POV character *feel* about the chase? Whatever side he's on, we need to know how the action is being experienced. This will help you to avoid clichés and the feel of writing a "generic" chase scene.
3. A chase is a great opportunity to stretch the tension. Use various beats (action, dialogue, inner thoughts, description) to accomplish this.

Fight Scenes

For a fight scene to work in a novel you need three things:

1. The fighters
2. A closed environment
3. An emotional component

The following is from my novel *Try Dying:*

Ratso took a Barry Bonds swing at me with a baseball bat. I ducked. The bat slammed into the inner doorjamb.

I stumbled backward into the homeless camp. Hit the shopping cart. Saw Ratso get ready for another swing.

Spinning, I whipped around to the other side of the cart as the bat whammed down on the cart stuffings. It made a sound like a fist hitting a pillow. A big fist.

I could keep the cart between me and Barry Bonds now. Like kids playing tag around a car. But that couldn't last forever.

Ratso's eyes gleamed like a rabid vermin wanting to bite something.

I needed a weapon. There was some furniture in the place. Old sofa. Tattered chair. An end table, scuffed and ancient. But with four legs.

"You die now," Ratso said.

"You don't want to do this," I said.

"Yeah I do." He smiled and again I thought he might be high. Or just crazy.

"Put it down and we talk about it," I said.

"You not leaving with your head," he said.

He started tapping the bat on the edge of the cart. *Chank chank chank.*

I took a step back, put my right foot on the side of the cart. Drove it into Ratso's middle. If he hadn't slipped on something and gone down I wouldn't have made it to the end table.

But he did. And I got it.

Held it up to him like a lion tamer. Or rat handler.

His eyes widened a little, then narrowed. "You got nothin', white boy." He laughed. "Fat white boy, you don't know how to fight."

I stared at him, not moving.

"What you say, white boy?"

Nothing.

"Say something!"

"I'm not fat," I said.

I charged, table up.

He sidestepped, but I anticipated that, guessing which side. He went to my left and drew back the bat.

I went left and high with the table. Caught his right cheek full on with a table leg.

He swung the bat but without anything behind it. It hit my shoulder but only enough for a dribbler up the first base line.

He screamed in pain.

Shoving with the table I got him back against the wall, pinning him with the table.

He kicked and almost got me flush between the legs.

I brought the table back and shot it forward again. Got him with a leg just below the right eye.

He cried out and his hands went to his face. He dropped the bat.

I slammed the table on top of his head, holding back about 25 percent. Didn't want him dead.

Not yet.

He crumpled to the floor like an old sleeping bag.

I picked up the bat and let him writhe a little. Then I poked him in his back with the knob end.

"Get up."

He put his hand behind him, rubbing the spot where I'd jabbed him.

I kicked his hand. He screamed again. I was glad about the rap thumping in the hallway. It would make it harder to hear him. "Get up or I take out a knee," I said.

"Who you think you are, man?"

"I'm a lawyer. Deal with it."

I poked him again. He struggled to his hands and knees.

"Sit there," I said, pointing to the couch.

In this scene the fighters are the narrator, Ty Buchanan, and a lowlife he has nicknamed Ratso.

They are in a close environment, Ratso's seedy apartment.

The emotion comes through in Ty's hurting Ratso once he's debilitated. There's an animal thing happening inside him at this point. Maybe he's even a little crazy. His thought is he's glad there's rap music blaring because that means he can hurt Ratso even more.

1. Be clear on the motives for your fighters to be engaged in combat.

2. Picture clearly the environment where the fight is taking place. A lot of writers actually map out their fight scenes, looking at the location and charting moves. It's not a bad practice.

3. Give us a glimpse into the emotions of the POV character in the fight scene. How does he feel about what's going on even as it's happening?

Setup Scenes

Even a scene that is a "setup" for other scenes will work if infused with conflict. Don't ever write a scene that is simply for the purpose of giving information.

In *Try Darkness* my lawyer hero, Ty Buchanan, an experienced civil litigator, is taking on a capital murder case for the first time in his professional life. He meets his opponent, Mitch Roberts, for the first time in court. The scene goes like this:

> His name was Mitch Roberts. He was my height and had toxic eyes. The prosecutors who handle capital cases are like that, I was told by a law school friend, one who worked for the Public Defender's office. They mean business, he said. They mean to put people on Death Row, on the gurney with the needle. They don't play around. And what are you doing trying criminal cases, you idiot?
>
> Good point. When Roberts came over to me and stuck his hand out, I thought this is a guy who owns courtrooms.
>
> "Buchanan?" he said.
>
> "How you doing?" I said.
>
> He smiled. "Saw you on TV." Lots of people saw me on TV when I was accused of murdering a hot reporter named Channing Westerbrook. That profile was not going to go away.
>
> "How'd I look?" I said.
>
> "Like you do now. Nervous."
>
> "Once I get going I'll be okay."
>
> "You were a civil lawyer. Ever do criminal?"
>
> "Some."
>
> "Trials?"
>
> "Once. Small company, a CEO cooking the books."

"Criminal's a different gig. Homicide's different than that. Capital is a world all its own. Think you're up to it?"

All right, the macho game had begun. Chest thumping. Looking for the advantage. That was right in my wheelhouse.

"Just call me Fast Eddie," I said.

"What?"

"Ever see *The Hustler?* Paul Newman?"

"What's that got to do—"

"There's a scene where he's going to play billiards with a guy, only he's never played it before. He plays the pocket game. So his manager, played by George C. Scott—"

"Look, Buchanan—"

"—tells him they're leaving, but Fast Eddie says, Hey, it's the same. It's a table and it's balls, you just have to get the feel of it. And he wins."

Roberts looked at me, eyes unimpressed. "You want to plead him out now?" he said. "We'll take off the special circumstances, he can do life."

"That's some sweet deal," I said.

"It's not going to get any better."

"Let's shoot some pool."

1. Look through your manuscript for scenes you wrote primarily to set up other plot points or scenes.
2. Have you left out the conflict?
3. List some possible ways you can add—or intensify—the conflict in the scene.
4. At the very least use dialogue to create a minor argument or back-and-forth between the characters.

Romantic Scenes

Love scenes are great fodder for conflict, and they should be. A love scene where everything is rosy is boring. There needs to be something happening that offers tension.

It can be outside or inside the characters, but it should interrupt the proceedings in some way.

Forces outside can be against the lovers. When Romeo climbs up to woo Juliet, she warns, "If they do see thee, they will murder thee."

That threat hangs over the couple for the whole play.

Inside, there are many ways lovers can doubt what they're getting into.

In Robin Lee Hatcher's *The Victory Club,* a World War II novel, Lucy is married to Richard, who is off fighting the war. At home she finds herself drawn to another man, Howard. The inner conflict is obvious and rendered this way:

> Lucy entered the market a few minutes before the store closed, knowing it was less likely any customers would be there. She was right.
>
> Howard stood behind the counter, writing in a notebook. He looked up as she approached. She suspected he'd been about to tell his last-minute customer that it was closing time.
>
> His eyes widened when he saw who it was, then he straightened, laying down the pen. "Lucy."
>
> "Howard."
>
> There was a world of unspoken sentiment in those two names, spoken in greeting, a confession of right and wrong, temptation and resistance, longing and regret. It wasn't until then that Lucy realized he wouldn't have pursued her if she stayed away. He wanted her, that she knew, but he would let her go.
>
> *Turn ...*
>
> *Run ...*
>
> *Resist ...*
>
> Oh, that wretched voice of warning. She wanted it to be silent.
>
> "I've missed you." Howard's smile was tentative. "Did you find a better place to shop for groceries?"
>
> She shook her head. "No."
>
> "How've you been?"
>
> *Lonely. I've been lonely, Howard, and I don't want to be lonely anymore.*
>
> He untied his apron, removed it, and laid it on the counter. "I'm hungry. Would you care to join me for supper?"
>
> *Resist ...*
>
> *Flee ...*
>
> "I was headed for Chloe's," he said, "but we could go somewhere else if you want."
>
> "Chloe's is fine."

He stared at her for what seemed a long while before he said, "Give me a few minutes to close things up, and then we'll go."

Richard...

She nodded. "I'll wait."

1. Utilize conflict in any romantic situation.
2. Look to both inside and outside obstacles. Make a list for each and choose which would work best for your purposes.
3. At the very least, employ the fear factor. What is it that each character fears in the passion of the moment?

Comedic Scenes

Comedy needs conflict as much as any other kind of writing.

In fact, without conflict you can't have funny.

Think about the great comedies, from *The Taming of the Shrew* to *The Odd Couple*. Those are all about characters thrown into conflict, usually over something trivial (see the discussion of *Seinfeld* in chapter one), although it can also be the opposite: an extreme. Here is a snippet from *Life, the Universe and Everything* by Douglas Adams:

> The regular early morning yell of horror was the sound of Arthur Dent waking up and suddenly remembering where he was.
>
> It wasn't just that the cave was cold, it wasn't just that it was damp and smelly. It was that the cave was in the middle of Islington and there wasn't a bus due for two million years.
>
> Time is the worst place, so to speak, to get lost in, as Arthur Dent could testify, having been lost in both time and space a good deal. At least being lost in space kept you busy.
>
> He was stranded on prehistoric Earth as the result of a complex sequence of events that had involved his being alternately blown up and insulted in more bizarre regions of the Galaxy than he had ever dreamed existed, and though life had now turned very, very, very quiet, he was still feeling jumpy.
>
> He hadn't been blown up now for five years.

The narration here is extremely "serious" in that it involves poor Arthur Dent alone in the vast galaxy, stranded.

The scenes then unfold with natural comedy based upon the situation.

Which is, by the way, the crucial component in all comedy writing. Danny Simon, Neil's older brother, is credited by both Neil and Woody Allen with teaching them how to write narrative comedy.

For many years Danny Simon taught a legendary comedy-writing class in L.A. I got into one of his last ones. And from the start he hammered into us that comedy was not a matter of jokes. It was a matter of a solid premise and natural character reactions, and finding the humor in those.

In that sense, don't ever write something just because it sounds funny to you. Make it come out of the conflict of the scene.

Once again, conflict is your friend.

Even if you write intense action, comedy can add much needed relief in short spurts. This adds to the layers of the reading experience and enables you to spring further conflict in a way that takes the reader deeper into the story.

Hitchcock was always using comic relief in his films. An example is the auction scene in *North by Northwest*. Cary Grant, trying to find James Mason (the villain) tracks him to a fancy auction in New York. But then Mason's henchmen show up and it looks like they'll be able to throw the net on him.

To get out, Cary begins to bid on items, and then bid against himself. This frustrates the auctioneer and the other people in attendance.

In my novel *The Whole Truth,* my lead character is in search of someone:

> They were dressed in blue smocks with yellow tags pinned on that said *Volunteer*. One of them had sleet-colored hair done up in curls. The other had dyed hers a shade of red that did not exist in nature.
>
> They looked surprised and delighted when Steve came in, as if he were the Pony Express riding into the fort.
>
> They fought for the first word. Curls said, "May I help—" at the same time Red said, "Who are you here to—"
>
> They stopped and looked at each other, half annoyed, half amused, then back at Steve.
>
> And spoke over each other again.
>
> "Let me help you out," Steve said. "I'm looking for a doctor, a certain—"
>
> "Are you hurt?" Curls said.
>
> "Our emergency entrance is around to the side," Red said.

"No, I—"

"Oh, but we just had a shooting," Curls said.

"A colored man," Red added.

"Black, Liv. They don't like to be called colored."

"I always forget." Red shook her head.

Steve said, "I'm trying to locate a certain doctor—"

"We don't do referrals here," Curls said. "But if you—"

Red jumped in: "We have a medical building just down the block if you'll—"

"He didn't ask for a medical building," Curls snapped.

"I know that, but if he's looking for a doctor that would be the place to start."

"Not any doctor," I said. "A specific doctor, named Walker C. Phillips."

A sudden silence fell upon the volunteers. Neither seemed eager to tackle that one.

"Is he still practicing?" Steve said.

Red leaned forward and whispered. "Lost his license to practice."

"Terrible tragedy," Curls said, shaking her head.

"He drank," Red added, and gave a tippling motion with her hand.

"When was this?" Steve asked.

"Oh, it's been, what, ten years, at least," Curls said. "His wife left him, you know."

"Ah, no, I did not know that."

The two women nodded.

"Can you tell me, is he still around?"

"Oh, he moved," Red said. "To Tehachapi."

"I thought it was Temecula," Curls said.

"No, Tehachapi."

"He moved where the prison is."

"That's Tehachapi."

"No, it's Temecula."

"Oh no. I have a granddaughter in Temecula."

"That doesn't mean—"

"I would have remembered."

"Excuse me," Steve said. "Maybe there's someone here at the hospital who would know for sure?"

To put comic relief in your stories:

1. Look at the most dramatic moments in your book. Can you find an opportunity, within those moments, or before and after, to inject a bit of humor?
2. Look to your minor characters. Can you intensify their eccentricities? Remember the grave digger in *Hamlet*. He is a complete personality. Look to your minor characters and to conflict between them, or between them and your main character.
3. Don't force it. Let the comedy arise naturally from the situation. Look for places where the trivial can be blown out of proportion.

The Sit-Down Scene

I know you like to sit down and have coffee or tea with your friends and talk pleasantly about many things. But don't let your characters fall into that trap. In a novel, you don't ever want just two characters talking.

You want conflict.

Here's a type of scene I've seen more than once in a manuscript:

> Don came in and sat at the table. "How's it going, Al?" he said.
>
> Al, a former NYPD detective, said, "Fine. You're looking fit."
>
> "What can I say?" Don rejoindered. "Good genes."
>
> "The only good jeans I have are in my closet, and I can't fit in them."
>
> Don laughed and motioned for the waiter and ordered a martini.
>
> "How's that girlfriend of yours?" Al inquired.
>
> "Melissa's great. I tell you, I've got a good one."
>
> "I've told you that for years," Al reminded.
>
> "I know. You've got it, right on. Did I tell you she's started her own clothing line?"
>
> "Really? That's very enterprising of her," Al encouraged.
>
> "She's a gem all right," Don agreed.
>
> They talked about the weather until the waiter came with the martini. Don and Al clinked glasses and drank. Don was drinking a Manhattan.
>
> "So what is it that you wanted to see me about?" Don asked.
>
> "I've got a little problem," Al expostulated. "I'd like to tell you about it."
>
> "Go ahead. I'm all ears."

"Well, it has to do with a woman I was seeing some time ago. She's gone missing and I'd like your help in finding her."

"Sure."

"Great. When can we start?"

"How about right now?" Don said, draining his martini.

"Sounds good," Al said, finishing his Manhattan.

The two friends got up. Al threw a twenty on the table. "It's on me," he said.

They walked out of the bar and into a pleasant New York evening.

This is a set-up scene, which means two people are talking just to "get the story rolling." Information is exchanged.

But doesn't that scene make you want to eat your own head?

Here's a suggested rewrite:

Don came in and plopped at the table. "You call me out on a night like this?" he said. "You nuts?"

Al, a former NYPD detective, said, "Last guy called me nuts I laid out on the sidewalk."

"Whoa."

"Order a drink and shut up."

Don motioned for the waiter and ordered a martini.

"Glad your girlfriend let you out," Al said.

"Leave Melissa out of this," Don said.

Al shrugged.

They sat in silence until the waiter showed up and delivered Don's martini. Don took a sip and waited for Al to talk.

"I got a problem," Al said.

"I know you do," Don said.

"Cut the jokes, will you? I'm serious."

"So am I."

"I have to find someone."

"Who?"

"A woman I used to know."

"Good luck," Don said. "I don't do that work anymore."

You get the idea. It didn't take much to add conflict to this scene, and while it won't win any literary awards, it sure is more readable than the original.

Note that we could have added even more conflict. Suppose the waiter had come back with the wrong drink or a weak one. Or he could have spilled it.

We could have added a third character to come in and make some noise. Maybe an old enemy of the NYPD detective. Maybe someone with a grudge against Don.

The possibilities are endless.

1. Look through your manuscript and find any scene where two or more characters are sitting and talking.
2. Make a list of ways to inject some conflict.
3. Make a list of ways other characters might add conflict.
4. At the very least, give one of them an inner conflict (based on fear) that keeps him from being perfectly comfortable in the scene.

CHAPTER 8
SUBPLOTS, FLASHBACKS, AND BACKSTORY

There are three areas where conflict may lag if you're not careful: subplots, flashbacks, and backstory. We want to have all of them filled with the same page-turning tension as any other part of the novel. This chapter shows you how to go about it.

SUBPLOTS FOR CONFLICT

It's helpful to distinguish subplots and parallel plots.

A *subplot* is that line of a story that interacts with the main plot, while a *parallel plot* runs along independently and intersects with the main plot at some point in the middle or near the end.

Let me illustrate.

We have our mistaken identity plot involving Roger Hill. He's suspected of being a serial killer and he has to keep from being captured. At the same time he has to gather evidence to prove who the real killer is.

When Roger is on the lam, it's the main plot.

But what happens when Roger is helped by the lovely and dangerous Eve Saint? They are drawn to each other. This development is a subplot. More specifically, the romantic subplot.

Now what if we cut to the POV of the real killer, and he is pursuing his next victim?

That is a parallel plot. The killer is not interacting with Roger. Indeed, Roger doesn't know who he is yet. So that plotline can run at the same time as the main plot.

We could also have a parallel plot involving the police detective as he follows the clues but also has trouble at home

In fact, we can lay out a general rule here: If the plotline involves the Lead and another main character, it's a subplot. If it does not involve the Lead but is in another POV, it's a parallel plot.

In general, a subplot adds to the conflict. A parallel plot adds to the suspense. Here's what I mean: A subplot, by interacting with the main story line, adds complications (at least, it should). It can serve a number of purposes, which we will discuss below.

For example, the romantic subplot involving Roger and Eve complicates both of their lives. Roger can't let his guard down for fear of being found. Eve has to be careful about getting involved with someone who might be guilty of murder.

The romance will bring out more feelings in Roger, a chance for inner conflict. And so on.

The parallel plot ratchets up suspense. When we see the serial killer performing his vicious acts, we grow increasingly worried about Roger. We worry the killer will soon come after him.

And from a structural standpoint, we can cut away from either plotline at a moment of great interest (see Cliff-Hangers on pg. 195) and keep those readers turning the pages.

In *Writing the Breakout Novel,* Donald Maass says that one of the most difficult tricks to pull off "involves creating story lines for two characters who at first have no connection whatsoever, then merging those plotlines."

> For some reason, this structure is particularly attractive to beginning novelists. While such a feat can be pulled off, again and again I find that novices fail to bring their plotlines together quickly enough. Beginners often feel the need to present scenes from each plotline in strict rotation, whether or not there is a necessity for them. The result is a manuscript laden with low-tension action.

Note what Maass says: Adding plotlines can actually lessen the tension.

Let's make up a simple example. Suppose your novel is about a police detective trying to solve a murder (how's that for a unique plotline? But remember, it's what you do with the character that makes it original, and in this case the subplot will help us).

So the main plotline will involve police procedure—the gathering and analyzing of evidence, interviewing witnesses, and so on.

But what about life at home? Let's create a subplot involving the detective's son. The son lives with his dad after a divorce. He's fifteen and getting into drugs.

This subplot involves the Lead character and one other major character, the son. It is going to be about challenges facing the father, like communication and influence and self-worth.

All good character work.

But if what happens in the subplot never "invades" the main plot, you've lost a huge opportunity for more conflict.

The ways in which the subplot can invade are various. It can be by way of emotion. If the detective-father brings, say, his rage with him to work, that could affect how he handles a witness. Maybe he crosses the line with that witness, all because what's happening at home complicates his life.

Or maybe the subplot comes in via physical means. What if the son shows up at the crime scene the father is working? What if the son is connected with that crime scene in some way?

Or what if the bad guy the detective is after kidnaps the son? There is an example of the subplot charging right into the main plot and wreaking all sorts of havoc.

Here's an exercise to use when working on subplots:

Make two columns. Title the left-hand column *Main Plot*. Give the main plot a label that describes it, then create rows of short sentences describing the main plot points.

On the right side of the page, create another column called *Subplot*, with an appropriate label. Only this time, instead of listing plot points, give a summary of the subplot. Now, draw two arrows from the right-side column over to the left. Put some space between the arrows so you can make notes. Label one arrow *emotional* and the other *physical*.

Under each arrow, brainstorm possible ways the subplot can shoot into the main plot. Your diagram could look something like this:

MAIN PLOT: TRACKING DOWN THE KILLER		SUBPLOT: RELATIONSHIP WITH 15-YEAR-OLD SON
Gets the case assigned	*Emotional*	There's trouble at home. Son might
First view of crime scene. Forensics.	←	be into drugs. There's evidence of lax
Interviews the eyewitness.		schoolwork and John is completely
Gets shot at. Who?		clueless how to handle it. He tries con-
Run-in with Captain.		frontation then listening (which is hard
Reporter follows him with camera.	*Physical*	for him) but nothing gets through. He
Bar fight.	←	decides to take major action by hiring
The first big clue, at the bridge.		a friend to follow his son, and what
		turns up is worse than he thought: His
		son is actually trafficking.

HOW MANY SUBPLOTS?

A subplot is not merely a plot complication. A subplot has its own reason for being, and weaves in and out of (or back and forth with) the main plot. Or it might go along on its own until it links up with the main plot later in the book. But here's the deal: Because it has its own reason for being, it's going to take up a significant chunk of real estate in your novel.

That being so, here is my formula for the maximum number of subplots, by word count, you can have in your novel (a novel being a minimum of 60,000 words).

> 60,000 words: One subplot (e.g., in a category romance, you might have the female Lead plotline and the love interest plotline, which intersect)
> 80,000: Two to three
> 100,000: Three to four
> Over 100,000: Five

There is no six. Six subplots is too many for any length, unless your name is Stephen King. If you ever go to this land, you go at your own risk. More subplots than suggested will tend to overwhelm or detract from the main plot.

FLASHBACKS

Flashbacks, by definition, interrupt the forward momentum of the story. So they had better contain enough conflict in and of themselves to sustain reader interest.

The first thing you have to ask yourself is whether the flashback is necessary. Are you using it only, or primarily, for exposition? Do you have a lot of background information on your characters that you are dying to share with the readers?

Don't do it. Unless there is a strong and compelling reason to do so. Reasons might include:

> Information essential to understanding fully the life of a character.
> Information essential to understanding the plot development.
> Information essential to understanding a setting.

What's not acceptable is that you have some really beautiful language you want to show off.

Once you have determined there is a flashback material, consider alternatives to a straight flashback scene.

For example, you might use what I call a *back flash*. This is where the character has a momentary thought in the midst of a scene, reflecting back on some significant incident in her life:

> She started running down the street. She remembered how she used to run, back in high school on the track team, when her father was alive and rooting for her. When she ran to please him.
>
> Now she felt the strain in her middle-aged legs. And the killers her father had hired were gaining on her.

How not to do a flashback:

> The crucifix reminded me of my childhood. Especially the first time I heard about hell. I was five and my stepfather, who was very strict, caught me in a lie. It wasn't a big one, but it was a lie all right. I'd taken two cookies instead of one, which was technically a violation of the rules. But they were small cookies.

Anyway, I told him I'd only taken one, but when he counted them we were one short. I never thought he'd count them!

That's when he told me about hell. That people went there for lying and were burned alive forever and ever. And that's where I was headed.

Instead, turn this into an actual scene with conflict:

The crucifix brought a memory rushing to the surface. When I was five I took two cookies from the jar, but was only allowed one.

My stepfather called me into the living room. "How many cookies did you eat today?" he said.

A little tremble ran up my body. I felt some gooseflesh on my arms. "One, Daddy," I said.

He took a step closer. His gray eyes burned into me. "How many?"

I tried to say ONE again, but my throat got stuck. I held up one finger.

He grabbed my ear and started walking me to the kitchen. I yelped but it did no good. I thought he'd tear my ear right off my head.

In the kitchen he pushed me down in a chair. "Don't move."

I held my breath so I wouldn't even move my chest. I held out as long as I could before sucking in air.

By then he was already pouring the cookies out on the counter ... and counting them.

The walls of the kitchen started squeezing in on me.

When he turned back to me I thought he might have a wooden spoon in his hand.

"Do you know what hell is, boy?" he said.

I shook my head.

"Do you know what fire is?"

I nodded.

"Do you know how hot fire is?"

Nodded again. The way he said FIRE made me think it was the worst thing in the world.

"What if your hand was in fire, boy. Would you like that?"

I shook my head.

"Answer me out loud. Would you?"

"No ... "

"Well you're going to be in fire someday, boy, and it will cover your whole body, and you'll scream and scream but the fire won't stop, and you'll never die, you'll just burn and burn forever. Do you want that, boy? Do you?"

This is a major event from the Lead's past (if not, it shouldn't be a flashback). Give us the beat-by-beat scene of it, not the summary.

CONFLICT AND BACKSTORY

When you reveal some of the character's backstory, you have the opportunity to do more than explain. You can create a sense of ongoing conflict within the character, with the past as a form of opposition.

Do not simply slip us information and details. Pack those details with a sense of menace for the character in the present moment.

One way to do this is to create a sense that darkness from the past might, at any time, be repeated in the character's present.

In Anne Lamott's *Imperfect Birds*, Elizabeth Ferguson is waiting for her teenage daughter, Rosie. Elizabeth's husband, James, is impatient and says they'll leave in three minutes if Rosie doesn't show:

> "When did you get to be so bossy?" But she knew the answer. He had become more anxious and vigilant in the last few years, since Elizabeth's little breakdown on the trampoline, as they still referred to it. Three years ago, while bouncing with Rosie on a neighbor's trampoline in Bayview, something had jiggled itself loose, all the suppressed loss and devastation she'd kept to herself after Andrew's death, and it poured forth without ceasing. She had spent a month dazed or crying in bed, on new medication, seeing her psychiatrist every two days. Then, two years ago, she'd had that brief AA slip, which is to say she had started drinking again after many years clean and sober. James hadn't a clue she'd been nipping at the bottle late at night for a week, until he'd found her that morning at dawn on the bathroom floor.

In this paragraph, Lamott gives us a quick but packed look inside Elizabeth's past. Her breakdown on the trampoline was sudden and eruptive. We feel that it could happen again.

And her "AA slip" is the sort of quiet and deceptive ghost an alcoholic carries around for life.

So we have two areas of inner vulnerability here, the past in conflict with the present. And it makes us wonder if it could happen again.

Which is what suspense is, remember: Will it happen again?

Sometimes the past itself can *be* the present. How? Consider Ken Grimwood's classic time travel novel, *Replay*. It asks some intriguing questions: What if you lived your life over and over again and remembered everything? Could you correct mistakes? And how long could this go on?

At the beginning of the novel, Jeff Winston dies in 1988 and wakes up in his college dorm room in 1963. His roommate comes in and says Jeff is late for a test:

> Martin stood in the doorway, a Coke in one hand and load of textbooks in the other. Martin Bailey, Jeff's freshman-year roommate, his closest friend through college and for several years thereafter.
>
> Martin had committed suicide in 1981, right after his divorce and subsequent bankruptcy.

Boom! How will Jeff handle his current "present" in the past, knowing what happens in the future? That's what keeps us reading the book as Jeff confronts more people, family, and events he's already been through.

A similar riff is in the film *Groundhog Day*, with Bill Murray repeatedly reliving the same day. The past itself is the conflict here, as it is in Grimwood's novel.

Past Guilt

John Harvey is one crime writer who has managed to please both readers and literary critics. It's easy to see why. In *Ash & Bone*, retired Detective Inspector Frank Elder must return to action to solve an old case. But life has not gone well for Frank the last few years.

His marriage fell apart. Bad enough. But worse was what happened to his daughter. The guilt haunts Frank still:

> Three years now since his marriage to Joanne had imploded and he had retired from the Nottinghamshire Force, off with his tail between his legs, almost as far west as was possible to go. More than a year since his daughter Katherine had been abducted by Adam Keach. Abducted, raped, and almost killed. Katherine, sixteen.
>
> *What happened to her, Frank, is your fault. You nearly killed her. You. Not him.*
>
> Joanne's words.

Because you had to get involved, you couldn't let things be. You always knew better than anybody else, that's why.

Of course, he had dreams.

But none so bad as Katherine's.

You'll get over this, Frank. You'll come to terms, find a way. But Katherine, she never will.

In the spring, before the trial, she had come to visit him, Katherine. They had talked, walked, sat drinking wine. In the night, he had been woken by her screams.

"These dreams," she said, "they will go, won't they? I mean, with time."

"Yes," Elder had replied. "Yes, I'm sure they will."

Wanting to protect her, he'd lied.

Now she refused to speak to him, broke the connection at the sound of his voice. Changed the number of her cell phone. Didn't, wouldn't write.

Your fault, Frank.

This emotional weight from Frank's backstory hovers over the present, complicating his personal life and affecting his work.

Past Secrets

In Cornelia Read's *A Field of Darkness*, Madeline Dare, a woman from old money and the upper crust, believes her very proper cousin may in fact be the killer of two young women—a crime that had gone unsolved for two decades. Talk about secrets.

But that's just the start as Maddie sets out to find the truth about what really happened.

Or take *Trail of Secrets* and *Garden of Lies* by Eileen Goudge. Both are built on secrets and lies that construct the plots.

Phyllis Whitney, the noted suspense writer, gave wise counsel in her gem of a book *Guide to Fiction Writing* (1988):

> "In the planning stage, I make sure that all my characters have secrets that will be revealed gradually during the course of the novel. Such secrets will motivate all sorts of unexpected action and furnish the surprise element that I'm trying for. Before I ever get to the writing, I examine my characters for those secrets they may be hiding, and I plan ways in which such secrets may affect the lives of other characters in

the story. Secrets make a wonderful source to draw on for the element of surprise."

Try it.

1. Make a list of the names of your primary and leading secondary characters.
2. Next to each name, list three or four possible secrets they might have. Look especially for secrets that could have an impact on some of the other characters.
3. Choose the best one from each list and brainstorm ways they might come out in dramatic, surprising, or shocking fashion in the novel.
4. Write three or four scenes where a secret is revealed. See if you can work one or more of those scenes into your manuscript.

INNER CONFLICT

The least interesting of Lead characters is the one who is absolutely sure of what he's doing. No doubt about it. And forward he goes. Because no one acts like that in life. We all have questions and doubts and fears. That's why inner conflict is such a powerful force for bonding reader and character. It humanizes the character and gives us an emotional connection.

DEFINING INNER CONFLICT

Think of this interior clash as being an argument between two sides, raging inside the character. Like the little angel and the little devil that sit on opposite shoulders in a cartoon, these sides vie for supremacy.

For inner conflict to work, however, each side must have some serious juice to it.

Here's what I mean.

Back to Roger Hill. He has learned a secret about some very bad guys, a secret that could lead to the destruction of the United States itself.

What should Roger do with this secret?

Go to the FBI, of course. Look up the number of the local field office and call this in pronto.

That's one side of the argument.

What's holding Roger back?

Well, what if they want him to come in and answer some questions? And Roger has a ticket to the Laker game that starts in a couple of hours.

If he goes in, that will make him late for the game. Maybe he'll miss the game altogether!

Is that inner conflict? Yes, but it's weak. Terribly weak. Because it's not strong enough to overcome the other side, unless Roger is an absolute loser of a hero (and you wouldn't have written him that way to begin with).

So let's jack up the other side a little.

Suppose the bad guys know Roger has the secret. And they immediately get a message to him via cell phone. *If you even think about going to law enforcement with this, we will kill your niece. You know, the pretty cheerleader with the bright future? We're watching ...*

Okay, now we're talking true inner conflict. It is a battle of *shoulds*.

On the one side are all the reasons Roger should call this in. He's a patriot. He loves America. He believes in law and order. He doesn't want to see people get killed.

On the other side are the reasons he should not. In this case, it's one very potent reason—the death of a beloved family member, an innocent.

EMOTIONS IN CONFLICT

A powerful technique is to put two competing emotions against each other in the same moment. There's a moment like that for Frank Elder in John Harvey's *Ash & Bone*. Elder is a retired inspector coming back to help on the murder of a woman he was once intimate with. Complicating that is his teenage daughter who is on a downward spiral Elder can't seem to stop. She won't let him get close to her, which tears him up inside.

When Elder gets the news his daughter has been arrested for selling heroin, he's at the limit. He calls his ex-wife:

> "How is she?"
>
> "She's all right. I mean, I suppose she's all right. It's difficult, Frank, you don't ..."
>
> "I'm driving up, leaving now. I just wanted you to know."
>
> "Don't, Frank."
>
> "What else d'you expect?"
>
> "She won't talk to you, you know."
>
> Elder wanted to hurl the phone into the far-flung reaches of the car park. Instead, he pocketed it carefully and made himself stand for

> some moments, perfectly still, controlling his breathing, before reaching for his keys.

Elder's rage is tempered by his controlled physical reaction. This inner battle of emotions is seen on the page in action terms as well as through interior description.

Do This:

1. Find the place in your manuscript where your Lead feels the most intense emotion.
2. Now, what is an emotion that would be in conflict with what the character is feeling? Where does it come from?
3. Write a paragraph in which your Lead feels the opposite emotion in conflict with the intense emotion, and provide a physical action to demonstrate the conflict.

For example:

> John exploded with rage. He picked up the hammer and started smashing the furniture. Every stick that reminded him of Mary he whacked.

Converts to something like this:

> John exploded with rage. He picked up the hammer. He raised it over the coffee table that had been their first purchase together. And froze. Smashing it would be like smashing the part of his life that had once been good. Killing the memory of love. A memory that was keeping him sane. His gut turned over like a pig on a spit. And then he brought the hammer down with all his might.

INNER THOUGHTS IN CONFLICT

In Stephen King's *Rose Madder*, Rose Daniels is married to a wife beater. A cop who knows how to hit her so it doesn't show up. For fourteen years she's lived with this, because he provides for her and because she knows that if she tries to get away, he can track her down. She has accepted her lot.

Until one morning when she notices a spot of dried blood from being hit the night before. A new thought hits Rose then. While she had considered that he might someday kill her if this went on, the new thought asked the question, What if he doesn't kill you? What if this will go on and on and on?

And then the "deep part" of her tells her to get out:

> "That's ridiculous," she said, rocking back and forth faster than ever. The spot of blood on the sheet sizzled in her eye. From here, it looked like the dot under an exclamation point. "That's ridiculous, where would I go?"
>
> *Anywhere he isn't*, the voice returned. *But you have to do it right now. Before...*
>
> "Before what?"
>
> That one was easy. Before she fell asleep again.
>
> A part of her mind—a habituated, cowed part—suddenly realized that she was seriously entertaining this thought and put up a terrified clamor. Leave her home of fourteen years? The house where she could put her hand on anything she wanted? The husband who, if a little short-tempered and quick to use his fists, had always been a good provider? The idea was ridiculous. She must forget it, and immediately.
>
> And she might have done so, almost certain *would* have done so, if not for that drop on the sheet. That single dark red drop.
>
> *Then don't look at it!*

The argument goes on, for another page, intensifying:

> She got up suddenly and with such force that the back of Pooh's Chair hit the wall. She stood there for a moment, breathing hard, wide eyes still fixed on the maroon spot, and then she headed for the door leading into the living room.
>
> *Where are you going?* Ms. Practical-Sensible screamed inside her head—the part of her which seemed perfectly willing to be maimed or killed for the continued privilege of knowing where the teabags were in the cupboard and where the Scrubbies were kept under the sink. *Just where do you think you're—*
>
> She clapped a lid on the voice, something she'd had no idea she could do until that moment.

Even as Rose grabs her purse and makes for the door, the inner voice of Ms. Practical-Sensible screams at her to stop. Not just that, she makes arguments:

It WILL hurt! Practical-Sensible screamed. *If you take something that belongs to him, it'll hurt plenty, and you know it! PLENTY!*

"It won't be there anyway," she murmured, but it was—the bright green Merchant's Bank ATM card with his name embossed on it.

Don't you take that! Don't you dare!

But she found she *did* dare—all she had to do was call up the image of that drop of blood.

The scene takes up almost four full pages. In lesser hands it would have been Rose Daniels grabbing her purse and the ATM card and marching out the front door. But King makes it a scene of conflict and suspense, conflict all within the mind of one character.

Crosscurrent emotions are almost irresistible in characterization. Inner conflict and opposing feelings are human and emotional, and connect us to the character in powerful ways.

Imagine this during the most intense physical and emotional circumstance known to us—the act of lovemaking. Anita Shreve renders an unforgettable and shattering moment through crosscurrent emotions.

The narrator of Shreve's *All He Ever Wanted* is a professor at a small New England college. Nicholas Van Tassel has finally won his obsession, the ironically named Etna Bliss. She has told him she does not love him but has consented to marry him anyway. Unaware of her past, Van Tassel now enters the marriage bed. The narration is in the heightened language of the period (the story is narrated in 1933, looking back to events in the early part of the century):

> Though one can never be absolutely certain about such a thing, human anatomy being as variable as it is, I was sure that entry into my new wife's body had been made easier by another before me. Even as I was experiencing those moments of the greatest physical pleasure a man can know, I was composing questions that would haunt me for years. *Who?* I cried silently. And *When?* I shuddered in the way that all men will do and then rolled onto my back. ... There would be no life conceived on this night. The act would, instead, give birth to jealousy—intense and fruitless and all-consuming. Love, which just moments before I had thought too domestic and tame a word for my nearly transcendent feelings for Etna, was replaced by something for which I have never been

> able to find a suitable name: the helplessness that descends when a
> cherished object has been stolen, the anger that one feels when one
> has been deceived.

A novel or film must move the emotions of the audience, or it is less than it can be. Or should be. Story is first and foremost an emotional experience. If it isn't, it's something else. It's words on a page or pictures on a screen.

Conflict, to have value and power in a story, must engage the emotions. Consider two openings:

> Paul Osborn sat a table sipping red wine. For no particular reason he looked
> up and saw a man he recognized. It was someone who knew his father.

Compare that to the actual opening of Allan Folsom's *The Day After Tomorrow:*

> Paul Osborn sat alone among the smoky bustle of the after-work crowd,
> staring into a glass of red wine. He was tired and hurt and confused. For
> no particular reason he looked up. When he did, his breath left him with
> a jolt. Across the room sat the man who murdered his father.

The difference is in the emotion, direct and indirect. Folsom tells us directly how Osborne is feeling—tired, hurt, confused. Telling us is not always the best way to get at emotions (see below), but in this case it's merely setup. At least it gives us something of an emotional peg to land our attention on.

Other words contribute: *alone* and *jolt*.

But it's the final line that hits us. We don't have to be told anything. We can fill in the blanks for ourselves. Pow! We need to see how Osborn will react.

SHOWING AND TELLING EMOTIONS

Everyone knows the age-old advice: Show, don't tell. It's solid, but needs explanation. You can't really show a whole novel, or it would be two thousand pages long. Telling is used as a shorthand when the action is at a lower intensity level.

Years ago, I came up with an intensity scale.

CONFLICT & SUSPENSE

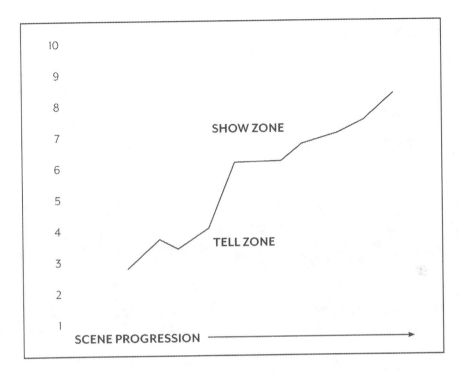

Here's what it means: When a scene is at a moment of lower intensity, you can get away with "telling" us what the emotions (or any beats) are. It's your choice. If Mary is entering a room where she'll get into a terrible argument with John, she might do it this way:

> Mary was nervous as she entered the apartment.

Or you could choose some showing:

> Mary fumbled with her keys as she unlocked the apartment door. Her hands were shaking.

The second way is more intense. If that's what you want, fine. That's why you choose according to the intensity scale:

But to create real emotional conflict for the reader, you have to show it. You cannot say that John was angry at Mary and expect that the emotion will translate to the reader.

To create an emotion in the reader, create the emotion on the page.

Don't name it, make it.

Here's a simple example:

John was angry at Mary. (Tell)

John slapped Mary. (Show)

In the novel we're constructing, let's say our hero, Roger, needs to talk to his old boss, a man he never really got along with. We can render it purely by showing:

Roger's pulse quickened as he knocked on Harrington's door. Heat rushed to his head. He saw Harrington's face in his mind that time Harrington chewed him out in front of everyone. The memory stirred all of Roger's nerve endings, sending him into a tremble. He opened and closed his fists. He took in a deep breath. His heart rate started to normalize. He had to talk to Harrington, so he clenched his jaw and knocked again, harder, hurting his knuckle. It throbbed.

Do we really need all that at this point in the story? Only if the past was much more dramatic than presented and only if those feelings were going to be a major part of the plot.

But if not, just do it this way:

Roger knocked on Harrington's door. He didn't like his old boss at all. But he had to talk to him. He knocked again.

Then when the scene with Harrington actually takes place, we will have the overview of conflict in place. The real attention—the place to show all of this emotion—is in the actual exchange with Harrington.

The Chair Through the Window Exercise

Imagine your Lead character in a nicely appointed room of an admirable home. There is a big bay window looking over an expanse of lawn with some pleasing trees and a blue sky.

Your character picks up a wingback chair and throws it out the window:

Now why did she do that?

What caused her to take such an action?

What emotion compelled her?

Find that emotion and name it. Then justify it.

What in her background could explain her doing this?

What does this emotion tell you about your character that's new?

Where can you place a moment of emotion this high in your manuscript?

It doesn't have to be a scene where she literally throws the chair out the window. But it does have to feel this intense.

What other scenes can you ramp up with emotion now?

Brainstorm answers to those questions, then pick the best answers and find ways to insert them in your novel.

Remember, conflict and suspense do not grip a reader unless and until she bonds with a character. Inner conflict is one of the great bonding agents. Explore deeply the inside of your Lead and give us glimpses of the psychological struggle. If you do, we will turn your pages.

CHAPTER 10
CONFLICT IN DIALOGUE

"**S**o tell me all about dialogue."

"In two pages?"

"Hey, you're the writer. Just do it!"

"Look, let's talk about this later when—"

"We'll talk about it now! Tell me about dialogue."

"Sure. You've just helped. Your dialogue adds to the conflict."

"How?"

"By arguing with me. Put two characters together who have different agendas. That should be revealed in their dialogue. In fact, that is one of the two primary goals of dialogue—to create conflict."

"Oh yeah? What's the other?"

"To reveal character. And you're doing that, too. Our readers will get the idea you're a rather brusque fellow."

"Says you!"

"See? And you don't talk like me. That's another key. Each character should have his or her own way of speaking."

"So I'm doin' somethin' right, is that what yer tellin' me?"

"Almost. I'd avoid overuse of idioms and accents, like *yer* and *tellin'*, unless they're absolutely necessary. They're too difficult to read. A mere suggestion every now and again is all you need. The reader's imagination will do the rest."

"So I'm *not* doing it right, is that it?"

"Calm down."

"I *am* calm!"

"At least you're a man of few words. Dialogue in fiction should be brief."

"What if I've got a lot to say?"

"Heaven help us. But if you must, avoid long speeches. Break the speech up, using other characters' interruptions and—"

"Interruptions?"

"Perfect. And with little actions that demonstrate emotion."

He paused, twirling the tiny revolver in his hand. "Like this?"

"Yes. You're catching on quick."

"Hey, how about those Dodgers, huh? And isn't it a nice day outside?"

"Hold on. Avoid small talk. You're not trying to re-create real life in a story. Remember, you want to use dialogue to move the story, create tension, interest the reader, reveal character."

"What if my character likes small talk?"

"Good point. If your character is supposed to be a bore, it will work, because that dialogue has a story purpose."

"Thank you." He pointed the gun at me. "Now give me your wallet."

"Very good! That is a surprise, a twist. It forces the reader to read on. That's often a good way to end a chapter, don't you think?"

"I mean it, give me your wallet, pal!"

"And there's another great tactic, the off-center response. You didn't answer me right on the nose. Work on that angle a lot. Have your characters give slightly off responses whenever they can. That helps make the scene tense. Listen, fella, why don't you give me the gun, huh?"

"Go ahead, make my day."

"Yech! Avoid clichés like the plague!"

"Is that supposed to be funny?"

"A little humor is always welcome in dialogue, so long as you don't force it. Now hand over the gun."

"Only if you tell me what I should do to make sure my dialogue works."

"Set it aside for a few days. Then read it aloud, in a monotone. Or get a friend to read it to you. Hearing it out loud gives you a different perspective. The gun?"

"Okay. Here. Now what do we do?"

"We figure out a snappy, interesting way to end this dialogue."

"You got an idea?"

"Yeah."

"Let's hear it."

I raised the gun. "Give me your wallet, pal."

Okay, a little bit of play, but with some content to consider. The main point is that dialogue is rich soil for sowing conflict and tension. Never waste it with small talk or throwaway lines. Sometimes even masters of dialogue, after a certain number of books, can seem to be stretching things out because, well, it's just so much fun to write.

Until you have that fortieth novel published (and maybe not even then) write compact dialogue with conflict.

The best tools for creating conflict in dialogue are:

1. Orchestration
2. Subtext
3. Opposing agendas
4. Sidestepping
5. Dialogue as weapon
6. Parent-Adult-Child

1. ORCHESTRATION

The concept of orchestration was covered in chapter three. Remember that great dialogue begins before you write it, with characters you create for contrast.

Pay special attention to how each of your characters sounds. Give them unique voices in your own mind, and that will play out in more conflict on the page. Do this for each main character:

a. Voice journal. Use this to give each character a distinctive sound.

b. A statement, in the character's voice, of their *reason for being in the story.*

> My name is Sam Gerard and I'm a U.S. Marshal. Why am I in this story? You have to ask? I'm the Big Dog, and I have one job. To bring in fugitives from justice. I don't care about their case. I don't care if they say they're innocent. Hell, they may be! That's not my job. Don't tell me it is. I want to catch guys. That's what I do. I love it. I love my team. And I will not accept failure as an option.

Try it for all major characters. Get to know them as individuals. Find back-story elements that will contrast with the other characters. Look especially at the *Big 5:*

1. Education
2. Religion
3. Politics
4. Type of work
5. Economic status

2. SUBTEXT

A scene should be about more than it is about. On the surface it is what the characters are doing and saying. But underneath the surface, other story deposits are bubbling up toward the top.

You have *previous character relationships.* This character web might be known to you but not the reader. Not yet. But the way the characters speak with this hidden knowledge will create uncertainty in the scene.

There is *backstory,* or events that have happened before the scene. You may have written about these events in previous parts of the novel, or they may have occurred before the novel's time line. But events from the past that affect the present create possibilities for conflict on the surface.

You may also be aware of the *theme* of your novel. Even if you're unclear about it, just giving it some thought will automatically offer subtextual elements. List several possibilities of what your book *might* be about.

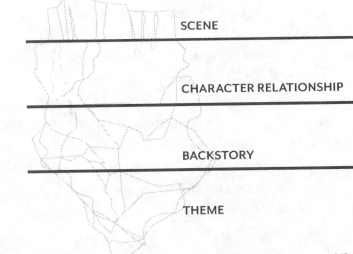

SCENE

CHARACTER RELATIONSHIP

BACKSTORY

THEME

3. OPPOSING AGENDAS

Always know what each character wants in a given scene.

If a character in a scene is just taking up space, give him an agenda or get him out of there. Or cut the scene entirely.

Scenes require conflict or tension, even if it's subtle.

Before you write the scene, note what it is each character wants.

Then spend a few moments playing with those motivations.

List three other possible motives for each of the characters, then mix and match to decide which ones will make for the best conflict.

It is also important to create tension among allies.

One of the danger points in fiction is when two friends, or people who are at least on the same side, have a talk about what's going on.

The trouble is there might not be any trouble between them. So much of the dialogue becomes a friendly chat.

This will violate Hitchcock's axiom, however, so we have to do something about it.

The fastest way to handle it is to make sure there is tension manifested from the start.

Create tension in at least one of the characters, preferably the viewpoint character.

For example, when you have Allison meeting Melissa, her college friend, for coffee, don't have them sit down and start talking as if nothing's wrong in the world.

Put the trouble of the story into Allison's mind and nervous system and make it an impediment to her conversation with Melissa.

In Melissa, place something that might be in opposition to Allison's needs. Allison needs to ask Melissa's advice about a crumbling marriage. Maybe Melissa is full of news about her sister's impending wedding to a wonderful man and gushes about the prospects.

Spend some time brainstorming about the ways two friends or allies can be at odds. Then weave those things into the dialogue.

4. SIDESTEPPING

You instantly create conflict in dialogue when you avoid "on the nose" responses. On the nose means a direct response, sometimes even echoing the previous line:

> "Are you ready to go, dear?" Bob asked.
> "I'll be ready in just a moment, darling." Sylvia said.

> "Want to play some catch?" Cody asked.
> "Yeah, let's play some catch," Jared said.

> "I didn't like what Collins did in there," Stan said.
> "Me either," Charles said. "It was nasty."

There is nothing inherently wrong with these responses. Indeed, we talk like this in real life and sometimes will do so in our fiction. But notice how you can create instant conflict with a slight sidestep:

> "Are you ready to go, dear?" Bob asked.
> "I saw you downtown today," Sylvia said.

> "Want to play some catch?" Cody asked.
> "What's on your chin?" Jared said.

> "I didn't like what Collins did in there," Stan said.
> "He that troubleth his own house shall inherit the wind," Charles said.

Notice the ways you can avoid direct response:

- A statement that is unrelated to the prompting dialogue.
- Answering a question with a question.
- A line of dialogue that is going to need some explanation.

Also consider using silence:

> "Are you ready to go, dear?" Bob asked.
> Sylvia said nothing.

Or use an action response:

> "Are you ready to go, dear?" Bob asked.
> Sylvia picked up the mirror.

5. DIALOGUE AS WEAPON

Look for places where you can use dialogue as a weapon, a means for your characters to charge ahead in order to get what they want. Keep in mind that dialogue is action. It's a physical act used by characters to help them get what they want. If they don't want anything in a scene, they shouldn't be there.

Note that not all weapons are explosive. They can be small and sharp, too.

Here's a well-known example from the classic film *Casablanca*. In this scene, a Nazi officer, Strasser, has come to Casablanca to capture Victor Laszlo, the underground fighter. It is rumored he will be showing up in Rick Blaine's saloon. The local French police captain, Louis Renault, allows Rick to operate because Rick takes no sides. He "sticks his neck out for no one."

Strasser wants to find out for himself where Rick stands. That's his agenda. See if you can pick up what the others want in the following exchange:

> RENAULT
> (calling to Rick)
> Rick!
>
> Rick stops and comes over to their table.
>
> RENAULT (CONT'D)
> Rick, this is Major Heinrich Strasser of the Third Reich.
>
> STRASSER
> How do you do, Mr. Rick?
>
> RICK
> How do you do?
>
> RENAULT
> And you already know Herr Heinze of the Third Reich.
>
> Rick nods to Strasser and Heinze.
>
> STRASSER
> Please joins us, Mr. Rick.
>
> Rick sits down at the table.
>
> RENAULT

We are very honored tonight, Rick. Major Strasser is one of the reasons the Third Reich enjoys the reputation it has today.

STRASSER
You repeat "Third Reich" as though you expected there to be others.

RENAULT
Personally, Major, I will take what comes.

Even before Rick enters the conversation, the positioning has begun. Strasser corrects Renault on a minor point to emphasize the dominance of the Nazi regime. Renault lets it be known that his agenda is to "take what comes." That's because (we find out later) he has a nice little setup here at Rick's. It's where he wins at the gaming tables and also selects distressed young women to dally with as payment for getting them and their husbands out of Casablanca. He doesn't want to upset the proverbial apple cart:

STRASSER
(to Rick)
Do you mind if I ask you a few questions? Unofficially of course.

RICK
Make it official if you like.

The first volley by Strasser is spoken in soft terms. Rick's rejoinder it intended to be a slightly harder parry. He's telling Strasser he has nothing of value for them:

STRASSER
What is your nationality?

RICK
I'm a drunkard.

RENAULT
That makes Rick a citizen of the world.

Rick's reply is sharp, a touch of the tip of a rapier. Renault knows this immediately and injects a line to deflate the impending tension. Rick's agenda is clear now: Don't be a patsy for strong-arm questions. Renault's agenda is to keep Rick's saloon from being closed down!

> RICK
>
> I was born in New York City if that'll help you any.
>
> STRASSER
>
> I understand that you came here from Paris at the time of the occupation.
>
> RICK
>
> There seems to be no secret about that.
>
> STRASSER
>
> Are you one of those people who cannot imagine the Germans in their beloved Paris?
>
> RICK
>
> It's not particularly my beloved Paris.

There is subtext in Rick's last reply. There's something about Paris he does not like. We don't find out until later what that is:

> HEINZE
>
> Can you imagine us in London?
>
> RICK
>
> When you get there, ask me.
>
> RENAULT
>
> Ho! Diplomatist.

Heinze, the humorless, charmless Gestapo man blunders in with a challenge. Rick knocks it right back at him. And once again, Renault tries to break the tension:

> STRASSER
>
> How about New York?
>
> RICK
>
> Well, there are certain sections of New York, Major, that I wouldn't advise you to try to invade.

Rick's response is priceless. Without giving up his pose of neutrality he jabs with a bit of American attitude:

> STRASSER
>
> Uh-huh. Who do you think will win the war?

> RICK
>
> I haven't the slightest idea.

> RENAULT
>
> Rick is completely neutral about everything, and that takes in the field
> of women, too.

So far, everyone is in roughly the same position as they were at the start of the scene. The initial jabs have all been met without lasting damage. Renault has succeeded in painting Rick as impartial. Now Strasser, frustrated in his initial queries, shows off a larger weapon—a dossier:

> STRASSER
>
> You were not always so carefully neutral. We have a complete dossier
> on you.
>
> (Strasser takes a little book from his pocket and turns to a page.)

> STRASSER
>
> "Richard Blaine, American. Age thirty-seven. Cannot return to his coun-
> try." The reason is a little vague. We also know what you did in Paris, Mr.
> Blaine, and also we know why you left Paris.
>
> (Rick takes the dossier from Strasser.)

> STRASSER
>
> Don't worry, we are not going to broadcast it.

> RICK
>
> Are my eyes really brown?

Rick meets the challenge with another sarcastic comment. The match is even to this point, even though the Nazi has the stronger power position:

> STRASSER
>
> You will forgive my curiosity, Mr. Blaine. The point is, an enemy of the
> Reich has come to Casablanca and we are checking up on anybody who
> can be of any help to us.

> RICK
>
> (looking at Renault)
>
> My interest in whether Victor Laszlo stays or goes is purely a sporting one.
>
> STRASSER
>
> In this case, you have no sympathy for the fox?
>
> RICK
>
> Not particularly. I understand the point of view of the hound, too.

The scene continues for a few more lines. The Nazi has failed to draw any blood from Rick. The confrontation has occurred but without it breaking into an overt fight (which Rick would have lost). Rick and Renault have won the exchange. Rick hasn't given the Nazi any reason to close him down. Renault has kept things light enough that Strasser isn't angered or suspicious enough of Rick to put him out of business.

The subtle use of weaponry above can be contrasted with a more overt duel. Mickey Spillane's Mike Hammer was never one for delicacy. Here he's talking to a cop he knows after being picked up for drunkenness in *The Girl Hunters*:

> When I looked up Pat was holding out his cigarettes to me. "Smoke?"
>
> I shook my head.
>
> His voice had a callous edge to it when he said, "You quit?"
>
> "Yeah."
>
> I felt his shrug. "When?"
>
> "When I ran out of loot. Now knock it off."
>
> "You had loot enough to drink with." His voice had a real dirty tone now.
>
> There are times when you can't take anything at all, no jokes, no rubs—nothing. Like the man said, you want nothing from nobody never. I propped my hands on the arms of the chair and pushed myself to my feet. The inside of my thighs quivered with the effort.
>
> "Pat—I don't know what the hell you're pulling. I don't give a damn either. Whatever it is, I don't appreciate it. Just keep off my back, old buddy."
>
> A flat expression drifted across his face before the hardness came back. "We stopped being buddies a long time ago, Mike."
>
> "Good. Let's keep it like that. Now where the hell's my clothes?"

> He spit a stream of smoke at my face and if I didn't have to hold the back of the chair to stand up, I would have belted him one. "In the garbage," he said. "It's where you belong too but this time you're lucky."
>
> "You son of a bitch."
>
> I got another faceful of smoke and choked on it.
>
> "You son of a bitch," I said.

Between the subdued tones of the *Casablanca* scene, and the Ali-Frazier punches of the Mike Hammer exchange, you have an infinite range of possibilities for conflict in dialogue when you see it as a weapon.

Using dialogue as a weapon is also a great way to give the reader *information*. Rather than clunky exposition (simply telling us, in narration or in dialogue, what the author wants readers to know), use a tense exchange. So long as it is organic—that is, true to the characters—it can work seamlessly. Here's what I mean.

In this first example, the exposition comes through narrative:

> Arthur Marks was her accountant. He'd come from Omaha a few years ago and set up a practice in Los Angeles. His troubles in Nebraska—a bit of local fraud leading to sanctions—prompted him to seek a new venue.

That's fine as far as it goes, but too much of this gets us out of the direct conflict of a scene. The enterprising novelist will then consider dialogue. But sometimes the dialogue looks like this:

> Mary opened the door. "Oh hello, Arthur, my CPA from Omaha. What can I do for you?"
>
> "I'm just trying to make it here in Los Angeles after my move from Nebraska. I thought I'd ask you for a reference."

Okay, perhaps not so clunky as that. But you get the idea. Many times, especially in the openings of manuscripts, I'll see this kind of slipping of information to the reader.

The simple and powerful solution is to make such dialogue *confrontational*. That renders the information through conflict, which is the best way to go. Here is the first example rewritten:

> "What are you doing here?" Arthur said.
>
> "It's not because of my tax return," Mary said. "I know about Omaha."

"I don't know what you're talking about."

"Really? Sears? Cooking the books?"

Arthur said nothing. His cheek twitched.

"Why didn't you come clean with me?" Mary asked.

"I just wanted a fresh start," Arthur said. "Is that so hard to understand?"

"It's my money we're talking about here."

"I'm clean! Honest."

A conference student once turned in a chapter to me. It contained the following (used by permission). A woman (Betty) has been planting bombs to avenge the death of her son. She now has a forensic investigator (Kate, who has been closing in on her) tied up and is threatening to kill her:

> Betty looked down at Kate. The triumphant smile on her face faded into a snarl at the mention of her son's death. "Why do you care?"
>
> "Because if my son had died as a result of finding out about something terrible that had happened to him that I had kept hidden to protect him, I would want to blame the person responsible." Kate thought she would try the empathy tactic. She did feel a great sorrow for Betty and her tragic story. She watched as Betty returned her statement with a hard stare.

In this tense moment, Kate has revealed to Betty facts about the case, but the dialogue sounds unnatural. The long line has information stuffed into it, but it feels more like it's for the reader's benefit rather than the character's.

I told the student to go back and cut all dialogue that is not absolutely true to the character and the emotional beats. What would either of them *really* say? Revised, it looks like this:

> Betty looked down at Kate. The triumphant smile on her face faded into a snarl at the mention of her son's death. "Why do you care?"
>
> "I do care."
>
> "Why?"
>
> "Because if my son had died like that—"
>
> "Don't talk about your son! He didn't die."
>
> "I would have protected him just like you."
>
> "You know nothing."
>
> "I wouldn't have told him. I would have made the same choice."
>
> "Shut up now. Don't you dare say another word."

6. PARENT-ADULT-CHILD

A great tool for creating instant conflict in dialogue is the Parent-Adult-Child model. I first read this idea in Jack Bickham's *Writing Novels That Sell* (1989). Bickham, in turn. picked it up from a school of psychology popularized in the book *Games People Play* by Eric Berne (1964). This school is called Transactional Analysis.

As I explain in *Revision & Self-Editing*, the theory holds that we tend to occupy roles in life and relationships. The three primary roles are Parent, Adult, and Child (PAC).

The Parent is the seat of authority, the one who can "lay down the law." He has the raw strength, from position or otherwise, to rule and then enforce his rulings.

As Yul Brynner's Pharaoh puts it in *The Ten Commandments*, "So shall it be written. So shall it be done."

The Adult is the objective one, the one who sees things rationally and is therefore the best one to analyze a situation. "Let's be adult about this," one might say in the midst of an argument.

Finally, there is the Child. Not rational, and not with any real power. So what does she do? Reacts emotionally. Throws tantrums to try to get her way. Even an adult can do this. We've all seen clandestine videos that prove this point.

So it is a helpful thing to consider what role each character is assuming in a scene. How do they see themselves? What is their actual role? (It may indeed be different than what they perceive it to be.)

Most important of all, how will they act in order to accomplish their goal in the scene?

Answering these questions can give you a way to shape your dialogue so there is constant tension and conflict throughout.

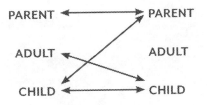

Also consider that the characters might change their roles (try something new) in order to get their way. Thus, this is a never-ending source of conflict possibilities and only takes a few moments to set up.

Do This:

1. Look at all of your dialogue exchanges, especially ones that run for a page or more.
2. Analyze what roles the characters think they're inhabiting.
3. Rework the dialogue by getting each character to be more assertive in their claimed role. (Also note that a character can change roles as a matter of strategy. For example, if the Parent isn't working, a character might switch to pouting like a Child in order to get his way.)

Much of the dialogue I see in manuscripts seems loose and without real purpose. That is a waste of potential conflict. When you follow the guidelines in this chapter, your dialogue will take on an added verve that agents and editors appreciate.

CHAPTER 11
CONFLICT IN THEME

I once read a blog post by an acquisitions editor for one of the big publishing companies. She was asked what it is that causes her to turn down a book. She gave several factors, then came to: *Not remarkable/surprising/ unputdownable enough.* "This one is the most difficult to articulate," she wrote, "and yet in many ways it's the most important hurdle to clear. Does the proposal get people excited? Will sales reps and buyers be eager to read it—and then eager to talk it up themselves? As my first boss used to warn us green editorial assistants two decades ago, the type of submission that's the toughest to spot—and the most essential to avoid—is the one that is *skillful, competent, literate, and ultimately forgettable.*"

Pretty telling, don't you think?

So is there a secret weapon for unforgettable fiction? Writers from time immemorial have searched for it, consciously or unconsciously.

Mark Twain found it. So did Charles Dickens.

Raymond Chandler used it. So does Michael Connelly.

Ayn Rand got it, and so did Jack Kerouac. That's why two of their novels, *Atlas Shrugged* and *On the Road,* continue to sell tens of thousands of copies a year, well over fifty years after they were first published. Even though they are about as different as two novels can be.

So what is this secret weapon?

I call it the *thematic argument.*

Most writers I know shudder at the word *theme.* I call it the "scary word" when I teach workshops. It brings to mind high school English papers that completely baffled you. Maybe you were told to coax out the theme of *The Red Badge of Courage* and what you came up with was completely wrong (you left out any mention of courage, a badge, or the color red).

You were clueless. And when the teacher gave his point of view on the matter, you thought to yourself, *I missed that completely. I must be a dunce.*

So now you're writing a novel and you are apprehensive about even thinking of theme. You want the story to just go. Let others worry about what your work means.

Maybe you're like so many writers who will allow the theme to work itself out. You'll find it at the end.

This is a perfectly legitimate way to do things, but what I'm going to suggest will be applicable to you whether you know your theme at the start or much later, upon rewrite.

If you can find the thematic unity of your book and present it in a way that is natural to the story, you will create a page turner no matter what your genre.

The key is to know what is of ultimate concern to you, and how to create conflict through "the argument."

This will create a unified story that transcends the immediate satisfaction of the reading experience.

THEME AS ARGUMENT

Think of theme as an argument the character has within himself. It's a bit like inner conflict, only it's a step above. It's an argument about life, how it should be seen, how it should be lived.

Let's take an example.

A Christmas Carol is about a misanthrope who is redeemed via the agency of three spirits. They show him his past, present, and future, just the right scenes to get Scrooge to turn his life around.

What is the theme of the story? One way to phrase it is, the life worth living is the life lived with generosity toward others.

So what is the argument going on inside Scrooge? *Money is the only thing that means anything in this life. People are untrustworthy schemers and liars, and you have to keep them all at arm's length. They'll rob you blind if*

you don't. And if the poorer ones die out at a rapid clip, that will reduce the
surplus population and make things much better for me.

And so on.

The "meta-argument" runs through the entire story.

In fact, a great move as an author is to have your Lead character, at some point in the first act of the novel, make an argument *against* the theme.

In *The Wizard of Oz,* for example, Dorothy argues to Toto that there must be a place where there is no trouble, the place she wants to live. Maybe it's a place over the rainbow. Let me sing a song about it.

At the end of the film, though, she has learned, there's no place like home.

In *It's a Wonderful Life,* what does George Bailey learn at the end? That no man is a failure if he has friends, and those friends are right there in his hometown, a hometown he's always wanted to get away from. So, early in the flashback sequence, we have young George in the drugstore with Mary and Violet, and he tells them he's going off on adventures, and he's going to have a couple of harems, and maybe three or four wives.

When you finish your novel and you have solidified your theme, find a place early on for that counterargument and put it in. This provides a nice arc for the story. It shows how the thematic conflict has been settled.

ONE THING

Curly in *City Slickers* said the secret of life was "one thing."

Some philosophers call that "ultimate concern."

A guy sitting at the bar might say it's what you'd die for.

Whatever you call it, it's the thing or belief that unifies your life and gives it meaning.

And even if you reject meaning itself, that's a viewpoint. You can't avoid it.

So why not battle some of this out in your fiction?

Do This:

1. Write down the one thing or person you would die for.

2. Write a diary entry, for your eyes only, on why this is so. What is it in your past that brought you to this point? Imagine a circumstance

where this choice is presented to you. What feelings does it evoke in you to contemplate death for what you have chosen?

This is the sort of feeling that is a clue to what your fiction should have pulsing through it.

3. Write down five characteristics you most admire in other people.

4. Under each of those, write a short paragraph on why you picked that trait. Is there someone you know who exemplifies these?

5. Write out your obituary. That's what I said. Write out what you would want to appear in a story written about your death. No, this is not morbid. It's one of the best ways to get at the beating heart of your own existence. This is the stuff thematic arguments are made of.

Use the *feelings* these items evoke and place them in your characters. Note this: Your characters do not have to be exact analogues of you. But when they care about something, it should be with the same ultimate concern you care. Lasting, memorable fiction is about extremes of passion. Those extremes may be controlled by the characters to one degree or another, but they should be running underneath the surface.

Now you're ready to put ultimate concern in your books.

KNOW THE QUESTIONS

One cannot get too far into the Harry Potter series without realizing it is a narrative treatment on the ultimate question of good vs. evil. How that resolves is a question that will be debated by readers, philosophers, theologians, and college professors. But it is obviously on the mind of J.K. Rowling.

Is Harry a Christ figure? Or is he a stand-in for all of us as we confront not some evil without but evil within?

Is the epic about the conquering of a dark force outside, or, as Susan Brooks Thistlethwaite put it in a *Washington Post* piece, "The Theology of Harry Potter," "an incredibly intimate struggle ... with the friend, the neighbor, and ultimately with oneself"?

What sorts of questions does a detective novel raise? They will vary by author, of course. But the best will have the questions clear in their minds. Raymond Chandler certainly did and expressed it in his famous essay "The Simple Art of Murder":

> In everything that can be called art there is a quality of redemption. It may be pure tragedy, if it is high tragedy, and it may be pity and irony, and it may be the raucous laughter of the strong man. But down these mean streets a man must go who is not himself mean, who is neither tarnished nor afraid. The detective in this kind of story must be such a man. He is the hero, he is everything. He must be a complete man and a common man and yet an unusual man. He must be, to use a rather weathered phrase, a man of honor, by instinct, by inevitability, without thought of it, and certainly without saying it. He must be the best man in his world and a good enough man for any world.

You may not be able to express your own thematic through-line as eloquently as Chandler, but the attempt will only help you as a writer.

Try it. As directly as you can, write down what questions your book is raising. This exercise may even help you find new streams to explore. As Madeleine L'Engle once put it, "Slowly, slowly, I am learning to listen to the book, in the same way I listen to prayer."

DON'T PREACH

But everything must ultimately be filtered through the characters. They should never be only a mouthpiece for you, the author. John Gardner, the novelist and writing teacher, explained it this way:

> [W]hen I write a piece of fiction I select my characters and settings and so on because they have a bearing, at least to me, on the old unanswerable philosophical questions. And as I spin out the action, I'm always very concerned with springing discoveries—actual philosophical discoveries. But at the same time I'm concerned—and finally *more* concerned—with what the discoveries do to the character who makes them, and to the people around him. It's that that makes me not really a philosopher, but a novelist

But what about Ayn Rand? Her novels are filled with speeches, most notably the long address of John Galt in *Atlas Shrugged*. Does that work?

For many it does, as continuing sales numbers attest. What this may tell us is that questions of ultimate concern do still matter to a large block of readers. Rand was only trying to fundamentally shift Western Civilization (that's all!). And a large portion of the reading public gave her a listen.

If you want to write philosophical rants like Rand, you can certainly give it a whirl. But almost always it is best to have the characters truly interacting with each other, not slyly preaching to the reader. So make sure:

1. You make each character a truly complex creation; and

2. Justify every position. That is, each character must have a reason, or motivation, for doing what they are doing. We may not like it, but they believe they are right. You have to make that clear. And you have to be fair.

Then, when the thematic argument breaks out between the characters, it will seem natural and not forced.

THE IMPORTANCE OF VOICE

But is there any room for a rant with thematic significance? Of course, if done with what people call "voice."

Teachers talk about it. Agents and editors say they are looking for it. But no one can truly define it. We'll cover it more in the next chapter. But for now consider the importance of voice and theme working together.

Jodi Picoult does this well in the voice of Anna, a teenager in *My Sister's Keeper* who has a most bizarre backstory. She was conceived to be a serial donor for her older sister, Kate, who has leukemia. This raises all sorts of bioethical issues. No wonder, then, that thirteen-year-old Anna is given to ponderings like this:

> Do you ever wonder how we all got here? On Earth, I mean. Forget the song and dance about Adam and Eve, which I know is a load of crap. My father likes the myth of the Pawnee Indians, who say that the star deities populated the world: Evening Star and Morning Star hooked up

and gave birth to the first female. The first boy came from the Sun and the Moon. Humans rode in on the back of a tornado.

Mr. Hume, my science teacher, taught us about this primordial soup full of natural gases and muddy slop and carbon matter that somehow solidified into one-celled organisms called choanoflagel-lates ... which sound a lot more like a sexually transmitted disease than the start of the evolutionary chain, in my opinion. But even once you get there, it's a huge leap from an amoeba to a monkey to a whole thinking person.

The really amazing thing about all this is no matter what you believe, it took some doing to get from a point where there was nothing, to a point where all the right neurons fire and pop so that we can make decisions.

More amazing is how even though that's become second nature, we all still manage to screw it up.

If you have a series character who has established a strong worldview and voice, you can even start a novel with a thematic refrain.

Take Burke, the hardest of hard-boiled protagonists, from the series by Andrew Vachss. Burke is obsessed with the protection of victimized children. And if you hurt any of his adopted family, you will not last long in the world.

Does Burke have a worldview? Oh my, yes. And it has a name. Here is the opening of the last Burke novel, *Another Life:*

Revenge is like any other religion: There's always a lot more preaching than there is practicing. And most of that preaching is about what *not* to practice.

"Vengeance is mine" translates to: "It's not *yours.*" The karma-ped-dlers will tell you how doing nothing is doing the right thing, reciting, "What goes around comes around" in that heavy-gravity tone reserved for the kind of ancient wisdom you always find in comic books.

Are you getting the sense Burke has an opinion?

Down here, we see it different. We don't count on karma. But you can count on this: Hurt one of us, we're *all* coming after you.

A defining philosophy might be a simple as lawyer Mickey Haller in Michael Connely's *The Brass Verdict.* Haller begins the novel with a reflection:

Everybody lies.

Does your Lead character have a defining philosophy? A way of looking at the world? An attitude? She should. She must.

Do a voice journal exercise. The voice journal is a free-form document you write in the character's voice, first-person POV. Even if your novel is written in third-person POV, do the voice journal as if it's the character speaking.

Prompt the character: What's your philosophy on life? Let her speak.

Probe a little deeper. Ask: Why do you think this way? What happened to you to make you think this way?

Here's a bit of journal I did in the voice of Terry Malloy, the character Brando plays in *On the Waterfront:*

> You wanna know my philosophy of life? Do it to him before he does it to you. I don't care what it sounds like. You don't get it. Down here it's every man for himself. It's staying alive. It's hanging with the right people so you can have a little change jingling in your pocket. That's what you need down here, other people to get your back, and you get the guys that wanna hurt you or your brothers.
>
> What? How'd I get this way? That any of your business?
>
> All right, if you'll shut up about it. I'm only going to say this once. When me and my brother were kids our old man got bumped off. Never mind how. I said never mind how. And they stuck me and Charlie in this dump they call the Boy's Home. Man, that was some home. The head guy had a whip, a real whip, and he'd tie you down and let you have it. He used to let me have it for nothin'. He just didn't like me, and I didn't like him and he liked to take it out on me. I couldn't do anything to him because I knew the law'd have me out of there and Charlie'd be alone. Charlie's the smart one, but I'm the tough one, and he needed me around. But boy, someday I'm gonna catch up with that guy and when I do, when I do ...

SYMBOLISM

Knowing the thematic unity of your book enables you to use symbolism to deepen the reading experience.

One of the most famous symbols in literature is the billboard in *The Great Gatsby,* advertising the services of Dr. T. J. Eckleburg:

But above the grey land and the spasms of bleak dust which drift endlessly over it, you perceive, after a moment, the eyes of Doctor T.J. Eckleburg. The eyes of Doctor T.J. Eckleburg are blue and gigantic — their retinas are one yard high. They look out of no face but, instead, from a pair of enormous yellow spectacles which pass over a nonexistent nose. Evidently some wild wag of an oculist set them there to fatten his practice in the borough of Queens, and then sank down himself into eternal blindness, or forgot them and moved away. But his eyes, dimmed a little by many paintless days under sun and rain, brood on over the solemn dumping ground.

What is Fitzgerald trying to tell us with this symbol? Clearly something. A feeling. The eyes are huge and "brood" over the "dumping ground." Could this be a symbol of God looking at the waste the world has become? Or does the advertisement point to the fading of a society based on commerce?

You may argue about that in your lit class, but surely Fitzgerald meant it to convey something that points to the matters of ultimate concern we've been talking about.

Time spent in pursuit of the thematic argument should not distract you from the writing of the book, or cause you endless rounds of frustration. *I'm just writing to entertain,* you might say.

Well, even that is a reflection of what's going on inside you. I'd urge you to broaden your horizons as a way to accomplish both purposes—to entertain and to capture more readers who begin to see that your book is more than just by-the-numbers scenes.

CHAPTER 12
STYLING FOR CONFLICT

That elusive thing we call "style" or "voice" is another tool you can use to heighten conflict. It basically comes down to language and how we use it. We have choices over words and sentence length. We can adjust the volume in how we put the words on the page, how they look and sound to the reader.

What this means is simply this: The more distinct and variable your style, the more choices you have. And with more choices come more ways to weave conflict into every page.

Can style be developed? Can voice be trained? There are doubters. "No, I don't think that style is consciously arrived at," wrote Truman Capote. "Any more than one arrives at the color of one's eyes. After all, your style is you."

On the other hand, many famous novelists, such as Somerset Maugham, trained themselves by copying passages of writers they admired. It was all a matter of getting the sound into their heads.

My own opinion is that style and voice are like your golf swing. You can change it. You can find a way to make it better. You can practice and drill so your muscles remember how to do it. But when you get on the course, you don't think about it. You just play.

No one has come up with an all-encompassing definition of voice. But I've heard agents and editors talk about it, and here is some of what they say:

- It's a combination of character, setting, page turning.
- A distinctive style, like a Sergio Leone film.
- It's who you are.

- It's personality on the page.
- It's something written from your deepest truth.
- It is your expression as an artist.

Clear enough?

Okay, how do you get there? How do you develop a voice and a style that will help in the creation of conflict?

You look at constituent parts of the novel and *go for it.*

Here are some suggestions.

THE TELLING DETAIL

"One well-placed detail can save you half a page of description," writes Monica Wood in *Description* (Writer's Digest Books). "Telling details can be come upon accidentally in the rush of a first draft, or they can be deliberately crafted, puzzled over, and inserted into places where either your character or plot requires a certain kind of image."

A telling detail is a single, descriptive element—a gesture, an image, an action—that contains a universe of meaning. Such details can illuminate, instantly, a character, setting, or theme.

In Thomas Harris's *The Silence of the Lambs*, FBI trainee Clarice Starling has been dispatched by the head of the behavioral unit, Jack Crawford, to interview the notorious killer Dr. Hannibal Lecter.

Lecter, in his cell, asks to see her credentials. The orderly slips in Starling's laminated ID card. Lecter looks it over, then:

> "A trainee? It says 'trainee.' Jack Crawford sent a *trainee* to interview me?" He tapped the card against his small white teeth and breathed in its smell.

The tapping of the teeth is a telling detail, relating of course to the their use in eating people like census takers. Also, the smallness of the teeth gives off a feral vibe, adding to the menace.

But it's the smelling of the card that really hits home. It tells of Lecter's longing for a previous life, on the outside. It is a whiff of freedom.

Not only that, it signals his strange power to get to know people intimately without really knowing them at all. It's a sign that he's going to try to pull some power away from Clarice Starling. There is conflict to come.

It's creepy, touching, and dangerous all at once.

The telling detail can give us a glimpse of inner conflict, too. In Raymond Carver's story "Will You Please Be Quiet, Please?" a husband and wife are having an intense conversation in the kitchen. The wife is reluctantly going over details of what happened at a party years ago, when another man took her for a ride in his car and kissed her. The husband's reaction as he listens:

> He moved all his attention into one of the tiny black coaches in the tablecloth. Four tiny white prancing horses pulled each one of the black coaches and the figure driving the horses had his arms up and wore a tall hat, and suitcases were strapped down atop the coach, and what looked like a kerosene lamp hung from the side, and if he were listening at all it was from inside the black coach.

What is going on in the husband is revealed completely in the images and in how he relates to the images. There is no need for Carver to *tell* us how the husband feels.

That's the power of the telling detail.

How do you find them?

- Identify a highly charged moment in your book.
- Make a list of possible actions, gestures, or setting descriptions that might reflect upon the scene.
- List at least twenty to twenty-five possibilities as fast as you can. Remember, the best way to get good ideas is to come up with lots of ideas and then choose the ones you want to use.
- Write a long paragraph incorporating the detail, then edit the paragraph so it is lean and potent. The telling detail works best when it is subtle and does all the work by itself.

VARYING RHYTHMS

In Cornelia Read's *A Field of Darkness,* Maddie Dare is trying to solve the mystery of a decades-old murder of two young women, with her cousin a suspect.

Most of the book is written in full paragraphs. But this scene is rendered in compressed form to heighten the tension. I'm leaving out some details so there won't be a spoiler:

I pushed against the scarred wood, expecting to find it locked. Instead it swung inward, easily, so I stepped into the darkness.

The door closed behind me.

I couldn't see. I blinked.

There was no sound, only a smell.

Thick and rancid. Sweet.

I was alone in the dark with something dead.

I backed toward the door. Didn't want to see, didn't want my pupils to dilate in the gloom.

Too late. Shapes emerged, sharpening.

The walls ... the bar's solid length ... The mass laid out along it – ...

Compressed sentences. Sentence fragments. And they're set off all the more because it's not Read's usual style.

The same effect can be delivered in dialogue. Here is an exchange between Will Graham, the forensic specialist, and Dr. Hannibal Lecter in *Red Dragon:*

"Your hands are rough. They don't look like a cop's hands anymore. That shaving lotion is something a child would select. It has a chip on the bottle, doesn't it?" Dr. Lecter seldom holds his head upright. He tilts it as he asks a question, as though he were screwing an auger of curiosity into your face. Another silence, and Lecter said, "Don't think you can persuade me with appeals to my intellectual vanity."

"I don't think I'll persuade you. You'll do it or you won't. Dr. Bloom is working on it anyway, and he's the most—"

"Do you have the file with you?"

"Yes."

"And pictures?"

"Yes."

"Let me have them, and I might consider it."

"No."

"Do you dream much, Will?"

"Good-bye, Dr. Lecter."

"You haven't threatened to take away my books yet."

Graham walked away.

"Let me have the file, then. I'll tell you what I think."

Notice how the clipped dialogue feels like a sparring match. There is the "sidestep," too, as discussed in chapter ten. These are tools you will become familiar with as your writing career continues.

Here's a simple exercise. Look at the pages of your manuscript where the conflict is supposed to be at a high level. Does this section contain large blocks of text? See if you can shorten sentences or dialogue exchanges in order to increase the sense of opposition.

WORD SELECTION

Look at the imagery Robert Crais chooses in the first chapter of *L.A. Requiem:*

> That Sunday, the sun floated bright and hot over the Los Angeles basin, pushing people to the beaches and the parks and into backyard pools to escape the heat. The air buzzed with the nervous palsy it gets when the wind freight-trains in from the deserts, dry as bone, and cooking the hillsides into tar-filled kindling that can snap into flames hot enough to melt an auto-body.
>
> The Verdugo Mountains above Glendale were burning. A column of brown smoke rose off the ridgeline there where it was caught by the Santa Anas and spread south across the city, painting the sky with the color of dried blood. If you were in Burbank, say, or up along the Mulholland Snake over the Sunset Strip, you could see the big multiengine fire bombers diving in with their cargoes of bright red fire retardant as news choppers crisscrossed the scene.

Notice: *buzzed with nervous palsy; freight-trains in; dry as bone; cooking the hillsides; tar-filled kindling; melt an auto-body; dried blood; bright red.*

Your word choices ought to be just right for the tone of your book and the individual scene.

How do you get at the right words?

Stephen King has stated that any word you have to pluck from a thesaurus will be the wrong word.

There's more than a little bit of wisdom in King's admonition. If you are substituting words that are unfamiliar to most readers, or even to you, because they sound good, the stuffy-reading-experience alarm may sound.

It's also been said that you must write to an eighth-grade reading level, or thereabouts, in order to have a popular book.

But there is an exception. If you know the words you are using, if they have become part of you, a little elevated usage in the right place is not a bad thing.

You don't want to have readers running to the dictionary. But you don't have to spare them a little brain power if the context calls for it.

The more words you know, the better able you'll be able to select the right ones for the conflict at hand. This is what style comes down to: the shaping of words for your desired effect.

Certain practices can expand your style world:

- **READING POETRY:** Ray Bradbury advocates reading some poetry every day. It expands the mind and the rhythms in your mind. You have an inexhaustible supply of poetry to choose from. Here is a starter kit: Billy Collins, Robert W. Service, Lawrence Ferlinghetti, Maya Angelou, Theodore Roethke, Tom Clark, Shakespeare, Lewis Carroll, Dr. Seuss, Robert Frost, Edna St. Vincent Millay, Stanley Kunitz.

- **REWRITE GREAT PASSAGES:** New writers can learn their craft by typing out, word for word, passages from their favorite writers. This is not in order to become copies of the masters who came before, but to learn what it feels like to write effective prose. And each author model has a particular strength to demonstrate.

- **LISTEN TO AUDIOBOOKS:** Hearing words read to you is a valuable way to get them into your head. You don't even have to listen to whole books, unless you want to. Find audio of authors you admire and listen to scenes several times. Let the cadence of the words take over and do their work in your writer's mind.

- **READ OUTSIDE YOUR GENRE:** Challenge yourself. Read some nonfiction and the type of fiction you don't normally favor. Get out of your comfort zone and keep up the mental calisthenics. Then sit back down and write the best story you can. You'll have all sorts of new ways of doing so. You'll have style.

CHAPTER 13
REVISING FOR CONFLICT

Revision presents you with a platinum opportunity to find ways to increase the conflict measures of your book.

When you write, write. Head down, plugging away, letting the words and scene unfold.

Get a first draft done as quickly as you comfortably can.

Revise the previous day's work if you like, smoothing rough spots, making the conflict clearer. Then get to today's work.

When you've completed your novel, put it away for at least two to three weeks. Get away from it. Work on another project. Take a vacation. Concentrate on your day job or your long-suffering friends or loved ones.

Finally, print out a hard copy. A complete revision strategy is presented in my book, *Revision & Self-Editing*. Here's what you can do to revise for conflict.

CHARACTER WORK

The characters in your story, especially the main characters, should not be passive. Another way to put this is that things need to *matter* to the characters. They need to be taking action.

The proceedings must be meaningful even from the perspective of the minor characters.

There will be times for the characters to pause and reflect, but those should be within the context of the *confrontation* discussed in chapter three. And, at certain points along the line, the characters ought to be in overdrive.

Are your characters *active*? Are they pressing the issues in a way that shows they truly care about the conflict?

1. Character Introductions

In this aspect of revision, go to the introductions of each main character. At what point do you show the intense interest they have in their story situation? When is it clear that they have a stake in the narrative?

If it is not in the first two pages of their introductory scene, put it there. And demonstrate how this results in initial conflict.

In Greg Iles's *24 Hours*, chapter two gives us the introduction of Will and Karen Jennings, whose lives are about to be shattered by some bad guys. We see them in the car, as Will is driving to the airport where he'll catch a plane for an out-of-town trip without Karen and their five-year-old daughter, Abby, who is in the backseat.

In less-skilled hands, this could have been a Happy People in Happy Land scene (see chapter six).

But Iles is better than this, and by the second page of the chapter, there's a small argument about insulin, which their daughter needs. This develops into a larger argument about Will's trip, during which we get his thoughts:

> There wasn't much use in pressing the issue, but he felt he should try. Things had been tense for the past six months, and this would be the first trip he had taken without Karen in a long time. It seemed symbolic, somehow.

Thus we have, in the introductory chapter, a small picture of the conflict that is based upon family tension. But it's enough to get us interested in the threesome. We see how much they care about each other, too, even as the tension hangs over the scene.

So go back to all your main character introductions and open with a disturbance. Then make it clear that the character is heavily invested in the actions going on around her.

2. Overdrive Scenes

Find the most intense scene, emotionally, in your novel. Is it intense enough? Have you held back because you, the writer, are afraid of melodrama or writing "too hot"?

Forget that. Ratchet up the scene intensity by 10 percent. Look to interior life, dialogue, and action descriptions as ways to indicate the higher level.

For example:

> Roger balled his hands into fists.

Could be one of these:

> Roger balled his hands into fists. His nails broke skin.

> Roger balled his hands into fists, his nails breaking skin. He thought he felt blood.

Which one is too much and which just right? Now you have some options, like dialogue:

> "You make me want to puke."

Could be one of these:

> "I want to spit you out of my mouth."

> "I'd love to tear your liver out and eat it raw."

Which is too much, which just right? Come up with alternatives.

3. Orchestration

Make sure your cast of characters is differentiated enough so there are possibilities for conflict. Look for ways to accentuate the differences (see chapter three). Look to:

- Physical makeup
- Mannerisms
- Dialogue (each character should have a unique "sound")

SCENE WORK

When looking at your individual scenes, have a checklist handy and remind yourself to look for the following:

- Scenes where there is a lot of dialogue without conflict or tension.
- Scenes that give too much exposition.
- Scenes where a character is alone, thinking.
- Scenes where characters are on the same side, not in conflict.

Each one of these areas can be "heated up" using the principles in this book.

Use Motion

Alfred Hitchcock hated scenes of people just talking. He never allowed that to happen. He always had something else of interest in the frame.

Character movement is a good way to avoid "talking heads." Look for ways to have characters move physically in keeping with their particular agendas. Ever notice in the show *Law & Order* how the cops are always going to a workplace to question someone? And that person is in the midst of doing his job? This is to keep the scenes from being static, always a wise choice. People at work have to work. People at home have duties to attend to.

Keep things moving like ping-pong balls all over the table.

Dialogue

Refer to chapter ten, on dialogue, especially the section on using dialogue as a weapon.

Go over all your dialogue exchanges and make sure you are clear on what each character wants in the scene. Put the agendas in opposition to each other.

Are the words your characters using the sharpest they can come up with? Be consistent with their makeup but give them strong verbal action in the scenes. The words do not have to be directly confrontational. They can be devious, clever, off-putting, charming, obscure, nervous—anything at all so long as they are in service of a certain agenda.

Make sure every character in every scene has an agenda, even if it is just not to be noticed.

Cut and Elevate

When going over your draft you should always be asking yourself a key question: Is there any place in my manuscript where a tired, overworked editor might be tempted to put the manuscript down?

Cut that scene. And keep cutting until there are no more weak scenes.

Next, find three scenes to elevate into greatness. This doesn't mean the rest of your book will have mediocre scenes. Every scene must work by itself, adding to the whole. Every scene needs tension and a strong readability quotient.

But three scenes should be elevated relative to the rest. These scenes need to be packed with conflict, emotion, and surprise.

All three. *Conflict. Emotion. Surprise.*

Conflict is the engine of fiction, of course. Crank up the conflict. How?

Through *emotion.* Make sure readers see the stakes to the inner life of the character.

Finally, give us something *surprising,* the unexpected setback, twist, revelation, or new question raised by the events.

Beginnings and Endings

A final thought on revising for conflict is to look at all your scene openings and endings. A very simple strategy can increase the readability of the scenes.

For beginnings, *start closer* to the main conflict in the scene. Can you begin your scene "farther in"? Can you cut some sentences, maybe even whole paragraphs? Just take a look at each scene opening and see how it feels to cut.

At the other end, see if you can cut the last few lines, or even paragraphs, of the scene. Many times you write to a natural resolution point. But if you cut away before that it will often leave the impression of conflict left "hanging in the air" (like a cliff-hanger; see chapter sixteen). It will prompt the reader to find out what happens and turn the page.

And that's always a good thing.

CHAPTER 14
TOOLS FOR CONFLICT

In so many ways you are like a good auto-body guy.

That's right. You create this mess of a manuscript (at least that's what you'll think of it at times) and now you've got to shape it into something that looks good and actually runs.

So you use tools.

That's what the writing craft is all about. Tools. And the more you use them, the better you become at using them. The more tools you're exposed to, the greater your skill.

So herein are some tools for you in this matter of creating conflict. Use them to build a great-looking book with plenty of horsepower.

THE NOVEL JOURNAL

I picked up one of the best ongoing writing tools for conflict from Sue Grafton. It's the novel journal. This is a document you keep, almost like a diary, jotting things in it every day before you begin to write.

"One of my theories about writing," Grafton says, "is that the process involves an ongoing interchange between Left Brain and Right. The journal provides a testing ground where the two can engage."

Grafton begins by writing a few lines on what's happening in her own life. Next she writes about any ideas that occurred to her in the dead of night.

Then she writes about where she is in her book. She talks about the scenes she's working on, or trouble spots.

And that begins the *"What If…"* game. She writes down story possibilities and the pros and cons for these possibilities. Then she lets those ideas simmer for a day or two. When she checks back on them, she can determine which ones have stood the test of time.

This journal idea works for both OPs (Outline People) and NOPs (No Outline People).

For the NOPs, it's pure gold because you're tiptoeing through the tulips of your imagination. "Every day I fall in love again with my writing," you say right before an OP slaps your face.

You OPs, on the other hand, are practically military in your position. You scoff at the NOPs from your structurally sound edifice of steel girders and industrial wiring. But the NOPs shake their heads, lamenting the beauty you might have created if you were in the tulips, too.

Strike back by using the novel journal to coax out deeper scene ideas, to discover surprises that you can work into your outline, and to find solutions to problems that inevitably arise in the writing of a novel.

The journal may be the item that enables NOPs and OPs to get along.

Here's what a NOP journal entry might look like for the novel we're writing about Roger Hill. Notice how I'm asking for more trouble—from the book, not life:

> Okay, Jim, you're feeling pretty good today aren't you? Pretty chipper you'd think you've got this thing nailed. But you don't. You don't think there's enough trouble for Roger. You better come up with some things.
>
> Fine. Don't talk smack.
>
> Hey, it's your butt that's got to be kicked. Look, Roger has just walked out of the bank and nobody has recognized him. What if you change that? What if he runs right into the worst possible person at this time? Maybe that cop from chapter one?
>
> Or maybe his old friend from high school who wants to hold him up. Like that Ned character in *Groundhog Day*. This could be a little comedy but also tension because Roger has got to get out of there.
>
> Good, good. What else could we do with this high school friend?
>
> Maybe he's got another assignment he's keeping secret from Roger. Maybe this wasn't a chance meeting at all.

Could said friend, we'll call him Ned for now, be CIA? Or something of that nature?

Or would that be too predictable?

Come on, Jim, you're the writer here. Make it unpredictable.

Show Ned to be just as boring and incompetent as the guy in the movie. Make him seem like comic relief, truly. And then maybe he dispatches an assassin with cool quickness in one shocking scene.

Or maybe Ned is married to an "ordinary" woman and SHE is the one with the skills.

Keep thinking, Jim. Give this to the boys in the basement [the writer's subconscious] and sleep on it tonight.

Now, while the NOPs are falling in love with their journals, you OPs can be using it to give depth and surprises to your well-thought-out plans. Your entry might look something like this:

Okay, Jim, you finished that scene yesterday with Roger about to leave the bank. Just like you pictured it. He's got all that fear inside him now.

By the way, did you exploit that moment? Did you give enough description there of Roger's emotions? You better look at that, because here's a real chance to deepen reader sympathy with ol' Rog. He's got the plot thing going on pretty good now. Make the reader wait a little longer before he leaves the bank.

Now he's going to meet Ned outside, and Ned is going to appear to be his old friend from high school. Of course, he's a CIA-trained killer who is living what seems a mild suburban life in Sherman Oaks, a total front.

What are you going to do to sell the surface story to the reader? You have Roger stepping out of the bank and Ned recognizing him.

What if you change that? Have Roger be the one to recognize him and make the first move? Have that be Ned's plan all along, to avoid suspicion? Also it will help convince the readers that this is a chance meeting with Ned, not something Ned has set up.

Man, you're good. Have I told you that lately?

Yes, a little pep talk never hurts.

So there you go. The novel journal. A tool that helps you to keep your mind in the book, no matter how you approach the material.

You'll find it also stimulates your thinking when you're not writing. Ideas will start popping like cameras at the Oscars.

QUESTIONS TO BE ANSWERED

Keep a running list of questions to be answered. This is, primarily, for research purposes.

Writers differ in their approach to research.

Some believe that research done up front reveals areas of conflict you never would have come up with on your own.

Others like to write the story and, as research areas pop up, save them for later.

Like the NOP and OP approaches, each has its strengths.

If you like research, by all means go for it. But don't do so much that you never get around to writing.

If you like to wing it, put a symbol in your text where you are going to need research and keep writing. Make your best guess about what should go there.

When in doubt, make it up and make it seem real.

You write fiction, after all. You're a liar by trade.

If it is a fact you must ultimately get right, keep writing and come back to it later.

When you have the chance to interview an expert, go beyond the standard issue questions. Ask things like:

What makes your job hard?
What conflicts do you face day to day?
What "war stories" can you tell me?
What kinds of people complicate your work?

Look for the friction points of a profession and not just the duties.

DREAMS

Dreams in fiction are often misused.

One way they are misused is when they open a novel. The writer thinks, Wow, I can write this really gripping opening, with all sorts of big-stakes conflict right off the bat! The reader will be totally sucked in and then I'll spring it on them—it's just a dream—but by that time they'll be hooked. Man, what a great idea.

Not.

It's a rip-off, a scandal, a con.

Do not open with a dream. (Yes, I know you can point to an author or two who has done this and sold a gazillion copies. And when you sell a gazillion copies, guess what? You can do it, too! And I know Daphne du Maurier did it in *Rebecca*, but that was first-person narration, and she *told us* it was a dream and related it to us in past tense, so we'll let Daphne get away with it, okay?)

Watch out for the *recurring premonition dream*. This is where the character has a mysterious dream that keeps repeating, and holds obvious significance the character can't figure out but is afraid of. As the dream repeats, we know that at some future moment all will be revealed.

It seems like a way to keep the reader's attention, but it's a bit like having the narrator (you) write, *Little did she know that danger lurked just up the road.* Yes, it gets the point across, but will the readers respect you in the morning? One reason they might not is that this type of dream has been used so many times in thrillers and speculative fiction. I'm not going to say you can never do it, but think twice before you do.

Almost as overused is the *past psychological mask* dream. This is where the character keeps having a dream about a traumatic experience in the past. All the symbolism is explained at some point in the proceedings. Hitchcock did this well in *The Paradine Case,* in 1947. But it was starting to show its age in *Marnie* (1964). Yes, you can do the same, but once again I'd consider alternatives.

The best way to use a dream is *sparingly* (once per novel as a general rule) and then only to give a window into what the character is experiencing, emotionally, at the moment. It is a method to get us inside the character and show us just how the conflict is getting to her:

> In the dream Sarah saw the figure in the distance, behind her, coming closer. It was dark, she could not see his face, but she knew who it was just the same.

It was him, and he wanted her.

She tried to run.

The sidewalk below her feet became hot tar. She tried to move but her feet wouldn't go.

She tried to scream but no sound issued.

Then the buildings, the tall glass buildings where her friends worked, began to melt like ice. The water gathered around her and came up to her knees, then her thighs.

The man was still there, walking on the water.

Dreams can be part of your toolbox but should be one of those that doesn't come out all that often.

ONGOING MYSTERY

Remember the woman in Starbucks wanting to know where Jimmy Hoffa was?

That's an ongoing mystery, isn't it? The ongoing mystery is a technique of suspense. It is the unanswered question that everyone is thinking about, is concerned with. The opening line of Ayn Rand's *Atlas Shrugged* is: "Who is John Galt?" That question haunts the characters in the book for quite some time (and I do mean *quite some time* in a book of that size). It's one of the elements that keeps us going.

Indeed, whole dramas can be built on the ongoing mystery. What else keeps us watching *Waiting for Godot?*

Can you work a mystery into your book that keeps the readers guessing for many pages to come? It's not that difficult to do and can pay big dividends in readability.

In du Maurier's *Rebecca*, the ongoing mystery is Rebecca herself, the dead wife of Maxim de Winter, whom the book's unnamed narrator has married. What is Rebecca's hold on this man? What is her hold on the imperious Mrs. Danvers? Was she so perfect that Maxim can never truly love another?

The new bride fights her way through all these doubts and expectations and youthful mistakes, until finally the mystery is resolved in a most shocking way. But until that point, the mystery has a hold on the narrator and thus the readers.

Try working a background secret of some kind into your story. It can be something in the Lead character's life or in the life of another. But the secret has to be asserting itself in some fashion, unexplained but very real.

IRRATIONALITY

When my son was about ten years old we were at a store and came out to the car in the parking lot. My son opened the door of the car, carefully, and slid into the passenger seat.

Out of what seemed like thin air a guy appeared, the owner of the Mercedes in the space next to ours.

"Hey!" he shouted at my son, "you hit my car!"

I whipped around the car and told the guy to hold on for a moment.

"He hit my car!" He took a step toward my son. I got in front of him and said, calmly, "He didn't hit it. I was there. You only thought he did."

He was not mollified. He started yelling at my son again.

I told him to back off.

He stopped shouting and looked at me. There was a moment there when I didn't know what this guy might do. He was completely irrational. And such people are dangerous.

Well, the guy gave a big huff and got in his car and drove away. My son was rattled. But I used it as a teaching moment, to tell him there are such people in the world. They won't listen to reason and they might just pop.

What if such a character walked into your story world?

He doesn't have to be violent, just irrational. Doing or saying things that don't have any relation to reality is unnerving. In my novel *Try Darkness*, the Lead character goes to a downtown hotel to find a witness:

> Afternoon light filtered in through the front windows, throwing weak beams of yellow on the black-and-white Chicklet floor. An old chandelier hung from a dark green chain in the beamed ceiling. A brown moisture stain spread out from where the chain was attached.
>
> I was making for the reception desk, enclosed in Plexiglas like a bank teller's window, when I heard *numbuddynomakenomubbamindGeneKelly* behind me.
>
> I turned around. A tall thin guy, maybe seventy years old, with beard stubble and a blue scarf around his head made wild eyes at me.

"MumbuddynomakenomubbamindGeneKelly," he said.

"Sure," I said and went back to my business.

The guy ran around in front of me. "Disco Freddy," he said.

"What?"

"Disco Freddy! Mr. Gene Kelly!"

His arms started whirly-gigging and his head shook like he was having a fit. Then he spun around three times fast and put his arms out in a *tah-dah* gesture.

"Gene Kelly!" he said.

An older gentleman in one of the chairs in the lobby clapped his hands.

"Terrific," I said and tried once more to go by him.

He jumped in front of me again. "Disco Freddy! Mumbuddynomakeno-mubbamindFredAstaire!"

"Oh, I get it. Now you're going to imitate Fred Astaire."

Disco Freddy smiled and went into the same helicopter routine with his arms, spun around three times, and finished just as before. It was not an imitation that would have been recognized as a dancer in any known universe.

"Mr. Fred Astaire!" he said.

"That's just great," I said. "You do Donald O'Connor?"

"Disco Freddy!" he shouted.

"Paula Abdul?"

I tried again to get past him. Disco Freddy was too quick. He put his hand out.

"You want me to pay you for that?" I said.

"Disco Freddy," Disco Freddy said.

"Got to pay the man," the old gentleman in the chair said.

Disco Freddy is a bit irrational, wouldn't you say? He provides a momentary bit of *What is this all about?* in the reader. The nice thing is, I used this character later on. Nothing went to waste.

GUY WITH A GUN

This was a Raymond Chandler idea. If you're writing along and the going gets dull, he said, just bring in a guy with a gun.

Justify it later.

It's a great trick (yes, it's okay to call these things "tricks of the trade." If you're angling for a position on the Yale faculty, you can call them "advanced literary operandi"). It brings instant conflict, and juices up your story.

Of course, it doesn't have to be a literal gun. It can be almost anything:

- An unexpected guest
- Someone from the past
- An upsetting phone call
- An accident
- A process server
- A cop
- A nun
- A con artist
- An animal
- Geraldo Rivera
- A news item
- A death
- A sudden shock ("You're fired!" or "Will you marry me?")

And so on. It's up to you, as always. Try stuff. See what happens. Let the justification come later.

Just continue to think *trouble, trouble, trouble. Make it worse. Turn up the heat.*

Let conflict come out and play.

PART TWO

Suspense

···············

CHAPTER 15
WHAT HAPPENS NEXT?

The greatest storytelling experience of my life occurred when I was in high school. A friend of mine ran the film club and arranged a showing of Alfred Hitchcock's *Psycho*. I'd never seen the movie before. Not on television or anywhere else.

For the screening, he booked the auditorium and showed the film at night. The place was packed.

And when the lights went down and the movie started, the place was electric with anticipation.

Some who had seen the movie before knew when to scream.

They screamed when Janet Leigh first arrives at the Bates Motel.

Of course, when she takes her infamous shower, the screams were all over the place. Maybe even I screamed. I couldn't hear myself. But I was so caught up in the movie by that point I didn't really notice anything else but my own pulse. I was gripped by the power of Hitchcockian suspense. I was in a dream.

When Martin Balsam started walking toward the house, the screams were intense. When Vera Miles started toward that same house, the screams could have cracked plaster. And they didn't stop till the end of the movie.

I'm telling you, that's the way to see *Psycho* for the first time. Not on television. Not alone. See it at night, in a crowded theater. If there is thunder and lightning outside, so much the better.

That's the feeling you should be going for. Not scream-out-loud suspense necessarily but the kind that holds you in its grip and won't let go.

The kind that has the readers asking, *What happens next?*

That's suspense. And every novel needs it.

In an interview, best-selling author Sandra Brown said, "Suspense is another essential. That doesn't necessarily mean the 'Boo!' kind of suspense. Every novel should have suspense. It's the element that keeps the reader turning the pages. I try and pose a question, subliminally, to my reader on the first page if possible, and I withhold the answer to that question until the very final pages. New questions arise along the way, and they're gradually answered as the story unfolds. But that main, overriding question, the one that makes a story out of a mere idea, is the last one to be answered."

Suspense in fiction creates a feeling of pleasurable uncertainty. The reader doesn't know what's going to happen, but is compelled to keep reading to find out. That feeling must, of course, permeate a genre thriller; but it is just as essential for a character-driven or literary novel. Unless readers feel pleasurable uncertainty, the story will drag.

Suspense is *the delay of resolution.* It's from the French, meaning to "cause to hang." You are letting the answer hang out there, and readers keep going to find out when the hanging thing will finally be resolved.

The more emotionally involved the reader is with the hanging question, the more worry generated about the characters and therefore the greater the degree of suspense.

A character might be looking for his pajamas. Where are they? That question is hanging in the air, but it's unlikely to generate a whole lot of reader concern.

Unless, of course, his pajamas are where he has the note that is the key to the mystery, and some cleaning service took them while he was asleep.

That's the goal: to create such a bond with the characters in a plot of high stakes that the reader has to know how the whole thing shakes out—and to do it for the whole length of the book.

In this section, we will take suspense apart and look at it from all angles.

THE DIFFERENCE BETWEEN MYSTERY AND SUSPENSE

Both mystery and suspense are tools of compelling fiction. It's helpful to know the difference so you can better judge your strategy. Here's a start:

Mystery = who did it?

Suspense = will it happen again?

Mystery is like a hedge maze as you go from clue to clue.

Suspense is like the trash masher in *Star Wars,* closing in.

Mystery is about "figuring it out."

Suspense is about "keeping safe."

Mystery is a puzzle.

Suspense is a nightmare.

Mysteries ask, *What will the lead character find next?*

Suspense asks, *What will happen next to the Lead character?*

There is a lot of crossover here. A thriller can have a central mystery, as in *The Da Vinci Code.* And a mystery can have plenty of suspense, as in *The Big Sleep.* A deft handling of both elements makes for a hugely pleasurable reading experience.

THE STRANDS OF SUSPENSE

In chapter four, I talked about the Golden Gate Bridge in San Francisco. You know those giant cables that drape over pylons? Those super-heavy-duty cables are actually made up of many smaller ones, twisted together.

And that's a good way to think of suspense, too. Different strands working together to support the whole.

I like to think of suspense in the following ways:

Macro Suspense

Since suspense is the withholding of resolution, your novel must hold a sense of suspense from beginning to end. The readers must be turning the pages because they *need to find out what happens.* If you have set up the story with the right stakes—death on the line—the big question is, *Will the character make it out of this alive?*

Without macro suspense, nothing else you do in your individual scenes will matter. The readers will simply not care.

You might have written the best chase scenes in the history of literature, but if there is no sense that the POV character is in real trouble, the chase is of little moment.

In *Velocity*, Dean Koontz sets up a dizzying dilemma for the ordinary guy Lead, Billy Wiles. Coming out to his car after a bartending stint, he finds this note:

> If you don't take this note to the police and get them involved, I will kill a lovely blond schoolteacher somewhere in Napa County.
>
> If you do take this note to the police, I will instead kill an elderly woman active in charity work.
>
> You have six hours to decide. The choice is yours.

What kind of sick joke is this? Billy, rattled by it, takes the note to his policeman friend, who says it's a prank. Forget about it. Billy tries, but when six hours has passed, Billy wonders, has someone been murdered? Surely not.

And we wonder, too. But Koontz doesn't give the answer. Billy goes into work the next day, and as he goes about his routine we can't help wondering if there has indeed been a murder.

Koontz can make us wait now, string us along as he will, because he has set up a hugely suspenseful premise.

Can you formulate a macro suspense sentence, one that sums up all the stakes for the Lead throughout the novel? If you've done your work on *death* as the stake, you should be able to do it.

Will Scarlett survive the Civil War, save her home, and find true love at last? (*Gone With the Wind* by Margaret Mitchell)

Will Dr. David Beck find his wife, thought to be dead for eight long years? (*Tell No One* by Harlan Coben)

Will Prince Albert be able to overcome his stutter in time to rally his people against the Nazi menace? (*The King's Speech*, screenplay by David Seidler)

Try it for your novel now and keep that sentence handy as a reminder.

Scene Suspense

Each individual scene should have suspense, and each can if you build upon the character's fears and worries. There is something unresolved in the scene, namely the outcome. The character has entered the scene with an objective (and this, in turn, is related to his overall objective in the novel). He encounters obstacles in the scene, so we wonder if he will come out of the scene successfully or unsuccessfully.

In the film *The Graduate,* based on the novel by Charles Webb, Benjamin Braddock has called Mrs. Robinson to meet him at a hotel. He has made the fateful decision to accept her offer—of herself.

In the scene at the hotel, Ben's objective is to meet with Mrs. Robinson without being noticed. But he has obstacles. Like the suspicious desk clerk who asks him if he's here "for an affair." Ben is aghast. "The Singleman party?" the clerk offers. Ben is relieved. But only for a moment.

Later, when he goes to the same clerk to get a room, there is more suspicion, such as Ben's only luggage being a toothbrush.

Here Ben knows what the obstacles are, and his fear factor is whether he'll be exposed as having an illicit tryst with an older woman, the wife of his father's partner, no less.

In *Gone With the Wind* there's a terrifying escape from the burning of Atlanta. The suspense comes from the questions, Will Scarlett get out of there with the pregnant Melanie? Get out before the mob steals her horse? Get out before fire falls on her and kills her? The suspense of this scene matters because we know the stakes for Scarlett in the overall story. This is her world coming apart, and she is the only one in her family who seems to have the strength to salvage some of it.

Hypersuspense

Hypersuspense happens when the character does not know what the forces are that oppose him—and neither does the reader.

You are part of the story along with the Lead, looking to figure out what's going on. When you write in first-person POV, it's almost automatic if you withhold answers from the Lead.

In du Maurier's *Rebecca,* the narrator recounts the story as it happened, not giving us the benefit of her knowledge right away (since she's the one telling it, she could have come right out and said, "Here's the deal on Rebecca ..." but where is the fun in that?).

Contrast that with one of the best-selling novels of the 1970s, *Love Story.* It begins with the first-person narrator telling readers that this is the story of a girl who died.

Does that dissipate the hypersuspense? No, it just shifts the focus. *How did she die?* We get the love story first, before we get to the death.

But you can also accomplish the same thing in third-person POV, just by keeping it close and limited. Follow one Lead throughout. Don't reveal anything else to the reader from another POV.

If you do use multiple POVs that clue the reader in, you can always keep the Lead in the dark as he tries to figure out who is opposing him.

Paragraph Suspense

The smallest unit for suspense purposes is the paragraph. Think of each one as having the possibility of withholding information or ramping up tension. For example:

> Roger turned the corner onto Spring Street. The day was bright and clear and he could see City Hall in the distance. The tower, with its pyramid-shaped cap, reminded him of something. Yes, that was it. The hood ornament he'd seen on Crandall's car. That night at the beach. What did it mean? Crandall was there all along!

Maybe that works for you and maybe it doesn't. But upon reflection you might decide you want to stretch out the suspense even further:

> Roger turned the corner onto Spring Street. The day was cloudy and dark. He could barely see City Hall. The pyramid-shaped cap, visible in the muck, reminded him of something. What was it? What? It was there, on the edge of his mind. Reel it in, bring it closer. It was *something*. Something important. But he couldn't get it.

Dialogue exchanges are also made up of paragraphs, and offer further opportunity for suspense and stretching tension. We'll cover that in chapter 18.

Every novel, of every genre, offers increasing possibilities for suspense. If you keep in mind the various strands available, it will soon become second nature for you to exploit them skillfully. You'll be writing page turners.

CHAPTER 16

CLIFF-HANGERS

The term *cliff-hanger* comes from the old movie serials that used to play in theaters. Back in the silent era, and up through the 1950s, movie going was usually an event. You didn't go out to see a movie. You went *to the movies*, which meant your local movie house. You'd go see whatever they were showing that week.

Many times it was a double feature. You'd have the B picture and the A picture. The B was the shorter, cheaper film. Then, before the main feature, the theater would have other small items, like a cartoon or a newsreel.

But the theater's main concern was to get you to come back next week. Every week. So the studios supplied the serial. This was a high adventure of some sort that would be shown in weekly installments between the features.

Perhaps the most famous of these was the silent serial *The Perils of Pauline*. Featuring actress Pearl White, it was the ultimate "damsel in distress" series. Pauline would be the prey of all manner of dastardly men who sought her demise. At the end of each installment, Pauline was usually in some form of mortal danger so the audience would *have to* come back the following week.

One such danger was Pauline hanging off a cliff, looking down at the vast crevasse below.

Thus cliff-hanger, which we will define as any moment of unresolved danger, either outside or inside the character. It can come at the end of a scene, but almost never at the end of a book. The latter is too frustrating for a reader who has invested so much emotion in a character.

The concept of a cliff-hanger in literature goes back at least to Charles Dickens, who wrote many works as serials. In this way, more readers could afford the installments and the publisher reached a wider audience. It was Dickens's job to create a hunger for the next installment by ending the present one with a need to read on. (This installment idea was famously mimicked by Stephen King in the original release of *The Green Mile*.)

The value of the cliff-hanger was picked up by writers in the old pulp fiction days. Back then there was a never-ending need for "novelettes," works of 20,000 to 30,000 words to fill up the pages of fiction magazines printed on cheap pulp paper. Americans gobbled these up, and many a fine writer cut his teeth on these entertainment vehicles.

One such writer was Dwight V. Swain, who went on to teach the craft of commercial fiction for many years at the University of Oklahoma. In his classic tome, *Techniques of the Selling Writer*, Swain quotes from a letter he received from the editor of one of these pulp magazines:

> Do these stories in the style Burroughs used to use; you know, take one set of characters and carry them along for a chapter, putting them at the end of the chapter in such a position that nothing can save them; then take another set of characters, rescue them from their dilemma, carry them to a hell of a problem at the end of the chapter, then switch back to the first set of characters, rescue them from their deadly peril, carry them along to the end of the chapter where, once again, they are seemingly doomed; and rescue the second set of characters ... and so on. Don't give the reader a chance to breathe ...

That is the value of the cliff-hanger.

Does that mean every novel has to have scenes, back and forth, of characters in physical danger? Of course not.

But it does mean that when you reach the end of a chapter you want to have something there that compels the reader to turn the page.

The art and craft of using a cliff-hanger is in "hiding" the technique from the reader. You don't want the reader to stop reading and mutter, "Hey, this writer is trying to manipulate me!"

How do you hide cliff-hangers?

1. You get the reader fully bonded with the Lead character and his death struggle *first*. This way, you have the reader thinking about the character and not about your technique.
2. You vary the type and intensity of the cliff-hanger.

Let's take a look at the different types of cliff-hangers.

PHYSICAL CLIFF-HANGERS

In a physical cliff-hanger, some circumstance happens on the page that we can see. There are three basic types of physical cliff-hangers:

- A bad thing happens.
- A bad thing is about to happen.
- A bad thing might happen soon.

A Bad Thing Happens

You can end a scene with something bad happening to your character. If you stop there, you have readers wondering just how bad it was. They read on to find out.

Or, in some cases, it can end with the worst possible thing: the death of a character. If that's so, you want the reader reading on to find out who killed her, or why she was killed, or what the consequences of her death are going to be.

Take the scene in Raymond Chandler's *Farewell, My Lovely*, where private detective Philip Marlowe is driven to a remote location by a couple of toughs. They tell Marlowe to get out and start walking:

> I started to get out of the car and put my foot on the running board and leaned forward, still a little dizzy.
>
> The man in the back seat made a sudden flashing movement that I sensed rather than saw. A pool of darkness opened at my feet and was far, far deeper than the blackest night.
>
> I dived in. It had no bottom.

So Marlowe has been knocked into unconsciousness. A bad thing.

Or the prologue of *Final Seconds* by John Lutz and David August. Will Harper, a NYPD bomb expert, is dispatched to defuse a bomb at a high school, along with his partner Jimmy Fahey. At the end of the prologue:

There was a roar in his ears and Harper went tumbling and spinning to the floor.

Stunned, he stared at a splash of red on the wall. It was his blood. He felt no pain in his hand, only in his ears. He looked down at his arm, at the shredded nylon, the burned and blackened skin.

Fahey was kneeling beside him. "Oh God!" he said. "Hang on, Will! Just hang on!"

Slowly, disbelievingly, Harper raised his arm and stared at what had been his hand.

Chapter one begins two and a half years later. How, we want to know, is Harper dealing with the bad thing that happened?

A Bad Thing Is About to Happen

This is perhaps the truest form of cliff-hanger, for it we leave our character hanging on a cliff, a very bad thing is about to happen—he'll fall!

In the aptly titled *Bad Things Happen* by Harry Dolan, David Loogan, who is a suspect in a murder, is renting a college professor's home. One night he is awakened from a nightmare. He thinks someone might be downstairs. He makes his way to the kitchen where he gets a knife.

He made his way to the living room armed with the longest knife from the drawer. He sorted out the black rectangles: one was the opening of the fireplace, one was the doorway of the history professor's home office. He switched on a lamp and felt the chill again. The air grew colder as he approached the window that looked out on the front porch. The sash was raised about an inch. There was a screen on the outside. There were two long cuts in the screen, corner to corner, forming an X.

Loogan heard movement and felt sure someone was behind him. He spun around, slashing with the knife. The blade whistled faintly in the air. It struck nothing; there was no one for it to strike. He lowered the knife until the blade pointed at the floor.

Just then the figure of a man seemed to materialize in the doorway of the office.

Bad thing about to happen? Dolan makes us wait, for the scene ends right there.

A Bad Thing Might Happen Soon

This is where you end with something like a premonition. Often a description of setting can do that for you, as it does here, in this excerpt from *Strangers* by Dean Koontz:

> "Honey? What's wrong?"
>
> "Nothing's wrong. Come see," Marcie said softly, dreamily.
>
> Heading toward the girl, Jorja said, "What is it, Peanut?"
>
> "The moon," Marcie said, here eyes fixed on the silvery crescent high in the black vault of the sky. "The moon."

Koontz does not always hit us with the *bad things*. But quite often he will leave the impression that they are just around the corner.

And so should you at various points. Feelings, moods, thoughts, premonitions, dialogue, and the way the setting looks to the characters are all tools for this type of cliff-hanger.

THE DIALOGUE CLIFF-HANGER

A line of dialogue can operate as a cliff-hanger, too. In fact, in the scene in *Bad Things Happen* directly after the passage quoted earlier, Ann Arbor police detective Elizabeth Waishkey gets a call from her partner:

> "You're calling me on the wrong phone," she said.
>
> "I tried your cell and got kicked to your voice mail," said Carter Shan.
>
> She picked up her cell phone from the coffee table and flipped it open. "The ring tone's off. I shut it off for the funeral."
>
> "I'm glad we got that settled," Shan said. "I'm taking a drive to the country. North Territorial Road. Thought you might want to come."
>
> "What is it?"
>
> "Body in a car. White male. Gunshot wound to the head. I think you'll be interested."

Now, that last line would have worked out all right. A murder report. The hint that Elizabeth might be interested. But the dialogue continues:

> "Who is it, Carter?"
>
> "Can't be sure yet, but the car belongs to someone we know."

That's where it ends. Now the stakes are higher. Who is this someone? How do they know him or her? It's a bad thing all right, and we want to find out.

Of course, Dolan now cuts back to the scene with David Loogan and the man in the doorway ...

EMOTIONAL CLIFF-HANGERS

Leaving a character at the height of an emotion is another way to hang them off a cliff. You leave the reader wondering how the character's inner life will be brought back to some equilibrium, as Stephen King does in this scene from *The Stand*:

> Surfacing briefly in the three o'clock darkness of the living room, her body floating on a foam of dread, the dream already tattering and unraveling, leaving behind it only a sense of doom like the rancid aftertaste of some rotten meal. She thought, in that moment of half-sleeping and half-waking: *Him, it's him, the Walking Dude, the man with no face.*
>
> Then she slept again, this time dreamlessly, and when she woke the next morning she didn't remember the dream at all. But when she thought of the baby in her belly, a feeling of fierce protectiveness swept over her all at once, a feeling that perplexed her and frightened her a little with its depth and strength.

It's the height of emotion here, with an expectant mother in the midst of the world-shattering events. How can we not read on?

IN MEDIAS RES CLIFF-HANGERS

Writers often talk about *in medias res* (Latin for "into the middle of things") as a way of opening a scene. That is, the closer you are to the action and the central point of the scene, the faster things take off.

But you can also use the principle at the end of scenes simply by cutting the last paragraph or two. Try it and see. It doesn't always work, but you may find that leaving a scene in the middle of things gives the feel of forward momentum. For example:

> "You'll regret it," Charlie said. He picked up the shoe and looked like he might throw it.

> "Put that down," Eve said. She was hoping he would run to her, throw his arms around her.
>
> Instead, he dropped the shoe. It hit the floor with a thud.
>
> "I'm leaving now," Charlie said. "Don't try to contact me." He turned and walked to the door. He didn't look back as he walked out and slammed the door behind him.
>
> Eve looked at the shoe. Single and alone it was, like her.

Nothing wrong with that. It's an emotional cliff-hanger. But what if the scene ended this way:

> "You'll regret it," Charlie said. He picked up the shoe and looked like he might throw it.
>
> "Put that down," Eve said. She was hoping he would run to her, throw his arms around her.
>
> Instead, he dropped the shoe. It hit the floor with a thud.

This gives an entirely different impetus for the reader. The scene hasn't really ended yet. There's got to be more coming. Eve's reaction. Charlie's next move.

You, the writer, can answer that early or late. You could begin the next chapter at the very same spot:

> "I'm leaving now," Charlie said. "Don't try to contact me." He turned and walked to the door. He didn't look back as he walked out and slammed the door behind him.

Or you could jump to another POV scene and make the reader wait. The point is, you have lots of choices and ways to put your friend Suspense to good use.

Cliff-hangers are one of the best suspense techniques you have. Every chapter in your novel can end with a little bit of "hang time" for readers. And why not do that? Don't leave them comfortable. Give them that pleasurable uncertainty that makes them need to flip the page.

CHAPTER 17
STRETCHING THE TENSION

Every scene in your novel should have tension in it, whether that comes from outright conflict or the inner turmoil of character emotions.

You create tension by giving the viewpoint character a scene goal. What does he want, and why? It has to matter to him or it won't matter to the readers.

Next, what keeps him from the goal? It may be the opposing action of another character or a circumstance he finds himself in.

Finally, make most scenes come out with the character suffering a setback. This ratchets up the tension for the scenes to follow because he's getting farther from solving his story problem.

Even in scenes that are relatively quiet, characters can feel *inner tension* in the form of worry, concern, irritability, anxiety.

In Evan Hunter's *The Moment She Was Gone*, Andrew Gulliver's twin sister, a schizophrenic, is missing. Andrew and his mother, brother, and sister-in-law take stock. The sister-in-law tries to lighten things:

> "Then maybe she's hiding out in St. Patrick's Cathedral," Augusta says. "Or the Museum of Modern Art."
>
> I hate it when my sister-in-law tries to be funny about Annie. I think she does this only to gain further favor with Aaron, who by the way has never thought any of our sister's little escapades were in the slightest bit comical, even when they really were. As for example, the time she peed on a cop's shoes in Georgia.
>
> "Or maybe we ought to go look for her guru," Augusta adds, compounding the felony.

"Augusta, you're not being funny," I say.

By throwing Andrew's irritability against Augusta's "humor," Hunter increases the overall tension in the story.

So put a sympathetic character into a situation that is life or death, and maintain tension in all your scenes. That's how you create that pleasurable uncertainty that makes readers love novels.

I've already noted that fiction is not reality, but the stylized rendition of reality for emotional effect.

A corollary is that real time is not fictional time. Nor should it be.

You are free to slow down time anytime you like, and the time to do it is when you can *stretch the tension.*

When you have any moment of action, conflict, or tension, consider the various ways you can keep it going.

Slowing time, like slow motion in the movies, is one way to go. In fiction, however, you have a lot of other options. Here are a few of them.

STRETCHING THE ACTION

In Lee Child's *Worth Dying For,* Jack Reacher throws a punch. No surprise there. Reacher has many ways to mess up another human being. How long does a punch take to throw? From decision to landing, a second maybe? Or even less?

Why waste the moment? Lee Child takes over *two pages* to render that one second. He starts with an observation and reaction in Reacher's mind:

> Reacher saw the dark blue Chevrolet and instantly linked it through Vincent's testimony back at the motel to the two men he had seen from Dorothy Coe's barn, while simultaneously critiquing the connection, in that Chevrolets were very common cars and dark blue was a very common color, while simultaneously recalling the two matched Iranians and the two matched Arabs he had seen, and asking himself whether the rendezvous of two separate pairs of strange men in winter in a Nebraska hotel could be just a coincidence, and if indeed it wasn't, whether it might then reasonably imply the presence of a third pair of men, which might or might not be the two tough guys from Dorothy's farm, however inexplicable those six men's association might be, however mysterious their

purpose, while simultaneously watching the man in front of him dropping his car key, and moving his arm ...

And on it goes, one thought, for several more lines. Note that this is all supposed to be firing off in his mind in a single instant. Then Reacher acts:

> He twisted from the waist in a violent spasm and started a low sidearm punch aimed at the center of the Iranian's chest. Chemical reaction in his brain, instantaneous transmission of the impulse, chemical reaction in every muscle system from his left foot to his right fist, total elapsed time a small fraction of a second, total distance to target less than a yard, total time to target another small fraction of a second, which was good to know right then, because the guy's hand was all the way in his pocket by that point, his own nervous system reacting just as fast as Reacher's, his elbow jerking up and back and trying to free whatever the hell it was he wanted, be it a knife, or a gun, or a phone, or a driver's license, or a passport, or a government ID, or a perfectly innocent letter from the University of Tehran proving he was a world expert on plan genetics and an honored guest in Nebraska just days away from increasing local profits a hundredfold and eliminating world hunger at one fell swoop.

Whew! And the punch hasn't even landed yet! When it does:

> Two hundred and fifty pounds of moving mass, a huge fist, a huge impact, the zipper of the guy's coat driving backward into his breastbone driving backward into his chest cavity, the natural elasticity of his ribcage letting it yield whole inches, the resulting violent compression driving the air from his lungs, the hydrostatic shock driving blood back into his heart ...

We'll leave it there for now. To see what happened to the poor Iranian who had the bad fortune to cross Jack Reacher, you can read the book.

The point is that Lee Child squeezes an amazing amount of tension out of a few seconds because he's not at all afraid to make us wait.

And that's the key to tension. It is waiting. The longer the better.

Can you write a whole book like this? Of course not. You pick your spots, and you don't do it the same way all the time.

1. Find a scene in your novel where you have the moment of highest tension.

2. Refer back to the material in "Action" on page 203.
3. Now, stretch your scene out another 25 percent. You can do it. Use all the techniques we've discussed: slow motion, inner thoughts, dialogue, description (which does double duty), and so on.
4. Analyze the scene for readability, trimming or adding as you see fit.
5. Find the next most intense scene. Repeat steps 2 through 4.
6. Repeat the process with yet another scene in your novel.

Note: The more intense the tension, the longer you can draw it out. But even a scene of relatively low tension can be expanded, even if it's just by one paragraph. Consider a simple moment like this:

> Our cook ordered me to the kitchen. She was furious. "There's some folks who don't eat like us," she whispered fiercely.

In *To Kill a Mockingbird*, however, Harper Lee does not let this skate by so quickly. Scout, six years old at the time, embarrasses Walter Cunningham, a boy from school who pours molasses on his food:

> It was then that Calpurnia requested my presence in the kitchen.
>
> She was furious, and when she was furious Calpurnia's grammar became erratic. When in tranquility, her grammar was as good as anybody's in Macomb. Atticus said Calpurnia had more education than most colored folks.
>
> When she squinted down at me the tiny lines around her eyes deepened. "There's some folks who don't eat like us," she whispered fiercely.

By delaying the payoff—Calpurnia's rebuke—Lee stretches the moment a bit more, letting us feel with Scout the anticipation of what is to come. She does it by giving us a bit of background and then a physical description of Calpurnia's expression. A few lines that create more tension.

1. Find ten places in your novel where you move quickly from a stimulus to a character's response. It may be the action of another character, something observed, or a line of dialogue.
2. Insert between the stimulus and response at least four lines.
3. Analyze and trim as needed, but keep something new in between the original stimulus and response.

Example:

> John slammed the door. "We have to talk," he said.

Change to something like:

> John slammed the door. Mary's heart kicked her chest. She dropped the magazine into her lap and pushed back against the chair.
>
> John crossed the room like General Patton. Mary knew that walk. It was part of his military, take-the-hill style. There was no arguing with it. It was always submit or get out of the way.
>
> When he got to within five feet of the chair he stopped, his frown lines deep enough to hold loose change. He pointed his finger at her face. "We have to talk," he said.

STRETCHING EMOTIONAL TENSION

The same principle holds for tension within a character. When there is a strong emotion to be portrayed, take your time.

Jennifer Weiner's *Good in Bed* is the story of Cannie Shapiro, a "plus size" woman who finds out that her ex-boyfriend has written about his love life with her in a woman's magazine for all to see.

Weiner slows the action and ups the physical reaction. She even cleverly slips in a cliché by having the narrator make reference to it:

> You know how in scary books a character will say, "I felt my heart stop?" Well, I did. Really. Then I felt it start to pound again, in my wrists, my throat, my fingertips. The hair at the back of my neck stood up. My hands felt icy. I could hear the blood roaring in my ears as I read the first line of the article: "I'll never forget the day I found out my girlfriend weighed more than I did."
>
> Samantha's voice sounded like it was coming from far, far away. "Cannie? Cannie, are you there?"
>
> "I'll kill him!" I choked.
>
> "Take deep breaths," Samantha counseled. "In through the nose, out through the mouth."
>
> Betsy, my editor, cast a puzzled look across the partition that separated our desks. "*Are you all right?*" she mouthed. I squeezed my eyes shut. My headset had somehow landed on the carpet. "Breathe!" I could

> hear Samantha say, her voice a tinny echo from the floor. I was wheezing, gasping. I could feel chocolate and bits of candy shell on my teeth. I could see the quote they'd lifted, in bold-faced pink letters that screamed out from the center of the page.

Study the word choices in that excerpt. The forward momentum is slowed in order to enhance the singularity and emotion of the moment.

SLOWING DOWN THE TERROR

Still another strategy comes when there is a feeling of outright terror. In real life it might pass by in a moment but not in fiction, which pulls the reader along for a ride. The following is from *24 Hours* by Greg Iles:

> When Abby turned away from the bedroom, something gray fluttered in front of her eyes. She instinctively swatted the air, as she would at a spiderweb, but her hand hit something solid behind the gray. The gray thing was a towel, and there was a hand inside the it. The hand clamped the towel over her nose, mouth, and one eye, and the strange smell she'd noticed earlier swept into her lungs with each gasp.

Notice the senses Iles uses in this one paragraph: sight, touch, and smell. Notice what he leaves out: sound. Have you ever seen a scene in a movie where the terror happens silently? It's often more menacing that way. Here is the literary equivalent.

Now Iles slows down the scene and ramps up the feeling:

> Terror closed her throat too tightly to scream. She tried to fight, but another arm went around her stomach and lifted her into the air, so that her kicking legs flailed uselessly between the wide-spaced walls of the hallway. The towel was cold against her face. For an instant Abby wondered if her daddy had come home early to play a joke on her. But he couldn't have. He was in his plane. And he would never scare her on purpose. Not *really*. And she was scared. As scared as the time she'd gone into ketoacidosis, her thoughts flying out of her ears as soon as she could think them, her voice speaking words no one had ever heard before. She tried to fight the monster holding her, but the harder she fought, the weaker she became. Suddenly everything began to go dark, even the eye that was uncovered. She concentrated as hard as she could on saying one word,

> the only word that could help her now. With a great feeling of triumph,
> she said, "Mama," but the word died instantly in the wet towel.

This is a fairly large block of text, especially for a thriller. But Iles knows he has a moment worth exploiting. Readers will not notice because they are in the terror right with the character.

Another strategy to accomplish the same thing is to use lines and lines of clipped language. One of the chapters in Ray Bradbury's *Dandelion Wine* has three women walking to a movie, then home again, in the dark. It's a warm summer night, but the town is in the grip of a special fear. Someone they have dubbed the Lonely One has been killing women in the town. The chapter is all about the suspense—will he strike again at one of these ladies?

Bradbury sets up the terror with the chiming of a courthouse clock. Sound becomes very important in creating the mood. Throughout the section the courthouse clock rings out the time, telling us it's getting later and darker.

> "Listen!" said Lavinia.
>
> They listened to the summer night. The summer-night crickets and the far-off tone of the courthouse clock making it eleven forty-five.
>
> "Listen."
>
> Lavinia listened. A porch swing creaked in the dark and there was Mr. Terle, not saying anything to anybody, alone on the swing, having a last cigar. They saw the pink ash swinging gently to and fro.

A little bit later:

> The courthouse clock struck the hour. The sounds blew across a town that was empty, emptier than it had ever been. Over empty streets and empty lots and empty lawns the sound faded.

Finally, Lavinia is alone walking home:

> She froze again.
>
> Wait, she told herself.
>
> She took a step. There was an echo.
>
> She took another step.
>
> Another echo. Another step, just a fraction of a moment later.

Bradbury uses staccato line structure here to stretch the terror. You can, too.

Do This:

1. Find a moment of terror in your novel. If it's a character-driven novel, you can find an inner terror that is meaningful to the Lead: terror of being exposed, of losing a love, of being ostracized, etc.
2. Write a page-long paragraph, stretching this tension out.
3. Now write a page of short sentences, one after the other, doing the same thing.

You will now have plenty of material to work with to the benefit of your scene.

Can you stretch the tension too far? Will it snap like a rubber band?

Yes, but the length of the stretch is farther than you think. Go for it. You can always cut it back later.

When in doubt, stretch it out.

CHAPTER 18
DIALOGUE AND SUSPENSE

The use of conflict and dialogue is covered in chapter ten. Here I want to focus on ways dialogue can carry suspense and stretch tension.

When you read the masters of dialogue—Hemingway, Elmore Leonard, Robert B. Parker—you will find they do this all the time. Dialogue for them becomes another means of heightening the stakes.

Remember, dialogue is an expression and extension of *action*. It is a physical act by a character in order to serve his purposes in a scene.

With that in mind, you have several options in your toolbox.

SPARE DIALOGUE

In chapter one of Lee Child's *Worth Dying For*, Eldridge Tyler, a seemingly benign Nebraska grandfather, gets a call. He and his rifle might be needed.

Immediately we're hooked. A grandfather and his rifle? What for? Child uses spare dialogue to develop it for us. Tyler asks, "What's going on?"

> "There's a guy sniffing around."
>
> "Close?"
>
> "Hard to say."
>
> "How much does he know?"
>
> "Some of it. Not all of it yet."
>
> "Who is he?"
>
> "Nobody. A stranger. Just a guy. But he got involved. We think he was in the service. We think he was a military cop. Maybe he didn't lose the cop habit."

"How long ago was he in the service?"

"Ancient history."

"Connections?"

"None at all, that we can see. He won't be missed. He's a drifter. Like a hobo. He blew in like a tumbleweed. Now he needs to blow out again."

"Description?"

"He's a big guy," the voice said. "Six-five at least, probably two-fifty. Last seen wearing a big old brown parka and a wool cap. He moves funny, like he's stiff. Like he's hurting bad."

"OK," Tyler said. "So where and when?"

"We want you to watch the barn," the voice said. "All day tomorrow. We can't let him see the barn. Not now. If we don't get him tonight, he's going to figure it out eventually. He's going to head over there and take a look."

"He's going to walk right into it, just like that?"

"He thinks there are four of us. He doesn't know there are five."

"That's good."

"Shoot him if you see him."

"I will."

"Don't miss."

"Do I ever?"

Here we get a ton of information, explicit and implicit. We know Tyler is a skilled sniper who has killed before, seemingly without a mistake. We know there's an unwitting victim (Jack Reacher, it turns out) walking around about to get his head blown off. We learn about his background in the military, and a bit of what he looks like. We don't know who is talking to Tyler, and that fact ratchets up the mystery.

Do This:

1. Find a high-tension section of your novel that is dialogue heavy.
2. Make a copy of the scene and open it in as a new document.
3. Compress as much of the dialogue as you can. Cut away at words, use fewer complete sentences.
4. Compare the two scenes and rewrite your master scene utilizing as much of the new material as you deem appropriate.

STRETCHED DIALOGUE

You can stretch the tension in dialogue, too. Remember to use the techniques of nonresolution and withholding information.

In *Velocity* by Dean Koontz, Billy Wiles is being played by a clever killer who seems to know Billy's every move. Threatening notes tell Billy what to do, or else.

In this scene, Billy is outside on his porch, as per instructions, to listen to a man named Cottle, sent by the killer with a message.

What is it?

> [Cottle says] "You'll have five minutes to make a decision."
>
> "What decision?"

Instead of telling us what it is right away, the dialogue continues:

> "Take off your wristwatch and prop it on the porch railing."
>
> "Why?"
>
> "To count off the five minutes."
>
> "I can count them with the watch on my wrist."
>
> "Putting it on the railing is a signal to him that the countdown has started."
>
> Woods to the north, shadowy and cool in the hot day. Green lawn, then tall golden grass, then a few well-crowned oaks, then a couple of houses down-slope and to the east. To the west lay the county road, trees and fields beyond it.

Now we get a paragraph of description, setting the scene but, most of all, making us wait for the answer:

> "He's watching now?" Billy asked.
>
> "He promised he would be, Mr. Wiles."
>
> "From where?"
>
> "I don't know, sir. Just please, please take off your watch and prop it on the railing."
>
> "And if I won't?"
>
> "Mr. Wiles, don't talk that way."
>
> "But if I won't?" Billy pressed.

His baritone rasp thinned to a higher register as Cottle said, "I told you, he'll take my face, and me awake when he does. I TOLD YOU."

Billy go up, removed his Timex, and propped it on the railing so that the watch face could be seen from both of the rocking chairs.

As the sun approached the zenith of its arc, it penetrated the landscape and melted shadows everywhere but in the woods. The green-cloaked conspiratorial trees revealed no secrets.

"Mr. Wiles, you've got to sit down."

Brightness fell from the air, and a chrome-yellow glare hazed the fields and furrows, forcing Billy to squint at numberless places where a man could lie in the open, effectively camouflaged by nothing more than spangled sunlight.

Still no answer! More description. Koontz knows exactly what he's doing. The tension grows from the delay.

In fact, the dialogue goes on for another full page before we get the information. Which I won't give to you here. This section is about suspense, after all.

Do This:

1. Find a dialogue exchange in which information is being revealed.
2. Can you stretch this section out so the information comes later, even in another scene?
3. Try adding an interruption to the scene so the information is held up.

THE UNEXPECTED

One of the surest ways to create instant conflict or tension in dialogue is to avoid the "on the nose" response (see also "Sidestepping" in chapter three). That refers to the statement >> direct response >> further direct response sequence:

"Hey Joe, let's go to the store."

"Great! I was just thinking of going to the store."

"You want to go now?"

"I sure do."

"All right! Whose car should we take?"

"Let's take my car."

> "Good idea. Mine's in the shop anyway."
>
> "Sorry to hear about that. What's wrong with it?"
>
> "I don't know, that's why I took it in!"

You get the idea. Now, this is not to say you should avoid all direct response in your dialogue, because it wouldn't be real. We do talk this way, and so do your characters. Scenes like the above scene should be cut because there's no conflict at all. You certainly can redo the scene with different agendas and so on. Direct responses can be full of conflict:

> "Hey Joe, let's go to the store."
>
> > "I don't want to go to any store."
> >
> > "How come?"
> >
> > "That's my business."

So there you have direct responses with conflict.

Now let's turn to the unexpected. Throughout your novel, look for places where you can insert "off the nose" responses.

One way is through simple avoidance:

> "Hey Joe, let's go to the store."
>
> > "How 'bout those Dodgers?"

Seemingly innocuous answers can take on tension if they are avoiding what seems like a simple statement or request. Why would Joe not want to talk about going to the store? What's going on in his mind? Immediate interest is created.

A stronger form of avoidance is to answer a question with a question:

> "Hey Joe, you want to go to the store?"
>
> > "Why don't you give it a rest?"

Instant conflict.

An interruption also creates conflict on the spot:

> "Hey Joe, let's go—"
>
> > "I've had enough, okay?"

The unexpected creates a freshness that elevates the writing. One of my favorite movie examples is *Moonstruck*. Loretta has just agreed to marry Johnny, a likable lug but no great catch. She wakes up her mother, Rose, to tell her:

CONFLICT & SUSPENSE

ROSE

Do you love him, Loretta?

LORETTA

No.

ROSE

Good. When you love them they drive you crazy cause they know they can.

What's funny about the exchange is that you would expect Rose to protest that Loretta should marry only if she loves Johnny. But she quickly and plainly lays out the exact opposite case.

Later in the script, Ronny, Loretta's true love, is trying to convince her to come into his abode after a night at the opera. How does he do it? By declaring how great love is? No, he says this:

But love don't make things nice, it ruins everything, it breaks your heart, it makes things a mess. We're not here to make things perfect. Snowflakes are perfect. The stars are perfect. Not us. We are here to ruin ourselves and break our hearts and love the wrong people and die!

Not exactly *Romeo and Juliet*, is it? But the unexpected makes it fresh and full of tension, if for no other reason than the audience doesn't know what the heck to make of it.

Now some of you may have a question bubbling around in your writer's mind. We usually hear that it's a good idea to cut in order to make our books more readable. That is not quite correct.

The idea is to cut the parts that don't hold the reader to the page. Clunky exposition, bloated dialogue, interchanges with no tension, and so on.

But when you have the reader nailed to the page because something major is happening, keep them there by adding—so long as what you add keeps the moment hot with suspense.

What would a roller coaster be if you got one climb and one dip? A rip-off, that's what. Give your readers the full ride by stretching tension.

CHAPTER 19
SUSPENSE IN SETTING

Conflict in setting (see chapter two) is important and suspense in setting is equally so.

Overall, you want the setting to operate similar to a character. That is, a good deal of the time, you want the setting to be opposed to your Lead character.

Your goal in a suspenseful scene is to keep the reader feeling as if circumstances are closing in on the character. Shoot for a sense of foreboding, a feeling that, at any moment, the trap could snap shut and take the character out, physically or psychologically.

Your setting should do double duty in getting the reader into the experience of the scene as perceived by the viewpoint character.

Perhaps no one is better at doing this than Stephen King. In his story "1408," Mike Enslin enters the Hotel Dolphin. At first, it's benign:

> The Dolphin was on Sixty-first Street, around the corner from Fifth Avenue, small but smart.
>
> There was a Persian carpet on the floor. Two standing lamps cast a mild yellow light.

But then Enslin is let off on the thirteen floor (called the fourteenth, of course) and the haunted room he's investigating:

> His problems with 1408 started even before he got into the room.
>
> The door was crooked.
>
> Not by a lot, but it was crooked, all right, canted just the tiniest bit to the left.

Not a big thing, but enough askew to begin the mounting suspense. A small visual that is in keeping with the mood King is building, slowly. A bit farther on:

> Mike bent, picked up his overnight case with the hand holding the minicorder, moved the key in his other hand toward the lock, then stopped again.
>> The door was crooked again.
>> This time it tilted slightly to the right.

Inside the room, continuing the theme of something not being quite right:

> What Mike had noticed at that point were the pictures on the walls. There were three of them: a lady in twenties-style evening dress standing on a staircase, a sailing ship done in the fashion of Currier & Ives, and a still life of fruit, the latter painted with an unpleasant yellow-orange cast to the apples as well as the oranges and bananas. All three pictures were in glass frames and all three were crooked ... .
>> There was dust on the glass covering the pictures. He trailed his fingers across the still life and left two parallel streaks. The dust had a greasy, slippery feel. *Like silk just before it rots ...*

And then some seriously weird things start to happen. Like an old menu supernaturally changing languages right in front of his eyes. Then:

> He turned around and very slowly edged himself out of the little space between the wall and the bed, a space that now felt as narrow as a grave.

And this being a Stephen King short story, things get even worse. I won't give away any more. Read it and watch how the room is described near the end.

Think of your prose in these sections like the score of a great suspense film. In the build-up sections, the theme is rather muted. It gets more intense as the scene progresses. There might even be a shock and a strong uptick, like the screeching violin in the shower scene in *Psycho*.

It's all part of the score, the mood you're trying to sustain.

AVOID CLICHÉS IN SETTING

You can create suspense in any setting, not just the dark ones. In fact, the fresher the setting the better.

The grand master of suspense, Alfred Hitchcock, knew this. In an interview, in *Focus on Hitchcock* by Albert J. Lavelley, Hitchcock described coming up with the famous crop duster scene in *North by Northwest*:

> To give you an example of avoiding the cliché ... I had occasion to use a situation (which is a very old-fashioned one) of sending a man—in this case Cary Grant—to an appointed place: He's what they call "put on the spot." And there, probably, to be shot at. Now, the convention of this situation has been done many times: He stood under a street lamp at night in a pool of light, waiting, very sinister surroundings, the cobbles are all washed by the recent rain—you've seen that in many pictures—then we cut to a window and a face peers furtively out, then you cut to the bottom of the wall and a black cat slithers along, then you wait for the limousine to arrive. This is what we've been used to seeing.
>
> So, I decided, "I won't do it that way"; I would do it in bright sunlight, not a nook or a cranny or a corner of refuge for our victim. Now we have a situation where the audience are wondering. A mad tension. And it's not going to come out of a dark corner. So, not only do you give them suspense, but you give them a mystery as well. He's alone and then a man arrives across the other side of the road, and he crosses to talk to him and this man suddenly says, "Look, there's a crop duster over there, dusting the field where there are no crops." Now that's the first thing that you give to the audience: this sinister, mysterious comment. But, before it can be discussed, you put the man on the bus and he drives off, so you and Cary Grant are now—because you are identified with him—left alone. And then suddenly the airplane comes down and shoots at him all over the place ... So there you see an example of ... rejecting the obvious and then, out of that, you will find new ways of doing the same thing.

Let's review that scene, shall we? Cary Grant arrives at the crossroads of a desolate cornfield. The shot is wide and the scene is bright sunlight. And Cary Grant is a little dot in the middle of the picture. In other words, he's quite alone.

He gets to the side of the road and starts waiting, looking around, but there's no one there. Empty fields. Fence posts. No sound. He waits a little more. Finally a car comes by, but it just whizzes on past. Cary looks a little confused.

A moment later another car approaches. Hitchcock takes his time, letting the suspense build. But that car runs by, too.

Cary looks around in the silence, hands in his pockets. Still another car approaches and then recedes.

Cary waits some more. Hitchcock is stretching the tension. In the distance another vehicle heads for him. This time it's a truck. Grant looks hopeful. But then the truck goes by without stopping. It kicks up dust, too, all over Cary and his nice suit.

Now what?

Off to the side, coming out of the corn patch, is another car. This one winds its way down a dirt road toward the highway. Cary watches. The car finally stops at the main road. A man gets out and walks to the side of the road opposite Cary, and stands there.

Could this be the guy? The mysterious contact?

Hitchcock is going to make us wait.

The two men just stand there looking at each other. This goes on for a couple of beats. Then Cary decides to take matters into his own hands and walks across the road to talk to the man.

They make small talk. The man gives no indication that he is the one Cary is supposed to meet. And then the man, looking off into the sky, makes mention of a strange thing. A crop duster in the distance, flying low where there aren't any crops.

This remains a mystery for the next several moments.

A bus arrives and the man gets on it. The bus takes off. Cary Grant is once again alone at the crossroads, waiting.

All this time, the setting's desolation keeps building a feeling of menace.

As he waits, Cary looks at the crop duster again. It's making a long lazy turn in the sky. Cary watches for a bit, unconcerned, until the plane starts heading his way.

Closer and closer it comes.

And then Cary realizes it's coming directly for him. He hits the ground as the plane zips right over his head.

Does Hitchcock waste this moment? Does he have Cary flee into the cornfield? Or get help from a car? Of course not.

A stunned Cary gets up and dusts himself off as the plane makes a strong turn and comes right back for him. Where is he supposed to run? Everything is wide open.

But he does run. He runs until he finds a ditch. He dives into the ditch, and as the plane flies over him it fires bullets. Machine gun bullets!

How much worse can it get? What's Cary supposed to do now?

The setting has revealed itself to be an absolute curse. Nowhere to hide.

The scene continues, with Cary trying to stop cars, hiding in the corn, getting poisoned, running out to the road to stop a truck, and the plane going out of control and hitting the truck in a burst of flame!

All this from a simple, wide-open field in bright sunlight.

Do This:

1. Look over the settings of each of your scenes. Have you selected the obvious or the overdone?
2. Consider changing it to the opposite. If it's a daylight scene, change it to night. If it's a scene in a desolate place, move the characters to where there's a crowd.
3. Test locations. The nice thing is you can travel anywhere you want in your mind and scope out places on your computer.
4. Try rewriting a couple of scenes in a new locale. Practice creating suspense where you least expect to find it.
    a. What sort of person might be part of or show up in this place? How can that person be opposed to the POV character?
    b. What sorts of physical items exist in this setting? Look deeply at each one and ask how someone could use it for menace.
    c. When all else fails, do a variation on Chandler's guy with a gun trick. Bring in a normal, everyday thing (like Hitchcock's crop duster) and make it do something unexpected.

CHAPTER 20

STYLE AND SUSPENSE

The basic sentence is the raw material of every novel. You put together sentences to form paragraphs, pages, and scenes.

They are your tools for every effect, including suspense. Handle them well and you'll be able to hold a reader in your grip. Get sloppy and the suspense drains out like oil from a leaky can.

In this chapter we'll look at sentences from different angles, which is exactly what you should do, mostly when you revise.

STIMULUS-RESPONSE TRANSACTIONS

In *Writing and Selling Your Novel*, Jack Bickham devotes a chapter to the stimulus-response unit. Simply put, "When you show a stimulus, you must show a response. When you want a certain response, you have to show a stimulus that will cause it. Following this simple pattern, you will begin to write copy that makes good sense, and steams along like a locomotive."

If you show a stimulus but fail to show a response to it, the stimulus becomes meaningless because it didn't make anything happen. Do this very often and readers lose interest in your book because nothing seems significant. If you show something happening (a response) without providing a cause for it (a stimulus), your transaction won't make sense and your readers will quit you out of confusion and/or disbelief.

Consider the following:

> Bob hit the ground. A bullet zinged past his ear.

> Bob ducked. Joe threw a right cross at him.
>
> Mary saw stars exploding behind her eyes. Tom placed his lips ten-
> derly on hers.

If these transactions stood alone, the reader would be jolted each time. The stimulus follows the response.

You probably are already thinking, *Hey, we can fix that.* We can either flip the two elements around … or make up a stimulus that precedes the first response. Like this:

> The sound of gunshots reverberated in the alley. Bob hit the ground. A
> bullet zinged past his ear.
>
> Joe feinted with his left. Bob ducked. Joe threw a right cross at him.
>
> Tom stroked Mary's cheek. She saw stars exploding behind her eyes.
>
> Tom placed his lips tenderly on hers.

Simple to understand, but you'd be surprised at how many times the less-than-careful writer subtly breaks the chain.

These considerations are especially important in sections where you want to ramp up the suspense. Concentrate on making stimulus-response units explicit and sharp. This will usually result in shorter sentence structure, which works toward your ultimate goal of keeping the reader on tenterhooks.

In David Morrell's *Creepers*, the Lead character, Frank Balenger, approaches a deserted hotel which he will soon be exploring with a team of "creepers," urban archaeologists who get into old boarded-up buildings. Notice how Morrell uses stimulus-response to build the suspense:

> In the darkness to Balenger's right, the crash of the waves on the
> beach seemed louder than when he'd arrived. [STIMULUS BY
> SOUND] His heart beat faster. [RESPONSE, PHYSICAL] The Oc-
> tober breeze strengthened, blowing sand [STIMULUS, PHYSICAL]
> that stung his face. [RESPONSE, PHYSICAL] *Clang. Clang.* Like
> a fractured bell, the strip of flapping sheet metal whacked harder
> against a wall in the abandoned building two blocks farther north.
> [STIMULUS, AUDITORY] The sound wore on Balenger's nerves.
> [RESPONSE, INTERNAL]

Getting these transactions right means your readers won't run up against small "bumps" in their reading experience. One thing to watch out for are *simultaneous action* sentences. The actions my not line up the way you intend. Here's what I mean:

> Grabbing his keys, Bob hit END on his phone.

Does he do everything at the same time? The reader is trying to picture it:

> Emerging from the car, Bob said, "This won't take a minute."

Is the person he's talking to still in the car? Does Bob have his back to her? What's the picture?

> Jumping away from the truck, Bob ran into the drugstore.

Violates the laws of physics, gravity, and good writing.

On occasion, if you make absolutely sure the two actions described can coexist logically in the same time-space continuum, you can use this construction for variety, e.g.:

> Grabbing his keys, Bob stormed to the door.

The grabbing can be part of the storming.

> Emerging from the car, Bob scanned the steps for the Mayor.

He can emerge and look at the same time.

Use the simultaneous sentence structure judiciously. As a rule of thumb, never more than once in the same section. Grab your keyboard and start there.

GRAMMAR

I'm no grammar hound. What I've learned about grammar I've had to pick up over the years. I know that my beloved high school English teacher, Mrs. Marjorie Bruce, now correcting papers in Heaven, would have plenty for her blue pencil to do on my stuff.

But there are some things worth pondering, especially when it comes to constructing sentences that will carry suspense for us. What we want to do is avoid words that take the reader out of the moment, even slightly.

First things to look at: adjectives and adverbs.

Adjectives

Adjectives just want to be helpful. As the old poem puts it:

> Adjectives tell the kind of noun;
> As, *great, small, pretty, white,* or *brown.*

And they often come in colorful clothes. There's nothing wrong with a solid adjective in the right place.

For example, your Lead is eating an orange. What kind of orange is it? Juicy? Dry? Tough?

Make sure the answer meets the mood.

Look out for flabby adjectives:

> He was a big man.
> He was a dull person.

If the description is not important to the mood or scene, if you just want to get on with it, those might work just fine. But maybe you want to enhance things a bit. Take some time:

> He was the size of a Buick. (direct)
> A hand I could have sat in grabbed my shoulder. (indirect)

Look at your adjectives on revision and see if you can't punch them up or replace them with a description. It's all in how you use them.

Adverbs

Adverbs describe other verbs, and sometimes other adverbs and even adjectives. Usually they end in *-ly.*

> Patiently
> Longingly
> Aggressively

That makes them easy to find using your word search function.

Search and destroy.

Unless they are absolutely (see that?) necessary to the sentence.

Always see if you can find a strong enough verb to stand on its own.

And whatever you do, keep those adverbs away from your dialogue attributions. Treat them as unwelcome visitors knocking at the door of your prose. You know what I mean:

"Stop!" he commanded abruptly.

"I ... love you," she said haltingly.

"Oh, I'm so sure," he said sarcastically.

"Back up, Junior," he ordered expressively.

"I shall bring down the house tonight!" he expostulated theatrically.

Be Very Wary of This Word

While you're hunting down adverbs with your word search, also do a search for the word *very*. This word is usually an adverb, though it can sneak into other categories. That's why it's so slippery. But almost always you'll want to cut this, because it doesn't do very much.

See? It would have been stronger to say: *But almost always you'll want to cut this, because it doesn't do much.*

I've used *very* on occasion for the sound of it, but most of the time I want it out.

Passive Voice

Here's the way to understand passive voice.

If the subject of the sentence *receives* the action, rather than *does* the action, it's passive.

Example: *A gun was fired.* (There's no one seen firing the gun. The subject of the sentence is the gun, and it is acted upon, *fired.*)

In passive voice, a person doing the action is most often simply not in the sentence.

The way to overcome this is to get someone *doing* the action, or *reacting* to it:

John heard the shot.

John fired the gun.

Does that mean you can never use a passive construction? Well, sort of. As long as you have rooted the reader in a point of view, we can sometimes understand that the action is being observed by or performed upon the character:

> Joe looked up. The door opened.

Or:

> The door opened. Joe looked up.

We understand Joe is seeing or hearing the door open.

But as a general rule, you'll want to write in the active voice as it is cleaner and stronger.

This is important for suspense purposes. Because suspense is rooted in a character in jeopardy, keeping the sentences active grounds the reader in that POV. A passive sentence dissipates the menace. It may be slight, but why settle for weaker constructions?

As Strunk and White profess in their invaluable classic, *The Elements of Style*: "The habitual use of the active voice ... makes for forcible writing. This is true not only in narrative concerned principally with action but in writing of any kind."

Periods

The period is the most helpful literary tool known to man. Use it.

Especially when writing suspense.

Which depends on strong units of expression.

Like shorter sentences.

This doesn't mean you can't vary the length and rhythm of sentences, but if you find yourself using a lot of commas, and writing flowery, lyrical, majestic language because you love it so, consider the old adage "Kill your darlings." Go back and look for places where you can cut commas and the word *and*, and insert that good old period instead.

Semicolons

When it comes to fiction writing, I think of semicolons the way I think of eggplant: avoid at all costs. As Kurt Vonnegut once said, "Here is a lesson in creative writing. First rule: Do not use semicolons. They are transvestite hermaphrodites representing absolutely nothing. All they do is show you've been to college."

The semicolon is a burp, a hiccup. It's a drunk staggering out of the saloon at 2 a.m., grabbing your lapels on the way and asking you to listen to one more story.

Not that I have an opinion, you understand.

But we're talking about suspense and how even little things can affect it.

Okay, I'll modify things a bit. For nonfiction, essays, and scholarly writing, the semicolon does serve a purpose; I've used them myself. In such writings you're often stringing two thoughts together for a larger point, and the semicolon allows you to clue the reader in on this move.

But in fiction—especially if you're writing sections of heightened suspense—you want each sentence to stand on its own boldly. The semicolon is an invitation to pause and think twice, to look around in different directions, to wonder where the heck you're standing.

Not that readers will notice this on a conscious level. Most won't think, "Why'd he use a semicolon here? I'm being taken out of the story!" No, but it will have that very effect on a subconscious level. It will weaken the reading experience in a small way. Not fatally, but why would you want even a small speed bump in your story?

The semicolon is especially grating in dialogue:

> "We must run to the fire," Mary said. "It is going to burn the town; that is a disaster!"

What's that semicolon doing there? Is it making Mary's dialogue stronger or weaker? Is it adding to the intensity of the moment or diluting it?

I know there are some novelists out there who insist that this bit of punctuation does serve a purpose. My advice to them is to get a semicolonectomy.

Exclamation Points

The old Hardy Boys mysteries could make you turn pages! They'd end most of their chapters with exclamation points! Easy, right?

Not for your fiction. Exclamation points must be used judiciously. Use them:

- when dialogue demands it
- to spice up an interior thought

As in:

> "Get out!"

Avoid the exclamation point in your narrative portions:

> She turned the corner. And saw Steve!

Instead, give us a reaction beat:

> She turned the corner. And saw Steve. Her pulse spiked.

Or set the sentence apart:

> She turned the corner.
> And saw Steve.

The stand-alone sentence feels like an exclamation. It's being given prominence, but without the punctuation.

When you're writing for suspense, you don't want to hit the reader over the head with that fact. The exclamation point can seem manipulative. Let the scene you are writing do the work. Let it *imply* the exclamation points!

Quotation Marks

Never put quotation marks around thoughts:

> "She's mad," he thought.

You can either italicize the thought, or give it an attribution:

> *She's mad.*
> She's mad, he thought.

Also, don't use quotation marks for *emphasis*:

> So she was in "love" with him.

Use this instead:

> So she was in *love* with him.

Sentence Shapes

Vary the way your sentences look.

Short sentences give the impression of forward motion.

They're fast. Like a jab.

Longer sentences generally give a slowing effect, so the reader may catch his breath and the mood of scene can be rendered in more shapely ways. This is how you control the pace of a scene.

Play with sentence variations. Try things. Become someone for whom style is a palette of colors.

Don't Gild the Lily

In suspense especially, the venerable rule against *gilding the lily* is especially apt. The saying goes back to the idea of adding unnecessary ornamentation to what is already a lovely work of nature.

In other words, don't pile it on. Don't *tell* us something we already know by *seeing* it on the page.

While most readers won't consciously notice it, each time you *tell* in this way, you take the reader out of the immediate experience, even if just for a moment.

Here are a couple of examples:

> Mark crept down the stairs, each creak a gunshot to his nerves. He was full of apprehension.

The last line is worthless. It doesn't increase the apprehension in the reader. It is a momentary blip in the beat-by-beat creation of the feeling:

> "Get out of here!" Mark threw the glass at Steve. He was livid.

See what I mean? We don't need you *telling* us how Mark feels because it's obvious. The suspense of that moment is diluted with the addition of that sentence.

Style is a matter of practice with awareness. So practice. Become conversant with these techniques. Your ability to hold readers will improve dramatically—and isn't *dramatically* the best way for a writer to improve?

CHAPTER 21
INSTANT SUSPENSE

I remember this suspenseful moment when I was dating my wife.

It had to do with Boston Cream pie.

Cindy and I had gone out for the evening, then stopped by a place for a late-night snack. I chose a nice big slice of the aforementioned repast along with a glass of milk.

I forget what Cindy ordered.

I do remember looking into her big blue eyes and thinking what a lucky guy I was. We were talking about whatever it was two people in love talk about.

And then the pie came.

I looked down for my fork.

When I looked up again I saw another fork. In Cindy's hand. Reaching across the table to snag a bite.

Time froze.

In that deep, slow-motion voice you sometimes get in cheesy movies, I went, "Noooooo …"

Cindy looked at me like I'd killed a baby seal by hitting it repeatedly with a baby dolphin.

"You aren't going to share?" she asked.

Of course I wasn't going to share! This was *my* pie. She could get her own pie. I'd lived alone and, in college, with four other guys. We hogged our food. Get your own food!

And so, in the stunned silence of a little late-night deli, suspense. We're incompatible after all? Was this the end of the dream?

We worked it out. But for a moment there …

That was *instant suspense*. Little things that you can do in the middle of a scene to create more of the page-turning momentum you want in your book.

MICROOBSTACLES

Alfred Hitchcock used to explain the difference between surprise and suspense this way: Surprise is when two people are sitting at a table in a restaurant, and a bomb blows up under the table.

Suspense is when the audience sees the ticking bomb under the table and wonders when it will go off.

This crucial distinction leads to a tremendous tool of increasing suspense and virtually any point in your plot: microobstacles.

A microobstacle is a seemingly small incident or object or character that enters a scene with the potential for huge ramifications.

Recently I was writing a scene where my Lead character had to get someone to an old priest in Hollywood. The priest was the only one who could help in this instance. He had been found in this little church that had its doors open 24/7.

My plan was to have my Lead drive up, run in, and find the priest bound and gagged. So that's where I headed … until she got to the door.

This is a great place for a microobstacle, I thought. So I locked the doors.

Since time was of the essence in this scene, this little obstacle added to the suspense. It kept the scene taut without much effort. Now my Lead had to overcome this hurdle in order to get to the next.

If she didn't, there was going to be even greater trouble for her.

These microobstacles enhance the pleasure of a reading experience if— and this is a big if—the readers already care about the characters.

If they don't, microobstacles become annoying speed bumps.

A case in point is a scene from the Ben Affleck movie *The Town*. It's the story of a crew from Charlestown, led by Doug McRay (Affleck), that robs banks. One of the other members is Doug's childhood friend, Jim (Jeremy Renner).

When the film opens, they rob a bank wearing skull masks. An assistant bank manager, Claire (Rebecca Hall), sees a tattoo on the back of Jim's neck. That's the only visual she has. And she's an FBI witness.

Trying to keep an eye on this witness, Doug ends up smitten with her. They start dating.

This is already a very thin piece of ice. In fact, Jim—who knows nothing of this budding romance—has suggested to Doug that they "take care of" this witness.

As Doug and Claire are at a sidewalk café one day, Claire leaves to use the restroom. At that moment Jim walks up and starts a conversation, asking Doug what's going on. Who is he here with? Doug tries to get him out of there, but Jim sits down to find out. He's suspicious.

He's also wearing a T-shirt and his tattoo is clearly visible.

Claire comes back to the table.

For the next two or three minutes, with camera shots of the tat thrown in every now and then, we wonder *Will Claire see the tattoo?* If she does, she'll know Doug has been lying to her, that he's part of the crew, and so on.

Even as the dialogue gets pointed, with Jim slyly trying to find out what's going on and signal his displeasure to Doug, we keep wondering about what Claire will see.

A small obstacle thrown into the mix, but one that carries the potential of blowing up.

Do This:

1. Look for scenes where you have more than two pages of low suspense. It might be two people talking in a restaurant, or allies conversing in the workplace.

2. Make a list of potential obstacles that could be introduced, from large to small. Keep going until you have nine or ten. Don't edit yourself. These can be other characters, sounds, weather, accidents (large or small), annoyances, and so on.

3. Choose *one* to insert into the middle of the scene.

After you do this a few times, your writer's brain will work on automatic and sense places to put a microobstacle. It's well worth the exercise.

RAISING THE STAKES

"To raise the stakes" is a saying that comes from the world of poker hustlers (obviously). Consider this scenario: A rube from the country comes into town, has a drink or two, then gets invited to a "friendly game of poker" in the back room.

"Why sure!" the country boy says and joins this group of men with pencil mustaches and beady eyes. After a few hands in which the country boy finds himself up a dollar or two, he feels confident. The beer his new "friends" have bought him doesn't hurt.

"I guess it's just not your night!" country boy exclaims as he pulls in another twenty cents worth of chips.

It's about this time that one of the mustache guys suggests they raise the stakes of the game, you know, just to make it interesting.

And you know the rest. Slowly country boy loses not only his winnings, but all the money he has on him, maybe his gold watch or even his suit of clothes.

When the stakes are raised, the risks are greater and the potential loss more severe.

In your novel, you can raise the stakes in three areas: plot, character, and society.

Plot Stakes

When the main action gets ratcheted up, you are dealing with plot stakes. The outer circumstances take on more danger and importance. Ask:

- What greater physical harm can come to my Lead? Think about the capacities of the opposition and what further tactics can be marshaled to make things worse.

- Think about introducing another character who brings more trouble. In the classic western *Shane*, the stakes are raised when well into the story the gunfighter Jack Wilson (played by Oscar-nominated Jack Palance) rides into the action. He's been hired by the villain as an enforcer. When you add a character, justify him with a real connection to the proceedings and opposition to the Lead.

- You can also add a character who is not necessarily opposed to the Lead but raises the stakes regardless. In *Casablanca*, a desperate young wife comes to Rick for help. Her husband is trying to win the money they need to buy their way out of Casablanca. But he's losing and the wife knows the only other option is to sleep with Louis, the French police captain, to get the papers they need. Rick doesn't want to get involved. Her plight is forcing him to make choices he doesn't want to make.

- Is there some professional duty at stake for the Lead? What is it about her work or vocation that can be threatened?

In William P. McGivern's classic noir tale, *The Big Heat,* a cop named Bannion is driven to get at the heart of the syndicate in his city. His superiors, who are part of the corruption, demand his badge and gun. He refuses to give the gun because he paid for it. Now his superiors have a reason to keep an eye on him, and he's lost his job.

Character Stakes

What happens inside the character to make the stakes more personal? What sends the Lead's emotions reeling?

In *The Big Heat,* a murder case for Officer Bannion becomes a personal vendetta when a car bomb kills his wife. Revenge becomes the personal stake.

Consider:

- How can things get more emotionally wrenching for your Lead?
- What threatens not just to defeat her but also to destroy her spirit?
- How is psychological death imminent?
- Is there someone the Lead cares about who can get caught up in the trouble?
- Is there a "ghost" from the past that can show up and cause the Lead greater inner grief?

Societal Stakes

Here you ask what are the consequences to the larger community? In *The Big Heat,* if Bannion doesn't bring down the syndicate boss, the town will suffer. The corruption that is going all the way to the top will remain. The citizens will be denied true justice.

So ask:

- How does my Lead character's problem extend outward to the larger community?
- What characters in that community can be brought into the plot to illustrate the societal stakes?

THE TICKING CLOCK

One of the greatest suspense writers of all time lived much of his life alone in a hotel room in New York, typing stories for the pulp magazines. Cornell Woolrich became synonymous with the art of suspense, even though his name is, sadly, little known today.

In his story "Three O'Clock," a man thinks his wife is cheating on him. So he plants a bomb with a clock mechanism in the basement. He's going to scoot out of the house, but two burglars surprise him and tie him up, with a gag, in the basement.

So he's left, unable to move. The bomb ticks, ticks, ticks away. Woorich gives us his thoughts, but his powerlessness to do anything ratchets up the suspense to unbelievable levels.

Until the twist ending, not to be revealed here.

In the Woolrich novel *Phantom Lady* (written under the pseudonym William Irish), the ticking clock is an execution date. A man has been falsely convicted of murdering his wife. His only alibi is a lady no one can remember or find. Will she be revealed before he gets the chair? The entire novel is divided by chapters with titles like, "The Ninth Day Before the Execution."

The noted TV writer and novelist Stephen J. Cannell put it this way: "Often, usually early in the story, a clever writer plants a time lock, a structural device requiring some specific event to occur, or some particular problem to be resolved, within a certain period of time. This serves to compress the story's tension. Of course, not all stories lend themselves to a 'ticking clock,' but the resourceful writer digs deep to locate a method and a place for integrating a meaningful one into the story."

Examples:

ONE MOMENT CAN CHANGE EVERYTHING: A man needs to get to the one he loves to tell her he realizes she's the one, but she's about to leave town to get on a plane. In *Manhattan,* Woody Allen runs through the streets of New York to get to Mariel Hemingway just as she's coming through the doors to get into a cab.

PILING IT ON: In *Back to the Future,* the ability of Marty McFly to get home to his own time zone is dependent on Dr. Emmett Brown hooking a conduit for lightning that will strike the town clock tower at precisely 10:04 p.m. and Marty driving the DeLorean into the wiring at the split second it happens.

- A) But a tree branch dislodges the connection with only a few minutes to go! Brown has to climb the tower to connect it.
- B) Marty positions the car and is ready to start at the right time, but it stalls.
- C) Brown almost falls off the tower.
- D) Brown connects the wires on the tower, but in doing so dislodges the wires on the ground. And Marty is coming!
- E) Brown slides down a cable and lands flat on his back.
- F) He has to disentangle the wire from the tree branch. Marty is almost there.
- G) The lightning strikes just as Brown makes the connection and Marty hits the wire.

Do This:

1. Set up something of importance and attach a time limit to it. It can be as simple as an appointment or as dire as a bomb.

2. Brainstorm obstacles that will prevent the character from relief within the time frame.

3. Relieve the tension at the last possible moment. Sometimes the most important ticking clock will happen in the climax, but don't overlook smaller time pressures in other parts of your story.

INTERRUPTIONS

Suspense can also be generated by a simple interruption. Remember, suspense means withholding resolution. So at any moment of tension, with the reader wanting to know how the situation will resolve, you can put a little more time. It's a way of stretching tension just a wee bit more.

Let's posit a scene between our example, Roger Hill, and Eve Saint, the woman he has met in an office (she hid him from some cops who had followed him in). She decided to do that because Roger looks a lot like Cary Grant, and she, as an icy blonde, thought that little circumstance needed some follow-up.

"Thank you," Roger said. "You didn't have to do that."

"No," Eve said.

"Mind if I ask why?"

"You have an interesting face."

"That's it?"

"Haven't you been told that before?"

"Not in such a charming way."

"Don't push your luck," Eve said. "I want to know exactly why the police are looking for you."

"It's all a mistake."

"Let me hear about it."

Roger gave her a long look. His gut told him she could be trusted for the moment.

"I'm accused of something I didn't do," he said. "And the proof of my innocence is right here in this office. I just don't know where to look."

"Wait a second. You're not the guy that's mixed up in this Baxter business, are you?"

"Good guess."

"Not a guess," she said. "I may be able to help you."

He took her shoulders. "Do you know where those papers are? The Baxter papers?"

"Yes. And if they are what you say they are, then you have nothing to worry about."

"Show me!"

> "This way."
>
> She led Roger into the adjoining suite.

So we are on to the discovery of some important clue that will help Roger. There will be many places in your manuscript that are like this. Think of them as Point A to Point B to Point C sequences. A logical order.

But why let the Lead off so easily? And, it should be added, the reader as well?

Let's add an interruption:

> He took her shoulders. "Do you know where those papers are? The Baxter papers?"
>
> "Yes. And if they are what you say they are, then you have nothing to worry about."
>
> "Show me!"
>
> "This way."
>
> She took a step but a pounding on the door stopped her.
>
> "Open up!" It was the cop's voice, the one he'd heard before.
>
> "What is it?" Eve said.
>
> "Somebody saw him come in there. Why is the door locked?"
>
> Eve motioned for Roger to get into the next room. But that was a problem. There was no way out of that room. Not that he'd seen anyway.
>
> "Open the door now," the cop said.

And on we go. Will Roger ever get his hands on the Baxter papers? That's up to you, but now he has to wait.

MINOR CHARACTERS
. . . .

Don't ever waste a minor character. They can do many things for your novel—add spice, extra beats, comic relief (see chapter seven). And suspense.

These minor characters can have lines or be, in theatrical terms, a spear-carrier (referring to the extras in a Greek drama who had no lines and merely took up space).

In either instance, look for ways to use these characters to *delay* matter for your Lead and increase suspense.

What if your Roger Hill needs to find a document he's lost? And he needs it *now*. He thinks he lost it at Union Station. So he hurries back to talk to the security desk, in charge of lost and found items. There's a guard who looks about twenty years old sitting at the desk:

"Excuse me," Roger said.

The guard looked up from what looked like a comic book.

"I lost a package," Roger said.

"Join the club," the guard said, tossing the comic book on the desk.

"What sort of package?"

"It was an envelope, a big one, you know the kind—"

"Manila?"

"That's it, manila."

"Uh-huh."

"Could you look?"

"What was in it?"

"Why do you need to know that? If you have—"

"Hey! You know what they put in envelopes? You heard of anthrax maybe?"

"Do I look like a terrorist?"

"We don't profile here, pal."

"Please just look. I'm in a hurry."

"So what is supposed to be in this envelope?"

"Just some papers I need, right now as a matter—"

"You a writer?"

"Excuse me?"

"We get a lot of writers pass through here."

"I'm not—"

"I'd like to be a writer. I got ideas. You get a lot sitting at this desk."

Meanwhile, the killers are getting away.

A minor character can and should be either an irritant or an ally, someone who frustrates or helps the Lead. Even in the case of the ally, there can be suspense built in depending on the moment.

Remember the scene in *It's a Wonderful Life* when the chronically absentminded Uncle Billy loses the bank deposit? He tries to find it but can't, and time is of the essence. Not having the money means ruin. And George reads him the riot act, screaming at him to remember.

They are allies. They are on the same side. But the clock is ticking and Uncle Billy provides the means for added suspense.

TWISTS AND TURNS

Twists and turns are nice subsets of conflict and suspense. By definition, they take the writing out of the ordinary and predictable. They work only when they add complications to the narrative, increasing the tension. In that way, they help us with our number one goal: Keep the reader turning pages.

We all know the experience of that breathless surprise in a book or film. Creating these moments is one of the pleasures of writing any kind of fiction.

So let's make some.

A twist is an event that changes the trajectory of the narrative. It puts an immediate stop to the expected direction and sends the reader off the road.

The twist may completely alter the story line, or it may add huge complications to it. In other words, the reader may be sent down a new stream toward an unknown destination. Or he may be on the same river, but with rocks and rapids—or even a waterfall—to suddenly contend with.

A twist can come in the middle of the story or near the end. It can create plot problems, character problems, or both.

A twist can be defined as a surprise that is unanticipated but justifiable.

That means the reader can't see it coming, but once it does come it makes sense. At least, once all the information is revealed.

A few examples below illustrate. I'll give the titles of the works, and if you don't wish to know the twist, don't read what follows—go experience the books for yourself.

Fair enough?

TWISTS: *THE CRYING GAME*

One of the most mind-blowing—and for the men in the audience, seat-squirming—twists in the history of film. It happens in the middle, as you recall. IRA soldier Fergus has fallen for a beautiful black hairdresser. Things get hot and heavy between them. Removing the clothes of his soon-to-be-lover, Fergus comes across an anatomical piece of information that sends him reeling with massive shock.

This is an example of a twist that happens in the middle of things and changes the trajectory of the story. And how.

The Sixth Sense

The famous twist in this film happens at the very end. Dr. Malcolm Crowe, a child psychologist, works with a boy named Cole who sees dead people. On and on it goes, until we discover that Crowe himself has been dead all the way through the movie.

This twist explains everything else that happens in the movie:

Star Wars

"I am your father!"

The Maltese Falcon

Sam Spade loves the lying, murdering Brigid O'Shaughnessy, but that is not enough at the end. He calls the cops and turns her over to them because:

"When a man's partner is killed he's supposed to do something about it. It doesn't make any difference what you thought of him. He was your partner and you're supposed to do something about it ... . I won't play the sap for you."

Rebecca

"I hated her!"

Murder on the Orient Express

All the suspects did it.

Gone With the Wind

Surely Scarlett and Rhett will end up together, after all they've been through. But then: "Frankly, my dear, I don't give a damn."

The Gift of the Magi

A young husband without much money sells his most valuable possession, his gold watch, so he can have enough money to buy his wife a Christmas present—a set of jeweled combs for her beautiful long hair. But then he finds out she has cut her hair and sold it, so she could buy him a beautiful watch chain.

Chinatown

"She's my daughter."

Slap.

"She's my sister."

Slap.

"She's my daughter *and* my sister."

Coming Up With Twists

Twists are fun to play with, harder to justify. It's like that old Seinfeld moment when Jerry is miffed that the rental car company doesn't have the car he reserved. He castigates the woman at the desk: "You know how to *take* the reservation. You just don't know how to *hold* the reservation. And that's really the most important part of the reservation, the holding. Anybody can take 'em."

We might say, then, that anybody can create a twist. But it's the justifying that's the most important part of the twist.

So what can you do?

1. Listen to Your Writer's Mind

As you write, even if you're writing to an outline, allow your subconscious writer's mind to deliver a message to you every now and then.

Sometimes that will happen without any prodding on your part. You'll be writing along, minding your own business—which means creating business for your characters—when all of a sudden you'll get this wild idea about the scene. It'll just happen, usually through the characters.

This is what some writers describe as the characters "taking over." That's a bit of an overstatement (you are free to remind those nettlesome creations that *you* are the one who taps the keys), but it holds a grain of truth.

When that happens, stop immediately and play with the idea.

Once I was writing a novel about a lawyer and his family, who get threats. I had planned a scene where the husband convinces his wife to move out of town to a safe location until the trouble is resolved.

When I got to that point in the dialogue the wife said, "No."

I blinked my eyes a couple of times and hit the backspace key.

She still refused to go.

I stopped and sat back and thought about it. I listened to her argument. She didn't want to leave her husband, wouldn't leave, and wasn't going to be forced.

I kind of liked that about her.

So I let her have her way, and both she and the book were the better for it. I had to do some new planning on the upcoming scenes, but it all worked out.

Sometimes it may not work out, though. Still, give it some rope. Let it play out a little in your mind and on the page. You can always go back to that point and reassert control.

But it pays to listen.

2. Play the Anticipation Game

At certain points in your writing you should stop and ask yourself a very important question: What will most readers expect to happen next?

This is the anticipation game, and to play it well you must find ways to un-anticipate.

So make a list of all the things a reader might expect to happen. For example, your Lead character has just been shot at in the street in broad daylight. What might he do next?

- Duck into a building.
- Run down an alley.
- Find someone with street smarts to help him.
- Get a gun himself and go looking.

And so on. Playing off that list, what are some things that a reader would not anticipate? Put some alternatives down:

- Steal a car.
- Get hit by a car trying to get away.
- Bump into a guy who decides to beat him up for it.
- Get help from a guy who then steals his wallet.

Play around and you'll come up with the new development you like best.

Make lists. That's how you get material to choose from.

3. Justify or Germinate

So now you've come up with a great twist. Very nice. You will have the reader's attention. And also raise a question in their minds, namely, "How can this be?"

In other words, they will be seeking a justification for the fabulous surprise you've sprung.

Now comes the hard part.

Your twist may have changed the entire complexion of the novel. It may require that what you thought you were going to write is going to have to be reimagined.

And it will have to make sense. Few things frustrate readers more than unanswered questions or answers that stretch credulity.

If a justification does not immediately occur to you, germinate on it. Let it stew in your writer's mind. Think about the problem just before you nod off. Give it a few days.

The answer will almost always come.

4. Layer in the Justification

The best way to get the loose ends tied up is by layering in the answers as you move toward the end.

That is, if you can avoid it, don't wait until the last chapter to dump all the answers in one spot.

Sometimes that is unavoidable. Remember *Psycho*? All the analysis of Norman Bates was contained in a long expository speech by a psychiatrist at the end of the film. But there would have been no other way to do it, since the big shock twist happened just moments before.

If you have to put in a lot of explanatory material at the end, put it in a scene with conflict and tension. Don't give up conflict when you're almost done! If you have one person with the explanatory power, turn it into an argument:

> Let me explain. You see, Bosley was regicidal. He believed it was his duty in life to assassinate as many kings and queens as possible. This is traceable to his childhood. When was four years old, he had found his sister's Pretty, Pretty Princess set and took a tiara. He thought that

would make him look like a king, and he put it on. But when his father saw him, he ripped it from Bosley's head and made him watch ten straight hours of *Tractor Pull*. All the while, his sister was taunting him, telling him he would never be the king of anything except his own little mind. To top it all off, she held him down and poured chocolate sauce on his hair.

Instead, make this a scene with tension:

Dr. Flywheel said, "Bosley was regicidal."

"In English, Doc," Roger said.

"He wanted to assassinate kings and queens."

"Come on!"

"It's true. A look at his childhood—"

"You're going to go Freudian on this?"

"Do you want to know about the incident with the chocolate sauce or don't you?"

"I'm not sure I do."

Modulate your major twists according to your needs and your genre. If you have too many you face the tremendous challenge of tying them all up in a justifiable way. There is nothing readers hate more than amazing story turns that aren't adequately explained. Or, on the other hand, require pages of explanation by some character at the end.

If the explanation is too outlandish, there are going to be complaints.

On the other hand, one well-placed major twist is often all you need to make the reading experience truly memorable.

REMOVING CAPACITY

Another way to increase suspense is to remove the capacity of the Lead to do something essential.

Like walk around.

In Hitchcock's classic *Rear Window,* James Stewart plays a photographer who has one whole leg in a cast. He's bound to a wheelchair in his apartment looking out into the courtyard. He can see the other windows and sometimes what goes on in those apartments.

Like murder.

When the neighbor he thinks is guilty figures out who his accuser is, he comes for him. And Jimmy can't get away. Hitchcock builds the suspense with the sound of the hall door opening and the shuffling of feet coming toward Jimmy's apartment.

Can you take something physically away from your character, either before the story or in the middle of it?

Or can you take away some device or person that is necessary for the Lead to solve his problems?

- The car is stolen.
- The road is closed.
- The friend or ally is delayed.
- The bridge is out.
- The police don't arrive.
- The phone is lost.
- The memory is wiped away.
- The alibi dies.
- The universe explodes.

What occurrences can you think up to make your Lead's desperate plight drag on? Continue to make lists throughout the writing of your book.

INCREASING THE STRENGTH OF THE OPPOSITION

You can also give the opponent greater strength as the story moves along.

What if:

- Allies of the opponent arrive to help?
- The opponent acquires more or better weapons?
- The opponent discovers a secret the Lead does not want revealed?
- The opponent holds a loved one hostage?
- The opponent gains access to the Lead's personal information?

Consider the plot from the opponent's POV, and what tactical plans he would come up with to gain the victory. Make a list of possibilities, like a general planning a battle, and use these for scene possibilities.

EMOTIONS AND THOUGHTS

Don't neglect the interior life of the character when you are creating suspense. Here's why. Any view inside the character delays resolution. It's a tool for stretching the tension (see chapter seventeen).

In Stephen King's *The Girl Who Loved Tom Gordon*, Trisha McFarland, nine years old, gets lost in the woods. For most of the book, that's where she is.

There is a lot of alone time then, and King fills it with varying shades of the interior life of the protagonist:

> When she got to her feet again (waving her cap around her head almost without realizing it) she felt halfway to being calm. By now they'd surely know she was gone. Mom's first thought would be that Trisha had gotten pissed at them for arguing and gone back to the Caravan ... Mom would be frightened. The thought of her fright made Trisha feel guilty as well as afraid. There was going to be a fuss, maybe a big one involving the game wardens and the Forest Service, and it was all her fault. She had left the path.

A little later on, King gives us some of Trisha's dream:

> Her mother was moving furniture—that was Trisha's first returning thought. Her second was that Dad had taken her to Good Skates in Lynn and what she heard was the sound of kids rollerblading past on the old canted track. Then something cold splashed onto the bridge of her nose and she opened her eyes.

Then a memory:

> Doing that made her sob briefly again, because she could see herself in the Sanford kitchen last night, putting salt on a scrap of waxed paper and then twisting it up the way her mother had shown her. She could see the shadows of her head and hands, thrown by the overhead light, on the Formica counter; she could hear the sound of the TV news from the living room; could hear creaks as her brother moved around upstairs. This memory had a hallucinogenic clarity that elevated it almost to the status of a vision. She felt like someone who drowns remembering what it was like to still be on the boat, so calm and at ease, so carelessly safe.

You can see the many ways to vary interior shots of the character's mind and heart, all in service of keeping open the suspense question, *Will she be found?*

Thoughts can also come by way of the first-person narrator, as in T. Jefferson Parker's *L.A. Outlaws.* The protagonist, a female thief, is about to do some robbing at a KFC, but first:

> When I was a girl my first job was for Kentucky Fried Chicken in Bakersfield. I told them I was sixteen and looked it, but I was barely fourteen. Back then girls were front store—filling orders and taking money—and boys worked back store doing the prep and cooking. I fell seriously in love for the third time in my life then, with a cook named Don.

She goes on to recount the manager, Ruby, with a son in prison, being very cool. And then how "corporate" sent in a new manager that gropes, and the whole staff quits:

> So I rob KFCs pretty much every chance I get.

Now you have a toolbox stuffed with ways to create page-turning suspense at every level. When you're looking at your manuscript and things seem a little slow (when you don't want them to be), refer to the strategies in this chapter. One of them will work for your situation.

And you'll become a master of the craft of storytelling.

CHAPTER 22

PUTTING IT ALL TOGETHER

R obert Heinlein said there are two rules for writers:

1. You must write.
2. You must finish what you write.

Not bad. I would only add that you should keep learning how to write better and apply what you learn, book after book.

You learn a lot by finishing your novel.

And you learn a lot by studying the craft.

Ultimately that's what "putting it all together" means. Everything you know, everything you feel, your passion and imagination, your craft and your discipline—all in the service of writing a novel that is conflict and suspense from cover to cover.

To help you along on this quest, let me offer you an approach that can be used whether you are an OP or a NOP, an outline person or a no outline person. At the very least, think through the following steps. They will save you a lot of frustration in the writing.

STEP ONE: GET YOUR STORY LOCKED DOWN

At the very least you need to know your LOCK elements before you start writing in earnest. You may say that you will "discover" these as you go along. That's fine if you see the "going along" as part of the planning process.

But a little thought up front can save you time better spent writing the actual story.

So, using the principles in chapter three, create:

A **L**ead worth following
An **O**bjective with death on the line
A **C**onfrontation where the opposition is stronger than the lead
A potential **K**nockout ending

The last element, the ending, is likely going to change by the time you get there. But having an ending point in mind helps with the actual writing process. It's a destination to aim for.

Brainstorm these elements for at least a couple of hours. Break those hours up over the course of two days. Let your writer's mind work on them overnight.

STEP TWO: A DISTURBANCE AND A DOORWAY

See chapter four and come up with an opening scene of disturbance. Work that disturbance into the first page.

Then plan your first Doorway of No Return. This is the incident that thrusts your lead into the confrontation of Act Two.

STEP THREE: TEN KILLER SCENES

The great film director John Huston (*The Maltese Falcon; The Treasure of the Sierra Madre; The African Queen*) once said that the secret to a successful film was three great scenes, and no weak ones.

Well, the same can be said for fiction, only I want you to come up with ten killer scenes. Here's how:

1. BRAINSTORM SCENES: Find yourself a nice quiet spot, or someplace you like to work (the local coffee joint, perhaps). Sit down with a stack of 3 × 5 cards (the reason will become clear) and a pen and give yourself at least an hour.

Now brainstorm away, writing your scene ideas on the cards. Don't do too much thinking about this. Let your mind give you all sorts of possibilities without censoring them. The ideas should be kept simple, as in:

Mary goes to a bar and gets hit on by a biker.

Joe is caught in the middle of a bank heist.

Mary discovers her mother has been lying to her.

Joe finds out Mary doesn't outline her novels.

And so on. Keep going until you have at least twenty scene ideas.

2. SHUFFLE YOUR WAY TO MORE: Shuffle your pack of twenty or more cards. Pick two cards at random and see what sort of connection they suggest. Write a new scene card based on the suggestion.

Set those cards aside and repeat this step five more times.

3. TAKE A STEW BREAK: You now have spent about an hour and you have thirty to forty scene possibilities. You need to let them stew. So put these aside and come back to them tomorrow.

4. CHOOSE YOUR TOP FIVE: Plan another session in another quiet spot (or chug coffee again). Look at your cards and choose the five scenes that excite you most.

5. DEVELOP THOSE SCENES: Use the scene outline principles in chapter seven. Come up with: Objective, Obstacles, and Outcome

Here is where you pack in the conflict and suspense. Brainstorm especially on the Obstacles. Come up with lists of possibilities and choose the ones you like best.

And one more thing: Stive for something surprising in each scene. A line of dialogue, a character action, an event. Any small thing that a reader would not anticipate.

6. REPEAT STEPS 4 AND 5 WITH FIVE MORE SCENES: And then you're done. Only a couple of hours of brainstorming, and you have ten killer scene ideas ready to go. Put them in a rough chronological order. It's okay not to know where a particular scene might end up. The important thing is you have ten scene ideas that are "signpost scenes." That is, you can write toward them and when you get to one, you can write toward the next.

Whether you outline or fly by the seat of your pants, these scenes are writer's gold. You can start writing knowing you have a solid foundation and plenty of great material for your book.

7. WRITE A NOVEL WITHOUT THE PARTS PEOPLE SKIP: This is one of Elmore Leonard's famous writing tips.

Once you've written your first draft, take a break. Then revise. Take out those parts people tend to skip. The dull parts.

As you read every page, ask: Could a tired agent or editor put this thing down?

If the answer is Yes, look at conflict and suspense, the two page-turning keys.

8. START PLANNING YOUR NEXT NOVEL EVEN AS YOU'RE FINISHING THE PRESENT ONE.

9. TAKE NOTES ABOUT EVERYTHING YOU LEARNED BY FINISHING YOUR NOVEL.

10. REPEAT THE PROCESS. Getting the words down is what makes a disciplined writer. Getting them down with the craft working for you is what makes a professional writer.

This ten-step process can help you get there.

Because, you see, we haven't come all that far from the days of Og and the fireside tale.

A great story has been, and always will be, about a character facing conflict and the suspense of not knowing what's going to happen next.

If you don't have conflict, you don't have readers who care.

If you don't have suspense, you don't have readers who finish.

If your story is dull and predictable, people will not want to buy it.

But if your story is packed with confrontation and tension and complications and surprises and twists and cliff-hangers and emotions, you just may have a shot at a writing career.

That's why, when all is said, done and written—*trouble is your business.* So go make some.

A CONFLICT ANALYSIS OF TWO NOVELS

L et's take a look at two novels in completely different genres. First the literary novel *To Kill a Mockingbird* by Harper Lee, then the suspense thriller by Thomas Harris, *The Silence of the Lambs*. The principles in this book apply to both.

TO KILL A MOCKINGBIRD

This novel by Harper Lee is, of course, a modern American classic and the basis for an equally beloved film. The story is narrated by Jean Finch, looking back at a portion of her life as a child, when she was known as "Scout." It gives us a couple of summers in her life, observing her father, Atticus, her older brother, Jem, and their new friend, Dill. The pace is leisurely in this character-driven story, tensing up considerably when the trial of Tom Robinson begins.

Lead

Remembering the foundations of conflict, we first need to ask, does the book have a Lead worth following?

Scout certainly qualifies. She is young and vulnerable, but tough. She's not afraid to get into fights with boys. Nor does she just accept the status quo. She asks questions and wants answers. She's honest about this. She's got a bit of a rebel in her. She exhibits courage.

Death Overhanging

Next, what is her objective? What are the stakes? How is "death" involved?

Certainly we're not dealing with physical death. There is the scene where Scout and Jem are in danger of getting knifed by Bob Ewell, but that only happens at the end of the book. Nor is this about professional death, though that does play a part in the subplot involving Atticus and the trial of Tom Robinson.

This leaves us with psychological death.

Remember our definition: *psychological death means dying on the inside. The character will never realize his or her true human potential.*

What does Scout need to become? Someone who is tolerant and compassionate about other people.

When the dirt-poor boy from school, Walter Cunningham, is invited by Jem for dinner, Scout has an instant reaction to one of the boy's practices. He asks for some molasses and proceeds to pour syrup all over his food—vegetables and meat included. Scout wonders out loud what in the Sam Hill he is doing.

This causes terrible embarrassment in Walter. Furious, the housekeeper Calpernia orders Scout into the kitchen:

> When she squinted down at me the tiny lines around her eyes deepened. "There's some folks who don't eat like us," she whispered fiercely, "but you ain't called on to contradict 'em at the table when they don't. That boy's yo' comp'ny and if he wants to eat up the table cloth you let him, you hear?"
>
> "He ain't company, Cal, he's just a Cunningham—"
>
> "Hush your mouth! Don't matter who they are, anybody sets foot in this house's yo' comp'ny, and don't you let me catch you remarkin' on their ways like you was so high and mighty! Yo' folks might be better'n the Cunninghams but it don't count for nothin' the way you're disgracin' 'em—if you can't act fit to eat at the table you can just set here and eat in the kitchen!"

And so Scout is given a crucial lesson in compassion and not being "high and mighty" with people less well off than she. Should she fail to learn that lesson, she would grow up to be one of those Southern women who are mean, cantankerous, intolerant. She would never grow into the full humanity she now inhabits.

Earlier in the day, Scout had been told by her teacher, Miss Caroline (a newcomer to the town), that she must stop reading with her father, because he didn't know how to teach properly. Scout gets in trouble, and gets some whacks, and then harbors harsh feelings for the teacher.

Later, after school and the incident with Walter, Scout sits with her father on the porch, telling him of her troubles. Atticus offers her a lesson:

> "First of all," he said, "if you can learn a simple trick, Scout, you'll get along a lot better with all kinds of folks. You never really understand a person until you consider things from their point of view—"
>
> "Sir?"
>
> "—Until you climb into his skin and walk around in it."

Again, this is crucial to Scout's growth. It is the key to her future life.

The entire novel unfolds from here, reinforcing this lesson to Scout. It will culminate with her seeing the "malevolent phantom" Boo Radley—and by extension people of any stripe—in a whole new light. It will save her from the psychological death of being an intolerant adult.

Opposition

In *To Kill a Mockingbird*, opposition to Scout's "becoming" is prejudice, but that is not enough. It has to be embodied in a character, or groups of characters. It is most specifically embodied in Bob Ewell. His opposition to Atticus Finch over the defense of Tom Robinson is the thematic threat of the whole book.

If Scout does not change, she will be no better than a Ewell. She could end up like Mrs. Henry Lafayette Dubose, the old lady next door who screams at Scout and Jem because their father has the temerity to defend a black man.

The Opening

Since this is a frame story—the narrator looking back at past events—the disturbance is given in past tense. In the first paragraph, Scout tells us about her brother Jem breaking his arm. Then the second paragraph:

> When enough years had gone by to enable us to look back on them, we sometimes discussed the events leading to his accident. I maintain that the Ewells started it all, but Jem, who was four years my senior, said it started long before that. He said it began the summer Dill came to us, when Dill first gave us the idea of making Boo Radley come out.

The ripple in Scout's ordinary world was the arrival of young Dill, who instigates the thread that is to run throughout the book, namely, get a look at the "malevolent phantom" Boo Radley. What exactly is happening to Boo in that house down the street? What sort of person is he?

That mystery, hinted at in the opening, is enough to keep us reading.

Doorways of No Return

The first doorway happens in chapter nine, when Scout finds out her father is going to defend a black man accused of rape. She's first clued into that by a boy at school and almost gets in a fight with him. But Atticus confirms it is so.

This forces Scout into a world where she will have to confront previous beliefs and form new ones. Because of her father's noble decision, the door to her old life slams shut behind her—in a coming-of-age novel, that's what it feels like. You have to leave the children's room and enter the real world. That world can be a dark and scary place.

The second doorway, a major setback, is the guilty verdict in the Tom Robinson case. It is incomprehensible to Scout and Jem. "It ain't right," Jem says, eyes filled with tears. "No, son, it's not right," Atticus says.

Scout has changed. When school starts up again (she's in third grade) ,she walks by the Radley place, but it no longer frightens her. Instead:

> I sometimes felt a twinge of remorse, when passing by the old place, at ever having taken part in what must have been sheer torment to Arthur Radley—what reasonable recluse wants children peeping through his shutters, delivering greetings on the end of a fishing-pole, wandering in his collards at night?

Resonant Ending

At the end of the book, when she has finally come face-to-face with Boo Radley, she has overcome psychological death. She is kind to Boo, and unafraid. She walks Boo home, holding his hand.

> Atticus was right. One time he said you never really know a man until you stand in his shoes and walk around in them. Just standing on the Radley porch was enough.

Later, as Atticus puts Scout to bed, the injured Jem asleep in another room, Scout reflects on the story Atticus was reading to Jem. It was about a misunderstood character who was, in reality, "real nice":

"Most people are, Scout, when you finally see them."

He turned out the light and went into Jem's room. He would be there all night, and he would be there when Jem waked up in the morning.

THE SILENCE OF THE LAMBS

This best-selling thriller by Thomas Harris became the basis of the hit movie. It tells the story of Clarice Starling, a young FBI trainee, who is suddenly thrust into a major serial killer case through her encounter with one of the most diabolical minds in the thriller canon, the flesh-eating Dr. Hannibal Lecter. Will she be up to the challenge? Can she win the cat and mouse mind game with a criminal mastermind? Can she do it in time to save another potential victim of the killer known as Buffalo Bill?

Those are the stakes.

Opening Disturbance and a Lead Worth Following

When we first meet Clarice Starling, she has been summoned to the office of the head of the FBI's Behavioral Science Unit. That is the opening disturbance, and it happens in paragraph two of the first page.

Thomas Harris does not warm up the engines. The story begins *in medias res,* the "middle of things." Clarice is in a meeting that will start a string of events that changes her life forever.

Page two begins to establish sympathy for our Lead character, Clarice.

We find out that she had been "spooked" by the summons, a bit of emotional jeopardy. Remember being called to the principal's office in school? Clarice has a twinge of that feeling.

Then we get a small snippet of backstory: *Starling came from people who do not ask for favors or press for friendship, but she was puzzled and regretful at Crawford's behavior.*

And then some inner conflict: *Now, in his presence, she liked him again, she was sorry to note.*

Two competing emotions add conflict automatically.

Then Harris gets back to the action. Remember: Act first, explain later. Concentrate on action in the first few chapters.

Further information about Starling (exposition) comes in via dialogue, so it is also contained within action (dialogue is a form of action):

"You have a lot of forensics but no law enforcement background. We look for six years, minimum."

"My father was a marshal. I know the life."

Crawford smiled a little. "What you *do* have is a double major in psychology and criminology, and how many summers working in a mental health center—two?"

"Two."

By the end of chapter one we know that Jack Crawford wants trainee Starling to interview the formidable criminal Hannibal "The Cannibal" Lecter. This is a further sympathy factor, because Starling is an obvious underdog.

Death Overhanging

We also know that this is a huge professional opportunity for her. The director himself will see her report. She will be on a fast track to success in the FBI.

The obvious implication being, of course, that fumbling the task will hurt her, perhaps irreparably.

Thus the "death" that is at stake for Clarice is professional.

The action moves immediately to the Baltimore State Hospital for the Criminally Insane. Here is where Starling will interview Lecter, but first she has to deal with the sleazy administrator, Chilton.

Harris masterfully orchestrates the casting. Chilton's attitude provides plenty of fodder for conflict with Starling. He drops a line about how attractive she is and refers to her as a "girl."

Starling ignores all this and tries to get on with business. Chilton keeps making inappropriate remarks and Starling has a thought that tells us exactly what she thinks of Chilton, even as she verbally stays even-tempered.

This shows us a couple of things. First, Starling is not a wimp. A wimp is someone who takes abuse but does nothing about it. Don't ever let your Lead be one of those.

Second, it shows that Starling has self-control, a hint that she is strong and able to meet challenges.

But, of course, the biggest challenges are yet to come.

Opposition

In chapter three she has her first encounter with Hannibal Lecter. He is polite to Clarice in an imperious way. But he very quickly shows his intimidating intelligence. He is the one in control of the conversation. Clarice shows guts by sticking with him, even when he delivers an entire psychological profile about her and her "rube" upbringing, information she can't deny.

Clarice comes right back at him, asking if he's strong enough to look at himself. And there seems a bit of admiration for her when he says, "You're tough, aren't you?"

But a moment later he dismisses her: "Go back to school, little Starling."

She did not get what she came for:

> Starling felt suddenly empty, as though she had given blood. She took longer than necessary to put the papers back in her briefcase because she didn't immediately trust her legs. Starling was soaked with the failure she detested.

At the end of the chapter, after Miggs (in the cell next to Lecter's) has insulted and humiliated Clarice in a disgusting way, Lecter is sympathetic, and gives her a bone: a clue about a past murder. He is offering her "advancement." That's his gift.

The clue Lecter gives her is to look in the car of an old murder victim named Raspail.

Scene Structure

This brings us to a scene that can be analyzed this way:

OBJECTIVE: Clarice wants to get in to the car belonging to one of Lecter's victims.

OBSTACLES: Time, bureaucracy.

To overcome the obstacle, Clarice uses cleverness (pretending to be a Ford recall person).

OUTCOME: Setback. No helpful information.

I have spent considerable time going over this first act, showing the various techniques Harris uses to establish a reader bond with Clarice and showing what a truly masterful antagonist Hannibal Lecter is.

Now we are about one-fifth into the book, where the first doorway of no return should happen, and it does.

First Doorway of No Return

In chapter nine, Lecter gives Clarice a key clue about Buffalo Bill, the serial killer. This leads to Jack Crawford pulling Clarice onto the case. Now her professional life is really on the line. She is part of the serial killer investigation. To fail here is to fail big time. "School's out, Starling," Crawford tells her.

We now enter Act Two. Starling is in the "dark world" of a real case, a notorious case, where innocent lives are on the line with every passing moment. One of those lives belongs to the daughter of a U.S. Senator.

We won't go through all the beats of Act Two. It's a series of scenes with organic unity. Clarice Starling trying to identify and eventually capture Buffalo Bill. Obstacles faced, actions taken to overcome the obstacles, setbacks and clues.

One of those actions is going back to see Lecter. He can help her, but he wants something in return. He wants to be transferred to another institution, and he wants a view from his prison cell.

He will give Clarice only bits of information until he gets his way.

She strikes a deal, but there will be a betrayal that upsets Dr. Lecter. He is not someone you should upset.

Second Doorway of No Return

The second doorway of no return makes possible the final battle of the ending. It's a crisis or setback, clue or discovery.

Clarice is on the hunt for Buffalo Bill. But she's been officially taken off the case. That setback doesn't stop her. She has been interacting with Lecter and her mind keeps working.

There is a ticking clock—the likely death of Buffalo Bill's latest victim, Catherine Martin, the Senator's daughter. It's probably just a matter of hours now.

Clarice has been given a bit of cryptic information from Lecter. He has suggested that Buffalo Bill *covets*, and that we covet what we see every day.

This proves to be the key clue, the doorway through which Clarice will pass so she can ultimately save Catherine Martin.

The clue causes Clarice to examine the background of Buffalo Bill's first victim, Frederica Bimmel. She reasons that he must have been seeing her, perhaps each day, until he finally decided to kill her.

Starling follows up. She goes to Frederica's house and examines her room, and finds out Frederica sewed her own clothes.

That discovery matches, in Clarice's mind, the observations she made of another victim, Kimberly Emberg, and the mystery of why patches of skin had been removed from her.

This gives Clarice a eureka moment: Buffalo Bill is sewing the skins of his victims together.

This, in turn, leads her to question a friend of Frederica's, who references a clothing store in town. The owner of the store has died, but Clarice goes to the store owner's family home to get more information.

The home is where the killer, Jame Gumb, is holed up.

Clarice doesn't know this when she first enters, but when a moth scurries into view (that being a key M.O. of the killer) she knows she's in the right place.

Which leads to the showdown with Gumb.

She kills him and saves Catherine.

Resonant Ending

Clarice has overcome professional death. In fact, she's moved on to a new level. Jack Crawford tells her, "Starling, I'm proud of you. So is Brigham, so is the Director."

Throughout Clarice had been haunted by a dream, a dream of lambs screaming when being slaughtered. Lecter posits to her at one point that she must think if she catches Buffalo Bill, and saves Catherine, the screaming will be silenced. Clarice admits as much.

The last line:

> But the face on the pillow, rosy in the firelight, is certainly that of Clarice Starling, and she sleeps deeply, sweetly, in the silence of the lambs.

INDEX

ABOUT THE AUTHOR

 James Scott Bell is the author of more than twenty novels and was a Christy Award winner for Final Witness in 2000. His fiction has been reviewed in *Publishers Weekly, Booklist,Library Journal*, and the *Library Review*. He's the author of *Write Great Fiction: Plot & Structure, Write Great Fiction: Revision & Self-Editing,* and *The Art of War for Writers*. He writes for *Writer's Digest* magazine. Bell taught fiction writing courses at Pepperdine University and is a regular on the conference circuit. His website is www.jamesscottbell.com. He lives in Los Angeles, California.

Printed in the United States
by Baker & Taylor Publisher Services